厦门大学
哲学社会科学繁荣计划
2011—2021

本书的出版得到厦门大学哲学社会科学繁荣计划的资助，特此鸣谢。

"欧亚裔的灵魂"——
伊顿姐妹、戴安娜·张、艾美·刘作品中的欧亚裔意识

王增红 著

外国文学研究丛书

厦门大学出版社
XIAMEN UNIVERSITY PRESS
国家一级出版社
全国百佳图书出版单位

图书在版编目(CIP)数据

"欧亚裔的灵魂"——伊顿姐妹、戴安娜·张、艾美·刘作品中的欧亚裔意识:英文/王增红著.—厦门:厦门大学出版社,2017.3
ISBN 978-7-5615-6452-3

Ⅰ.①欧… Ⅱ.①王… Ⅲ.①小说研究-美国-现代-英文 Ⅳ.①I712.074

中国版本图书馆 CIP 数据核字(2017)第 063049 号

出 版 人	蒋东明
责任编辑	王扬帆
特约编辑	刘文松
封面设计	李夏凌
美术编辑	李嘉彬
责任印制	许克华

出版发行	厦门大学出版社
社　　址	厦门市软件园二期望海路 39 号
邮政编码	361008
总 编 办	0592-2182177　0592-2181406(传真)
营销中心	0592-2184458　0592-2181365
网　　址	http://www.xmupress.com
邮　　箱	xmup@xmupress.com
印　　刷	厦门集大印刷厂

开本	720mm×1000mm　1/16
印张	10.25
插页	2
字数	216 千字
版次	2017 年 3 月第 1 版
印次	2017 年 3 月第 1 次印刷
定价	39.00 元

本书如有印装质量问题请直接寄承印厂调换

厦门大学出版社
微信二维码

厦门大学出版社
微博二维码

序

　　王增红博士的专著马上就要付梓了。在替她高兴的同时，也为她的刻苦认真和坚强意志所感动。

　　王增红博士从西南大学硕士毕业后到厦门理工学院任教。教学之余，她开始思考自己的未来：没有博士学位，想在高校立足很难。因此，她下定决心，认真备考。功夫不负有心人，她在众多的考生中脱颖而出，表现出色。但是，另一个现实问题又摆在她面前：厦门大学只招收全脱产博士生。这个政策意味着被录取的博士生必须放弃原单位的工作。没有工作也就没有经济收入，这对一个年轻人，特别是年轻母亲来说，压力是巨大的。但是，她在家人的支持下，毅然辞去环境优越的工作，成为我的第一个博士生。

　　人们戏称：要减肥，读博士。这句话说明，读博过程路漫漫，读博压力伤心神。但是王增红博士善于科学安排时间，正确处理生活和学习的关系。除了完成学业课程之外，她目标远大，积极申请国家留学基金，获得美国加州大学洛杉矶分校联合培养博士项目，为期一年。她利用那边丰富的第一手资料，广涉群书，勤做笔记，逐渐厘清自己的思路，聚焦欧亚混血儿作品，并以此作为博士学位论文的研究对象，认真写作，几经修改，终于顺利获得博士学位。

　　《"欧亚裔的灵魂"——伊顿姐妹、戴安娜·张、艾美·刘作品中的欧亚裔意识》的一大特点是视角新。关于美国少数族裔文学研究，国内外学者已有很多独到的见解，主要集中在本族群内部的研究，而跨种族研究则相对较少。同时，跨种族作品研究侧重于黑白混血族群。该书选取伊顿姐妹、戴安娜·张、艾美·刘四位欧亚混血儿的作品为研究对象，探讨欧亚混血儿的身份和意义。因此，该书选题新颖，对促进美国社会的混血儿研究有相当的学术价值和社会意义。

该书的另一大特点是内容新。它以后殖民种族视角为切入点，系统分析四位作家作品中的欧亚裔种族意识和身份认同。该书以文本细读为基础，通过对这些作家个人身份和作品主题的详细剖析，进而指出，她们在不同时代追寻欧亚裔意识，构建一个既独立于美国白人，又独立于美国亚裔的欧亚裔身份。她们一方面身处反对种族通婚的社会环境，体验了强烈的被排斥感和劣等感；另一方面，又苦苦追寻，试图找到一个适合她们自己的特殊属性，从而突显一种流动的跨种族身份认同的可能性。同时，该书从历史、政治、文化和地理等层面和维度出发，阐述这些作家及作品人物的欧亚裔意识形成过程和成因，指出欧亚裔"无处可归"的生活现实和内心对身份重构的渴望。经过层层分析，该书最后指出，在后种族时代的美国，以欧亚裔为代表的混血族群承载着打破种族界限构建多种族未来的希望。

人才成长有其内在规律。在刚刚起步的三十多岁这个年龄段是对人才成长最为严峻的考验。这个时候的年轻人上有老，下有小，既要考虑到现实生活中的柴米油盐，又要静下心来超脱世俗的纷扰。王增红博士经受住了考验。她一方面要照顾好父母和孩子，另一方面还要在女儿睡觉后抓紧时间，孤灯作伴，潜心科研。正是有了这样的超人毅力，她先后于 2015 年和 2016 年在《外国文学评论》发表两篇论文。

"宝剑锋从磨砺出，梅花香自苦寒来。"王增红博士在科研道路上已经迈开脚步往前走。希望她在将来也能够"撸起袖子加油干"，实现自己的人生价值。

张龙海
2017 年 1 月 13 日
于裕康斋

Contents

Abbreviations

The following abbreviations used in parenthetical citations in the text refer to the sources indicated below.

MSF: *Mrs. Spring Fragrance* (1912) (Urbana: University of Illinois Press, 1995)

ME: *Me: A Book of Remembrance* (1915) (Jackson: University of Mississippi Press, 1997)

MA: *Marion: The Story of an Artist's Model* (1916) (Montreal: McGill-Queens University Press, 2012)

HH: *The Heart of Hyacinth* (1903) (Seattle: University of Washington Press, 2000)

FL: *The Frontiers of Love* (1956) (Seattle: University of Washington Press, 1994)

FA: *Face* (1994) (New York: Warner Books, 1994)

前 言

　　有数据表明，美国跨种族婚姻在近20年增长了近4倍，进而一度形成了双重种族婴儿潮。混血人口的不断增加，引起了美国学术界对混血族的高度关注。与此同时，20世纪90年代，美国兴起了混血族运动。运动旨在问责主流的种族概念和单一种族论，呼吁重构混血族历史，主张视混血族为新世界秩序的开拓者，是种族主义的终结者。在这个背景下，许多学者纷纷从社会学、哲学、文学、艺术、医学、政治学等领域对混血族进行了大量研究。但是这些研究都主要集中于黑白混血族。就文学领域来讲，已有不少学者关注混血族和由混血作家创作的文学作品。同样地，文学领域的研究也大多集中于黑白混血族，而作为混血族中比较重要的一支欧亚混血族却由于种种原因没有得到应有的重视，研究成果寥寥可数。

　　本研究横跨20世纪约80年，以四位重要的欧亚混血作家及其代表作品为研究对象，以种族混杂这一概念为理论基础，历时性地考察欧亚混血作家通过文本讲述的欧亚裔意识以及她们一心想要构建的独立于华裔和白人之外的第三种身份即欧亚裔身份，揭示一种跨历史的族裔感性。

　　受种族混杂衰退论的影响，主流美国文学中对欧亚混血儿的描述常常以死亡、疯癫等悲惨结局收场，也因此形成了"悲惨的欧亚裔"这样的文学刻板形象。而在作家本身就是欧亚混血族的文学作品中，欧亚混血主人公虽然也经历身份迷失、找不到归宿的困境，但是在摆脱了白人刻板描述的桎梏后，欧亚裔作家将自身的经历与文学艺术糅合，创作了真实、形象的欧亚裔文学人物，突出了欧亚裔主体性。20世纪美国的种族话语植根于次血统种族论，这种观念依据"一滴规则"将美国种族二元化、等级化。欧亚混血族由于有非白人血统，被排除在白人外，又因为不是纯粹的亚裔，被亚裔排斥。因此，从世纪之交伊顿姐妹的自传和小说到20世纪50年代戴安娜·张的自传体小说，再到90年代艾美·刘的小说，尽管历史时期、地理、政治环境不同，但是欧亚混血主人公都承受了由双重种族身份带来的认同痛苦与"两边都不是"的异化感。

　　本书选取的四位欧亚裔作家在文学创作的过程中，都不遗余力地抵抗白人主流话语对欧亚混血族的刻板描述，通过自我表征来刻画欧亚混血儿"无处可归"的困境，表达一种欧亚裔意识。从世纪之交开始，作为一种全新的族裔主体，欧亚混血族就处于严苛的反对种族通婚的话语中，体验了强烈的被排斥感与自卑感。"二战"期间，中国上海战时语境下欧亚混血儿经历了自我迷失与身份危机。20 世纪 90 年代，欧亚混血儿则遭受到种族暴力与精神打击。本书认为，伊顿姐妹、戴安娜·张和艾美·刘反映欧亚裔人物现实的作品，都诉说一种强烈的欧亚裔意识。这种意识源于白人或者亚裔对欧亚混血族的种族主义歧视，也成为欧亚混血族构建其独立身份的根源。此外，四位作家都拒绝被限定在某一固定的族裔范畴，通过不断变换作者身份、创作主题等途径解构单一的族裔身份，构建欧亚裔身份。这种身份赋予欧亚混血族完整的自我概念，强调身份的机动性、开放性和即兴性。

　　本书主体部分以时间为线索，根据四位欧亚裔作家的创作特点，分三章依次讨论了四位作家如何通过文学创作叙述欧亚裔意识。第一章考察世纪之交伊迪斯·伊顿的自传和短篇小说。由于伊迪斯的半华裔身份，以及当时华人成为美国种族主义迫害的直接对象的残酷语境，她勇敢地打破主流话语对华人的刻板描述，客观、公正地刻画唐人街的华人和他们的生活，批评家们倾向于认为伊迪斯完全拥抱华裔身份，并将其定位为美国华裔作家。其实，伊迪斯对自我身份的定义是很复杂的。她同情华人，愿意为华人充当族裔解释者的角色；她看似围绕着华裔身份定位，但是她始终没有完全认同其华裔身份。事实上，伊迪斯始终自认是具有华人血统的欧亚裔。她在捍卫华人事业的同时，在短篇小说中有意通过刻画不同的华人形象，保持她与华人身份之间的距离，解构其纯粹的华裔身份。同时，伊迪斯的不少短篇小说直接关注跨种族婚姻，并将一些"摇摆的"、没有出路的欧亚混血人物的身份困境刻画得淋漓尽致。同时，在自传中，伊迪斯始终坚持她的双重性，不但讲述了由于她的欧亚混血身份而遭受的各种歧视与不公正待遇，而且还乐观地为欧亚混血族预设了一个没有种族差异的理想的未来。

　　第二章围绕温妮弗蕾德·伊顿和她的欧亚裔意识展开。本书避开批评界一贯的"好姐姐—坏妹妹"的批评模式，认为温妮弗蕾德和她的姐姐伊迪斯一样，虽然冒用一个日本身份获得了极大的文学声誉，但是同样抵制完全进入某一具体的族裔范畴。在整个写作生涯中，温妮弗蕾德游走于不同的作者身份之间，不仅没有将自己限定在一个族裔角色当中，而且使得以血统为基础的种族纯粹性毫无意义。因此，本书认定温妮弗蕾德为一个族裔流浪者，表面上她不忠于族裔事实，本质上反映的是她的欧亚裔意识。通过分析自传《我》的匿名性和欧亚裔小说代表作《风信子之心》中的种族跨越，本书探讨温妮弗蕾德如何通过变换作者身份、人物形象和种族跨越实践来凸显她的欧亚裔意识。温妮弗蕾德追求一种流动的、乌托邦式的欧亚裔身份，这种身份可以自由地跨越种族界限，打破族裔类别的稳定性。

第三章解读戴安娜·张的自传体小说《爱的边界》和艾美·刘的小说《脸》。同是欧亚混血儿的戴安娜·张和艾美·刘在文学创作上有一个共同点，即二者都在创作后期放弃了族裔主题，转而创作非族裔主题的小说。在戴安娜·张的六部小说中，《爱的边界》是唯一一部涉及族裔问题的小说。其他的五部小说均以白人为故事主人公，都与亚裔无关，因而受批评界冷落。同样地，艾美·刘的创作尝试为族裔作家提出一种新的可能性。她不主张通过叙述"统治的与受压迫的"的主题来迎合市场对族裔作家的期望，也不愿意通过描写异国风情来吸引读者。她坚持认为亚裔作家不必把自我限定在亚裔主题上，因此她的作品也没有受到批评界的热捧。尽管如此，本书认为，作为欧亚裔作家，她们的创作整体上发出的是一种声音，她们想要表达的是不同于亚裔和白人的欧亚混血意识。本章借助格洛丽亚·安扎尔朵的"中间地带理论"，认为戴安娜·张和艾美·刘分别把故事背景设定在"二战"时期的中国上海和纽约的唐人街，是为了更好地诠释欧亚混血主人公如何渴望种族的统一性和自我的完整性。在这两种特殊的环境里，欧亚混血主人公都经历了身体和精神上的不充分感，他们既不是完整的美国人，也不是真正的华人。两位作家都指出"不断地即兴改变"是解决身份困境的最合理的出路。

虽然四位作家的文本阐释了不同的历史、地理、政治和文化情形，但是作为针对种族主义的文本回应，它们都揭示了一种强烈的欧亚裔意识。这种意识形成于欧亚裔与种族主义交锋的过程中，突出欧亚裔"无处可归"的种族事实和他们想拥有完整、独立族裔身份的渴望。通过分析欧亚裔文学作品，本书认为尽管美国种族主义具有持久性，但是在后种族时代，以欧亚裔为代表的混血族不可否认地承载着打破种族界限、构建多种族未来的希望。

Introduction

"It's just because I'm half Chinese and a sort of curiosity that she likes to have me there. When I'm in her parlor, she whispers to the other people and they try to make me talk and examine me from head to toe as if I were a wild animal—I'd rather be killed than be a show.... Last week...she came up with an old gentleman with white hair and gold-rimmed glasses. I heard the old gentleman say, 'Oh, indeed, you don't say so! Her father a Chinaman!' and then he stared at me with all his might. Mrs. Goodwin said, 'Do you not notice the peculiar cast of features?' and he said 'Ah, yes! And such bright eyes—very peculiar little girl.'"

——Sui Sin Far, "Sweet Sin"

"There are so many people who are mixed like myself, who struggle with belonging just like me, who have to be chameleons and adapt to situations. There are people out there who understand what I am talking about and believe that the issues of the identity of mixed people is overlooked. My idea is, why not make a third option, where there is a community of mixed people and individuals who can choose to be mixed with other people and be proud of who they are?"

——Jonathan Ng, "Being Mixed in Today's America"[1]

The first quotation, excerpted from Sui Sin Far (Edith Eaton)'s short story "Sweet Sin" published in 1898, illustrates a half Chinese girl's anguish of being gazed at by racist eyes, while the latter, as the concluding part of an autobiographical article recently published by a mixed Chinese American in 2013, gives an account of the present struggling situation for mixed race in America, and further draws the outline of an idealized future.[2] This book begins with the above two quotations as a way to historically show the struggling experience of mixed race in America from the 1900s

---

1   This epigraph is excerpted from *Mixed: Multicultural College Students Tell Their Life Stories*, ed. Andrew Garrad, Robert Kilkenny, and Christina Gomez (New York: Cornell University Press, 2013), 125.

2   For consistency's sake, since there exists no popular critical consensus, this book uses "mixed race" as both an adjective (without hyphens) and a noun (without capitalization), and more or less synonymous with other common terms applied to and invoked by those interested in this phenomenon, which include "multiracial," "biracial," "interracial," and so on.

when mixed race appeared as a new ethnic subject to the present day when the mixed population has increased to a large number. As is shown, for the mixed people in America, no matter how time changes, the fact that they have no place to belong to remains changeless. This book, focusing on four Eurasian writers' literary texts, attempts to explore the plight of being Eurasian in the twentieth century.

By calling it "The Souls of Eurasians," this book invokes W. E. B. Du Bois' famous *The Souls of Black Folk* (1903) which as Du Bois stresses "show[s] the strange meaning of being black at the dawn of the twentieth century" (Du Bois 1). It is recognized that the problem for biracial and bicultural Eurasians is more complicated than bicultural but racially pure ethnic subjects such as Asian Americans, African Americans and the like. Because of the very concept of race and racism, Eurasians' soul state is much more tormenting and fragmenting. So quotation marks are used in the title as a reminder of appropriation as well as emphasis. This book spans the twentieth century, ranging from an examination of turn-of-the-century Eurasian characters in the short stories and autobiography of Sui Sin Far to the contemporary Eurasian heroine of Aimee Liu's in *Face*.

The book title's oblique summoning of Du Bois in particular is also significant because all the writers discussed here explicitly pay homage to Du Bois' theory of double consciousness as well as his fascination with the narrative possibilities of mixed race. Being Eurasians themselves, the four writers narrate a kind of Eurasian consciousness or Eurasian sensibility in the authorial practice and literary productions. In the matter of biracial identity, they stress the concept of fluidity, openness, and process.

I. Eurasian: Definition and the Plight of "with No Place to Be"[1]

The term "Eurasian" refers to people of mixed Asian and European ancestry. It was originally coined in the nineteenth-century British India to refer to the offspring of a European father and a Hindoo or Mussulman woman in India. According to the *Oxford English Dictionary*, it was first invented by Marquis of Hastings, who

---

1 Paul Spickard contends that the monoracialist impulses of both the majority and minority communities left Eurasians "with no place to be." See Paul Spickard, "Who Is an Asian? Who Is a Pacific Islander? Monoracialism, Multiracial People, and Asian American Communities," in *The Sum of Our Part,* eds. Teresa Williams-Leon and Cynthia L. Nakashima (Philadelphia: Temple University Press, 2001), 18.

coined the term to refer to the progeny of "white fathers and Hindoo or Mahometan mothers" at the advent of British colonization of the subcontinent in the seventeenth century. According to Shirley Geok-lin Lim, to facilitate the penetration of the East India Company into India in 1683, the first British soldiers and traders were encouraged to marry Indian women in order to populate the country with Christians. One hundred years later, however, in 1786, "because of increasing competition from British subjects coming out for employment into the colonies and the need for greater control of its employees, the East India Company passed repressive measures restricting the economic roles open to the children of these marriages" (Lim, 1994 xi). Consequently, popular portrayals of Eurasians became increasingly derogatory and the original Eurasian community in India referred to themselves as Anglo-Indian. With the spread of colonization to other parts of the globe, Eurasian was broadened in the nineteenth century to include the mixing of Dutch and Portuguese with the Malay. With the appearance of the first Chinese on the West Coast in the mid-nineteenth century, Americans adopted Eurasian to describe the mixing of these new immigrants with whites. Hence, its racial connotations intensified. In this book, Eurasians refer to individuals of mixed European and Asiatic descent (Chinese in particular), and describes a mixture based not on geographical origin (Europeans and Asians) but on racial origin (Caucasians and Orientals).[1]

Certainly, in addition to its meaning of racial mixing, Eurasian has many other modern usages in different fields. In fact, Eurasia is a place referring to the combined continental landmass of Europe and Asia, although its boundaries vary from the geographical to the geological to the political according to the person who is doing the research.[2] Thus, accordingly, the term "Eurasian" is a demonym usually meaning "of or relating to Eurasia" or "a native or inhabitant of Eurasia." In addition to this, for geopoliticians, the "Eurasian School" refers to the emerging Eurasian democracies in the area known as the Eurasian rimland or periphery; while a linguist of the Academia Eurasiana in Hungary might speak of the Ural-Altaic languages; and the geologists would specialize in tectonics studying the "Eurasian blocks."

---

1   Sometimes Amerasian or hapa is used interchangeably with Eurasian. Amerasian is a broader term describing the mixed American and Asian consciousness of Asian Americans and not simply a racial blend. Hapa, from the Japanese "half," is a colloquial usage. In *Between Worlds*, Amy Ling uses Eurasian interchangeably with Amerasian. For consistency's sake, this dissertation uses Eurasian to address issues of racial mixture between Caucasians and Asians.

2   For more information on Eurasia in a geographical sense, see Martin W Lewis and Kären Wigen, eds. *The Myth of Continents: a Critique of Metageography* (Los Angeles: University of California Press, 1997), 31–32.

In this book, Eurasian is a racial concept. It is a North American term describing a lack of genealogical consistency, like the terms "mulatto", "mestizo", "hapa" and "half-breed". The twentieth-century conception of race in the United States is rooted in the powerful, although scientifically insupportable rule of hypodescent. This famous one-drop rule defining any individual with any amount of "black blood" as black logically prevents the concept of mixed race identity. People are white according to historical definition, only if everybody in their family is not black; and people are black, or non-white, whenever anybody in their family is black, or non-white. This rule can also be extended to other races as well. This biracial caste system—white and raced—prevents mixed race from having any identity in the "official and public, legal, and social history of the United States" (Zack, 1993 73).[1] Ruth Frankenberg notes that "Chineseness," "Blackness," and "Whiteness" are states of being in theories of racial superiority, so that the "half" or "mixed person"… "does not belong anywhere" (Frankenberg 95). Therefore, Eurasian does not exist as a racial or ethnic entity. In other words, racially speaking, Eurasian is an impossible being. Naomi Zack in *Race and Mixed Race* has argued, "If the existence of certain human beings causes problems for certain concepts or systems of categorization, then it is the concepts or systems of categorization and not the human existents which need to be criticized and changed" (Zack, 1993 17).

However, the fact that the history of racial liberation in the United States is a history of adaptation to rather than interrogation of this binary structure testifies not only to the endurance of racism, but to the power and function of the systems of classification involved in its maintenance. Scholars have frequently asserted that American society prior to 1967 was rigidly monoracial, assigning people either a white or nonwhite identity without giving recognition to mixedness, with hypodescent operating as the normative convention.[2] Nowadays, though we live in the increasingly

---

1 Something approaching a distinct mulatto culture did exist in the colonial period before increasingly harsh anti-miscegenation laws came into effect and intermarriage was more common than it has been since 1865. In Louisiana, in particular, until the mid-nineteenth century, mulattoes could use their lightness to get free and achieve white culture; and gradation of color mixture, like quadroon, octoroon, indicated a social and racial structure similar to Afro-Caribbean. However, neither the number of mulattoes nor the variation of degrees of color among them undoes the fundamental caste structure which gives them their meaning. See Joel Williamson's *New People: Miscegenation and Mulattoes in the United States* (New York: The Free Press, 1980), 188.

2 See Carlos A. Fernandez, "Government Classification of Multiracial/Multiethnic People," in *The Multiracial Experience: Racial Borders as the New Frontier*, ed. Maria P. P. Root (Thousand Oaks, CA: Sage, 1996),16.

post-race world—a world concerned with struggles for ethnic, national, religious and cultural meanings—the irrational and corporeal ground of race can still be a powerful force in social relations. Although the concept of racial "blood" is used figuratively, the dichotomy of white and non-white is refortified in other forms. According to some scholars, it endures in the form of multiculturalism, which celebrates ethnic and racial distinctiveness, and is the form of contemporary racism.[1] An exploration of the mixed race identity reinforces these essential categories of race and also provides one of the best opportunities to see the limitations and absurdity of racial categories.

II. Theoretical Discussion of Hybridity in the Discourses of Race

The theoretical concept of hybridity as a metaphor for the new transcultural forms produced out of the colonizer-colonized relation has become fashionable in academic circles since the late 1980s, thanks to the influential work of Homi Bhabha among others. Bhabha's theorization of hybridity as a disruptive force with the power to subvert or undermine colonial authority has lent the concept as a critical tool. Indeed, hybridity has become one of the most widely employed concepts in postcolonial studies and has frequently been cited as a defining characteristic of "the postcolonial condition."[2] Hybridity, as certain theorists promise, allows us to evade "the replication of the binary categories of the past" (Ashcorft, et al. 183).

Whereas postcolonial theorists have largely conceptualized hybridity in cultural or discursive terms, mixed race studies focus on racial hybridity, analyzing the "mixed race experience" and "mixed race identity." Racial hybridity arises in part from the nineteenth-century preoccupation with the question of mono ~nesis and polygenesis— whether humans have a single origin or several origins ~cientific debate about the issue continued throughout the era, the polyr humans differed by species and race was synonymous with s rooted

检 验 员

3

1　See, for example, E. San Juan Jr's "Problematizing Multic. e 'Common Culture'; Alan Wald's "Theorizing Cultural Difference: A Critique of the 'L. School'"; and Joan Scott's "Multiculturalism and the Politics of Identity."

2　See Homi Bhabha, "Signs Taken for Wonders: Questions of Ambivalence and Authority under a Tree Outside Delhi, May 1817," *Critical Inquiry* 12.1 (1985): 144-165; Bhabha, "The Third Space" in *Identity: Community, Culture, Difference*, ed. Jonathan Rutherford (London: Lawrence & Wishart, 1990), 207-221; Ella Shohat, "Notes on the 'Post-Colonial,'" *Social Text* 31/32 (1992): 99-113; and Robert J. C. Young, *Colonial Desire: Hybridity in Theory, Culture, and Race* (New York: Routledge, 1995).

cultural belief, that is, the biological degeneracy of racial hybrid.

Etymologically, the word "hybrid" has developed from biological and botanical origins; in Latin it means the offspring of a tame sow and a wild boar, but it was scarcely in use until the nineteenth century. By Webster in 1828, a hybrid is defined as "a mongrel or mule; an animal or plant, produced from the mixture of two species." When applied to human, it was first used in the nineteenth century to denote the crossing of people of different races. According to the *Oxford English Dictionary*, a hybrid is the offspring "of human parents of different races, half-breed." Hence, "hybrid" is the nineteenth century's word referring to a physiological phenomenon. But today, it has been reactivated to describe a cultural one.[1]

Robert Young argues that Western culture carries within it the seeds of its own resistance, an "uneasy syncretism" or "inner dissonance" characterized by "an obsession with sexuality, fertility and hybridity; a furtive fascination with miscegenation and inter-racial transgression" (Young 25). One manifestation of this obsession is the belief in the biological degeneracy of the racial hybrid. One of the most prominent early proponents of hybrid degeneracy is American polygenist Josiah Nott. In "The Mulatto a Hybrid—Probable Extermination of the Two Races If the Whites and Blacks Are Allowed to Intermarry," he declared that "the Mulatto or Hybrid is a degenerate, unnatural offspring, doomed by nature to work out its own destruction" (Nott 255). Robert Knox, a polygenist like Nott, elaborated the laws of human hybridity in his influential book *The Races of Men*, declaring that "the hybrid was a degradation of humanity and was rejected by nature" (Knox 497). Asserting that hybridity was unviable, Knox argued that miscegenated subjects either were infertile or reverted to one of the parental types after a few generations. The polygenist physician John H. Van Evrie asserted in 1864 that the "facts proved, the crossing of distinct races produces a mongrel population, which … has less powers of virility, greater tendency to disease, and hence is shorter lived … that the condition is an abnormalism, and one of unspeakable wrong and suffering" (Evrie 25). If unchecked, Van Evrie warned that, miscegenation would lead to the inevitable downfall of American civilization. The theory of hybrid degeneracy even survived the revolution of evolutionary biology. The opinion that crossed races of men are singularly savage and degraded found support in no less than Darwin himself, who speculated that

---

1　While cultural factors determined its physiological status, the use of hybridity today prompts questions about the ways in which contemporary thinking has broken absolutely with the racialized formulation of the past. For detailed examination of the concept of hybridity, see Robert J. C. Young's *Colonial Desire: Hybridity in Theory, Culture and Race*.

the "degrade state of so many half-castes is in part due to reversion to primitive and savage condition, induced by the act of crossing, even if mainly due to unfavorable moral conditions under which they are really reared" (Darwin 21). Although Darwin explained "half-caste" degradation in terms of both environmental and biological factors, it was the latter notion that found most attraction during his time.

In the essay "*The Freedom's Bureau*," Du Bois has stressed that the problem of the twentieth century is the problem of the color line. Mixed race, for their color of being not fully white, yellow, or black, occupies no place in the racial hierarchy. Not only this, straddling between white and non-white, mixed race people are troublesome for disrupting the notion of a clearly delineated color line. Thus, they constitute a threat to essentialist theories of racial superiority because, as Nancy Bentley writes in relation to mulattoes in antebellum fiction: "the person of mixed black and white parentage stood precisely at the place where nature and culture could come unbound" (Bentley 35). Nancy Bentley's work on the mulatto identifies a cultural concern with how to classify the American subject who is neither black nor white and the underlying cultural anxiety this causes, which, she argues, is evident in the production of terms to classify the miscegenated subject like "octoroon" and "quadroon." Frankenberg further argues that this cultural anxiety is manifested in a discourse against interracial relationships which claims that mixed race children can't fit in. Conceived as a dangerous source of subversion, racial mixing is not only seen as a threatening force for rigid hierachizing and division, but also as an embodiment of American degeneration and moral decay because of the bad side in their blood. It is such cultural anxieties and hybridity degeneracy discourses that resulted in the anti-miscegenation laws, which were active from 1880 in California until they were finally declared unconstitutional in 1967 by the United States Supreme Court.

Nevertheless, mixed race obviously did occur, has existed, and will grow in number in the United States. In fact, about racial hybrid, apart from the notion of polygenist denial of viable human hybridity, there were other social scientists who were largely sympathetic to the social possibilities represented by mixed race, arguing that racial "crossing" would produce a new third race, a new form of humanity hitherto unknown. Cedric Dover's *Half-Caste*, appearing in 1937, envisioned an American mixing of races as the "portent of a new humanity," which freed from irrational forces would be a "major contribution to a productive state of universal brotherhood." Everett Stonequist, in *Marginal Man*, conceived of the hybrid as symptomatic of the "process of acculturation," namely, a product of the economic and cultural imperialism necessary for the growth of civilization. It was not until 1950, with the UNESCO "Statement on Race," that biologists publicly rejected the belief in hybrid degeneration.

However, compared with the more progressive thrust of social science, the literary representations of the racial hybrid seemed not to escape the nineteenth-century paradigm of boundary transgression. In terms of familiar images of half-caste degeneracy and degradation, typical stereotypes that circulated in literature and popular culture are invariably depicted like this, "he is mentally unstable, physically disfigured or degenerate; is sterile, is invested with magical powers; is licentious, corrupt, perverse, an outcast, an exile; is the embodiment of and a challenge to racial designations and the harbinger of a future without them" (Roh-Spaulding, 1996 57). Judith Berzon points out that the question of the "mixed blood" is always a problematic one in American literature. The mixed race figure is "both agent and victim, capable of polluting pure blood and yet demeaned or destroyed by blood distinctions" (Berzon 253).

In American literature, literary representation of mixed race has a long history, from 19th century black (mulatto) writer Williams Wells Brown's mulatrass in *Crotelle*, to Washington Irving's depiction of the half-blood, Pierre Beattie, in *A Tour on the Prairies*, to William Faulkner's tragic mulatto, Joe Christmas, in *Light in August*, to the Eurasian in Aimee Liu's *Face*, to the "breed" Pauline, in Indian American novelist Louise Erdrich's *Tracks*. Irrespective of their ethnic particularities, the literary trope of mixed blood in American literature shares important commonalities that traverse current racial and ethnic formations called African American, Asian American, Mexican American, and Native Indian American literature. All the terms—the octoroon, the "breed," the mulatress, the Eurasian, the Amerasian, the "blood," the hapa, the mestizo/a, the mongrel, the mutt—all bear the metaphorical weight of the culture's binary stratification. Whether the binary figuration is black/white, east/west, north/south, or native/non-native, ultimately, the insufficiency of racial designation to contain or describe biraciality except in terms of degeneration or alienation is what unifies the concept of mixed race. As Carol Roh-Spaulding summarizes in her study of mixed-race literary representations, there are four commonalities.

> First, mixed race is founded in the experience of marginality. The characters of mixed race experience internal racial conflicts between their white and "raced" sides. Second, mixed-race characters are always negatively defined—not "both/and" but "neither/nor." Third, the characters serve a kind of barometric function, revealing the racial tensions embedded in texts.[1] Finally,

---

1 For example, in Mark Twain's *Puddinhead Wilson* (1894), Han Suyin's *A Many Splendored*

> mixed-race protagonists come to a crisis point in the narrative when they are forced to confront in some manner their indeterminate racial status. While this crisis point is not always the denouement, it is still indispensable in order to narrate mixed race. (Roh-Spaulding, 1995 98)

Regarding Eurasian, specific stereotypes of Eurasians have been well-documented in Gina Marchetti's study of East-West interracial romances in film, *Romance and the Yellow Peril* (1993) and Elaine Kim's *Asian American Literature* (1982). Most portrayals are by Anglo American writers, who either romanticize the conflict of blood or invoke it as the explanation for cruel or stoic Oriental behavior or for valiant, superior Anglo behavior (Kim 9). Elaine Kim points out that the characters' white side is usually valorized over the Chinese (or Japanese) side, and the unresolvable dilemma of mixed blood usually ends in death.

III. The Rise of Mixed Race Studies and Critical Responses

In 1995, Maria P. P. Root hailed mixed race as the "new frontier."[1] In the next year, Stanley Crouch proclaimed that "race is over."[2] Since then, others also have rung race's death knell. Holland Cotter in a 2001 piece in the *New York Times* stated that the time for "ethno-racial identity" is past, and that we are now witnessing the coming of "postblack or postethnic art."[3] In other words, racial hybridity heralds a liberating "racelessness" (Naomi Zack)[4], a step "beyond race" (Ellis Cose)[5], the "end of racism"

Thing (1952), and Leslie Silko's *Ceremony* (1977), the mixed-race characters Roxy, Han Suyin, and Tayo serve as sites of racial contestation founded in the binary opposition between the white and the black (non-white).

1 See Maria P. P. Root, *The Multiracial Experience: Racial Borders as the New Frontier* (Thousand Oaks, CA: Sage, 1995).

2 See Stanley Crouch, "Race is Over," *New York Times*, September 26, 1996.

3 See Holland Cotter, "Beyond Multiculturalism, Freedom?" *New York Times*, Arts and Leisure, July 13, 2001.

4 Naomi Zack declares in *Race and Mixed Race*: "An American who identifies herself as mixed black and white race is a new person racially, because old racial categories do not allow her the option of identifying this way. It is such a person's very newness racially that gives her the option of racelessness. To be raceless in contemporary racial and racist society is, in effect, to be anti-race" (164).

5 Ellis Cose, *Color-Blind: Seeing Beyond Race in a Race-Obsessed World* (New York: HarperCollins, 1998).

(Dinesh D'Souza)[1], a gesture "against race" (Paul Gilroy)[2], and a "new racial order" (G. Reginald Daniel).[3] In December 2003, the *New York Times* celebrated "Generation E. A.: Ethnically Ambiguous" hailing racially mixed people as ambassadors to a new world order.[4] Stimulated by this, the subject of mixed people appears frequently in the popular press and in many books that flood the marketplace.[5] In fact, as a result of the 1967 *Loving v. Virginia*, which lifted states' bans on interracial marriage, till the 1990s, interracial marriage rates had increased almost fourfold.[6] Meanwhile, the rate of multiracial births had increased at an even faster rate. Consequently, as the news media declared, there existed a "mixed race baby boom" in the United States.[7] During the 1990s, "The Mixed Race Movement" emerged. The movement aims to interrogate dominant constructs of race and monoracialism, while also reclaiming the histories of mixed race. Therefore, since the 1990s, on behalf of the movement, many mixed organizations, like Eurasian Nation, New Demographics, Mixed Media Watch, mixedfolk.com, and dozens of podcasts, blogs have emerged.[8] Such organizations claim to be representative of and responsible to a large number of people eager and poised to be identified and rallied. Influenced by this, mixed people began to publish their life stories. Paul Spickard even identified a "boom in biracial biography" (Spickard, 2001 76). The monthly magazine *Interrace* features a book list containing

---

1   See Dinesh D'Souza, *The End of Racism: Principles for a Multiracial Society* (New York: Free Press, 1995). D'Souza argues that racism is no longer an important factor in American life, even suggesting a repeal of the Civil Rights Act of 1964.

2   Paul Gilroy, *Against Race: Imaging Political Culture Beyond the Color Line* (Cambridge, MA: Belknap Press of Harvard University Press, 2000).

3   G. Reginald Daniel, *More Than Black? Multiracial Identity and the New Racial Order* (Philadelphia: Temple University Press, 2001).

4   See Ruth La Ferla, "Generation E. A.: Ethnically Ambiguous," *New York Times*, December 28, 2003.

5   For example, Alon Ziv's *Breeding Between the Lines: Why Interracial People Are Healthier and More Attractive* (2006); "Mixed Race, Pretty Face?" *Psychology Today*, December, 2005.

6   See "Marital Status and Living Arrangements" March 1992, *Current Population Reports* (U.S. Department of Commerce, Bureau of the Census, Series P20-468, Washington, D. C., December 1992).

7   See "Interracial Baby Boom Refocuses Racial Identity," *Minority Markets ALERT: Critical Trends Among Non-European Americans* (Brooklyn, N.Y.: EPM Communications, March 1992), 2.

8   See Lisa Nakamura, "Mixedfolks.com: 'Ethnic Ambiguity,' Celebrity Outing, and the Internet," in *Mixed Race Hollywood*, ed. Mary Beltran and Camilla Fojas, 64-83 (New York: New York University Press, 2008). The complete name of the mixedfolks.com website is "MixedFolks. com Representing People" and it has links to "Our People" and the "MF Community."

about 25 titles (fiction and non-fiction) on the subject of mixed race. 2000 U.S. Census for the first time allowed people to check off multiple race boxes on the census, signaling the official end of the one-drop rule. Hybridity and multiracial chic are being packaged as a new trend in the West. Most significantly, President Barack Obama is a case study in the cultural invention of mixed race, for the self-described "mutt."[1] Obama is heralded by mixed race advocacy groups as proof that multiracial people will eventually inherit the earth. UC Berkeley now offers a course called the sociology of mixed race. Particularly, many contemporary discourses of celebratory statements about hybridity focus on mixed race peoples of Asian descent. "College campuses from University of Berkeley to MIT have established student groups for Asians of mixed heritage, while online forums dedicated to Eurasian issues have targeted virtual communities across the globe" (Teng xvi).

The dramatic increase in the public visibility and popularity of mixed race has also drawn academic attention in medicine, philosophy, political science, sociology, psychology, education, and literature among other disciplines. One feature distinguishing the new mixed race studies is that the majority of practitioners are scholars who self-identify as mixed themselves. Due to its association with activism and identity politics, mixed race studies have largely tended to construct racial intermixing as a socially progressive and liberal phenomenon. As in postcolonial theory, hybridity is treated as a disruptive or destabilizing force, with "mixed race" identity promising to break down racial boundaries and bring an end to racism, which is equated with the ideology of racial purity. Maria Root, one of the leading pioneers of the field, has asserted that

> the presence of racially mixed persons defies the social order predicated upon race, blurs racial and ethnic group boundaries, and challenges generally accepted proscriptions and prescriptions regarding intergroup relations. Furthermore, and perhaps most threatening, the existence of racially mixed persons challenges long-held notions about the biological, moral, and social meaning of race. (Root, 1992 3)

Hybridity, then, seemingly holds the promise of moving beyond the old identity politics of white and black, colonizer and colonized toward a boundary-less future where in-betweenness and ambivalence reign supreme. Mixed race studies tend to adopt a celebratory approach, often portraying hybridity as the key to a postracial

---

1   In a response to a reporter asking President-elect Obama at his first news conference on November 7, 2008, what kind of dog the First Family would get, Obama says they could get a dog from the pound that would be a "mutt" like himself. See also "Obama Checks Simply African American," Blackpolitics.com (April 2, 2010).

future.

The earliest mixed race criticism can be traced back to Edward Reuter's *The Mulatto in the United States*(1918). But most mixed race scholarships are developed more recently, such as Joel Williamson's *New People: Miscegenation and Mulattoes in the United States* (1980), F. James Davis' *Who Is Black?: One Nation's Definition* (1991), Paul Spickard's *Mixed Blood: Intermarriage and Ethnic Identity in Twentieth-Century America* (1989), Gloria Anzaldua's *Borderlands/La Frontera: The New Mestiza* (1987), Maria P. P. Root's *Racially Mixed People in America* (1992), Naomi Zack's *Race and Mixed Race* (1993), *American Mixed Race* (1995), and Suki Ali's *Mixed-Race, Post-Race: Gender, New Ethnicities and Cultural Practices* (2003). In particular, Maria Root (1992, 1996) and Naomi Zack (1993, 1995) have been at the forefront of writing about mixedness in the USA. Maria Root's *Racially Mixed People in America* even features a "Bill of Rights for Racially Mixed People," noting twelve "rights" which include the right "not to be responsible for people's discomfort with my physical ambiguity," the right to "identify myself differently than strangers expect me to identify," and the right to "change my identity over my lifetime—more than once" (a list that might be good for everyone).[1]

In literary field, there is a growing body of mixed race literary criticism, especially in the African American and native American literary fields. Because both of the fields are significantly marked by the work of mixed race writers, by work that attempts to represent a kind of mixed race subjectivity, critics in these fields have sometimes grappled with mixed race issues in their analyses. Of course, there have been many studies of mixed race writers which choose to explore the mixed writer's role within a single ethnic literary field rather than within a mixed race tradition. Thus, they are not included in this review. In the 1970s, William J. Scheick published a study of literary representations of mixed race Indians entitled "The Half Blood: A Cultural Symbol in 19th-Century American Fiction. *"* Scheick examines the depictions of half bloods in nineteenth-century popular prose fiction, argues for a set of "unique characteristics" of mixed race Indian subjects in literature, and concludes his study by comparing mulatto and half-blood literary representations. Published in 1978, Judith Berzon's *Neither White Nor Black: The Mulatto Character in American Fiction* was a study of the European-African mulatto in literature. Werner Sollors published a fascinating and very thorough study of African-European interracial literature in 1997:

1　For more, see "A Bill of Rights for Racially Mixed People," in *The Multicultural Experience: Racial Borders as the New Frontier*, ed. Maria P. P. Root (Thousand Oaks, CA: Sage), 1995.

Neither White Nor Black Yet Both: Thematic Explorations of Interracial Literature, in which he explores the origins of interracial themes, images, and texts. Samira Kawash published *Dislocating the Color Line: Identity, Hybridity, and Singularity in African-American Narrative* (1997) as an interrogation of the color line between black and white and an exploration of the geographies of literary productions that negotiate the color line.

Besides monographs, there are several collections of essays focusing on mixed race writers. *As We Are Now: Mixblood Essays on Race and Identity* (1997), edited by William S. Penn, focuses on the perspectives of nonreservation or urban mixed blood Indians. *Cross Addressing: Resistance Literature and Cultural Borders* (1996), edited by John C. Hawley, includes essays on American and international mixed race writing, and focuses "upon those whose 'hybridized' biology or shifting locale forces their ironic confrontation not only with uprootedness but also with rootedness, generally in two cultures" (Hawley 3).

Yet, throughout the above literature review, nearly all research focuses on mixed African Americans or native Americans or Mexican Americans. No matter in which field, book-length studies of Eurasians are very scarce, monographs even more so. Teresa Williams-Leon notes, "in the U.S., discussions of race generally center on matters of black and white; mixed heritage Asian Americans usually figure in conversations about race as an undifferentiated ethnic group or as exotic Eurasians" (Williams-Leon 2). However, in reality, according to Jonathan Brennan, "there is every indication that there will be growing numbers of Amersasians in the United States, for of the two million interracial households with children recorded in the 1980 census, 'the largest proportion live in Asian-White households'" (Brennan 13). According to 2000 U.S. Census, nearly one-third of all interracial marriages in the USA included an Asian-descent spouse. Why, however, is the Eurasian study so scarce?

Factually, the lack of Eurasian studies largely lies in that most scholars tend to follow distinct racial categories while doing research. They also often follow the long-established one-drop rule, examining people of mixed heritage who are part Asian in the light of Asian American history, cultural, literary, and sociological tradition. This is also why, actually, this book of Eurasian literary works is carried out from reading the anthology of Asian American literature. Scholars like Amy Ling, Shirley Geok-lin Lim, and Elaine Kim all classify Eurasian writers as a subcategory of Asian American writers. In part, this is correct. Many Eurasian writers do belong to an Asian American community. Yet in order to really understand these writers and what they create in their works, one must also examine their double or parallel heritage without denying either one. Therefore, in the sense of Eurasian consciousness or sensibility, this book reads Eurasian writers out of Asian American literature. Sui Sin Far, Winnifred Eaton, Diana Chang, and Aimee Liu all have addressed insight into the in-between condition of biraciality. Sui Sin Far/Edith Eaton is usually read as a Chinese American writer for her affinity with Chinese identity, but in fact she worked to undermine the concept of a totalized Chinese self. Winnifred Eaton/ Onoto Watanna and Diana Chang as well as Aimee Liu have sometimes been said to avoid their ethnic identity in an attempt to gain a larger audience, while in reality their works express a Eurasian identity which is distinct from Asian (Chinese) American identity.

Among the important book-length studies of Eurasians, Carol Roh-Spaulding's 1996 dissertation "Blued-Eyed Asians" is the only literary study so far, which examines the literary representation of Eurasians through the concept of Eurasianism, and discussies racial indeterminacy in the works of Eurasian writers. Like Said who studies Orientalism as a means of resistance to the hegemonic Western ideas, Roh-Spaulding coined radical Eurasianism to resist racism. In 2001, Teresa Williams-Leon and Cynthia L. Nakashimi edited *The Sum of Our Parts: Mixed Heritage Asian Americans*. It is the first collection of essays on multiracial and multiethnic Asian Americans by experts in the field. This unique collection of essays focuses on the construction of identity among people of Asian descent who claim multiple heritages. The contributors to this book disrupt the standard discussions by considering people of mixed Asian ethnicities. They also pay particular attention to nonwhite multiracial identities to decenter whiteness and reflect the experience of individuals or communities who are considered a minority within a minority. In 2013, Emma Jinhua Teng published a sociological monograph, *Eurasian: Mixed Identities in the United States, China, and Hong Kong,* 1842-1943. She compares Chinese-Western mixed-race families in the United States, China, and Hong Kong, examining both the range of ideas that shaped the formation of Eurasian identities in these diverse contexts and the claims set forth by individual Eurasians concerning their own identities. Teng argues that Eurasians are not universally marginalized during this era, as is often asserted. Inspired by and largely departing from the above studies, however, this book seeks to explore how Eurasian writers narrate a transhistoric racial similarity or sensibility throughout the twentieth century. By locating the readings of Eurasian writers in such a historical span, this project aims to disclose the viability of racism to which Eurasian writers made differing textual responses on the one hand; on the other hand, to highlight the commonality of Eurasian writers in their demonstration of

Eurasian consciousness as a branch of mixed race literature.

IV. Eurasian Consciousness and Eurasian Identity

With the rise of mixed race studies, mixed race literature acquired much attention. In view of the specialness of mixed race literary works, there formed two kinds of different sounds in literary academia. One sound, represented by Jonathan Brennan and Werner Sollors, calls for and presupposes a separate mixed race tradition in which to place mixed race literature. In *Mixed Race Literature*, Brennan insists that a mixed race writer's work must be considered within every single ethnic literature tradition corresponding to the writer's mix. According to Brennan, Langston Hughes is an "African-French-Cherokee-European American" (Brennan 29), and thus one should see his work as a "hybrid text" that is the sum of all those traditions, as if each were itself singular and internally homogeneous. Brennan defines "mixed race literatures" as "texts written by authors who represent multiple cultural and literary traditions. These authors are, in many cases, culturally mixed race themselves, and in other cases are attempting to represent a mixed race subjectivity in their literary text" (Brennan 6). In addition, Werner Sollors does argue in *Neither Black Nor White Yet Both* that "race mixing" has its own tradition, and an interracial tradition needs to be explored.

The critical and literary scholarships of David Palumbo-Liu, Amritjit Singh, Robert Young, and others suggest that we should better place the mixed race narratives, rather than reinvent a literary history.

> In addressing the issue of critical multiculturalism with regard to the canonization of ethnic literatures, three topics are of utmost importance. First, it is crucial to obtain a sense of the history of forming a "canon" of minority literatures and how the convergence of certain political claims (i.e. race and gender) had to be negotiated. It is also necessary to consider how the texts of a particular "group" may occupy specific institutional positions. Second, turning to specific texts, one needs to critique how ethnic "voices" are constituted within the interstices of dominant aesthetics and ideologies and minority discourses. How are minority discourses generated differently within the dialectic of dominant and ethnic discourses? And how are tribal and ethnic communities "represented" in these discourses? Finally, moving beyond U. S. national borders, how do ethnic texts become canonized and reconfigured as they move across national cultural spaces? And how do race, class, ethnicity, and gender intersect in the aggregation of an ethnic canon? (Palumbo-Liu, 1995 19)

Palumbo-Liu's argument is not to make narratives about mixed race less "special," but to suggest that their specialness might not require separation or independent status. The latter approach allows us to see how mixed race literature should be situated, and how it participates in respective ethnic literary traditions; it also, importantly, invites closer attention to the ways hybridity is narrated already within these traditions and where it can be more fully articulated and elaborated.

In fact, both of the two sounds cumulatively reinforce the idea that mixed race literature is an important field in need of special attention. The lingering cultural nationalist perspective prevents the fullest understanding of Eurasian. Therefore, if establishing a mixed race literary tradition is too radical, what a better place the Eurasian writers should be placed in Asian American literature is my biggest concern. Till now, this is a question without solution.

In this book, in a manner of speaking, Eurasian writers are read both in and out of Asian American literature. They are "in," because till now, the majority of the scholarships regarding the four writers that this project focuses on have been done within Asian American criticism, reading from the Asian American perspective. They are "out," because what the four writers want to express, explicitly and implicitly, is their Eurasian consciousness, which absolutely can not be equated with the sensibility of Asian Americans. Hence, to roughly include Eurasian writers within Asian American literature, to a great extent, is inaccurate. Thus, what is Eurasian consciousness? This question will be answered from the following two aspects, namely, the Eurasian themselves and the Eurasian characters in literary works.

First of all, the authors' Eurasian consciousness is mainly manifested in their Eurasian subjectivity and refusal to be fixed into one singular racial category. In the first chapter of Elaine Kim's study of Asian American literature, she explores the prevailing images of a variety of Asian American groups embedded in American literature by writers from non-Asian American communities such as Sax Rohmer's Fu Manchu. Moreover, Kim notes that stereotypes of Eurasian subjects in much of American literature are often applauded for their attributed "white" characteristics and accused of a racial reversion to purported "Asian" values.

> When a Eurasian girl longs for freedom, she is "white at heart." When a mixed-blood boy is cruel to animals, it is because he has "inherited his callousness from his stoic Eastern blood." A war is waged in the blood of the Eurasian in Achmed Abdullah's short story, "A Simple Act of Piety": "the Chinese blood in her veins, shrewd, patient, scotched the violence of her passion, her American impulse to clamor loudly for right and justice and fairness." The Eurasian character in Irwin's *Seed of the Sun* is tortured by the feeling that "the dragon's tail of the Orient is fastened to the

goat's head of Europe" in his being: "All the time the European in me is striving to butt forward, the dragon's tail is curling around some ancient tradition and pulling me back." (Kim 9)

To put it simply, Kim suggests, these texts are marked by the appearance of the tragic Eurasian, whose identity is always deeply conflicted, most often leading not to a new challenge to racial categories, but to a reinforcement of the legitimacy of existing categories through the death of the Eurasians. Defying these stereotypes, all the four Eurasian writers discussed in this project represent a Eurasian subjectivity through self-representation of Eurasian. According to Robert Solomon, subjectivity is "the condition of being a subject, namely, the quality of possessing perspectives, experiences, feelings, beliefs, desires, and power" (Solomon 900). The four writers strive to embody a Eurasian subjectivity in their texts. Sui Sin Far posits herself as a Eurasian subject who consciously maintains a mixed race identity as a Eurasian subject despite the pressure to choose either a European American or Chinese identity in her autobiographical essay "Leaves from the Mental Portfolio of an Eurasian." Winnifred Eaton defends the "enchanted fox woman of the provinces of Fuki" in her Japanese novel *Tama* and writes about the racial crossing of the Eurasian brother and sister, Hyacinth and Koma, in *Heart of Hyacinth*. The Eurasian protagonists in Diana Chang's *The Frontiers of Love* and Aimee Liu's *Face* tend to function in contradiction to the tragic mixed race characters so common in literary works. Elaine Kim notes that the protagonists "are not particularly restless; they neither wish to be dead nor white… no wars are waged in their veins" (Kim 14). Even when depicting the conflicting perceptions caused by biraciality, the Eurasian writers choose to provide an expression from personal understanding, real and direct.

The other aspect contributed to explain the authors' Eurasian consciousness is their refusal to allow themselves to be corralled into a fixed ethnic category. None of these writers regards "Eurasian" as a subcategory of Asian Americans. Through a variety of authorial practices they seek to articulate a strong Eurasian consciousness which neither capitulates to nor retreats from racial designations. Sui Sin Far clearly adopts the position of a deliberate, conscious mixed race writer, both as a literary strategy and in her decisions regarding her public and private identity. She resists any single ethnic categorization. When championing the cause of Chinese Americans, Sui Sin Far intentionally maintains a distance between herself and Chinese in short stories, in order to deconstruct the single Chinese identity later critics assumed to impose upon her. Meanwhile, in her autobiographical essay "Leaves from the Mental Portfolio of an Eurasian," Sui Sin Far insists on her doubleness, on her identity as an Eurasian when Eurasian was seriously despised by majority whites and minority Chinese.

In response to the limitations imposed on mixed race subjects, and in an attempt to overturn or escape such restrictions, Winnifred Eaton's literary texts are marked by the appearance of tricksters and trickery. She conceals, creates, and revises facts, particularly concerning the origins of her biracial background. When Edith Eaton took the name Sui Sin Far in publishing her literary works, Winnifred used the name Onoto Watanna and published "Japanese" romance novels. However, Onoto Watanna is only one part of her identity. Winnifred creates many identities throughout her writing career by adopting several authorial personas. Her constant shift in personas, in essence, is a strategy to express her Eurasian consciousness. Both Diana Chang and Aimee Liu refuse to settle into ethnic particularity. Among Diana Chang's six novels, only *The Frontiers of Love* is relevant to the ethic subject. All other five novels are less welcomed and criticized by Asian American critics for their preoccupation with white people. Similarly, Aimee Liu offers little cultural information in her earliest autobiography. Instead, she struggles to fulfill the standards of beauty defined by the dominant culture. In order to suggest a new possibility for an ethnic author, Aimee Liu seldom writes about the ethnic subject. As a matter of fact, as Eurasian writers both Diana Chang and Aimee Liu refuse to participate in a fixed identity. What they seek to articulate through their literary practice is a Eurasian consciousness. Shifting, temporary positioning, and endless movement indicate that there is nothing natural about the relationship between racial self-determination and racial designation.

Secondly, all the Eurasian characters in literary texts convey a strong Eurasian consciousness. In the essay "Of Our Spiritual Strivings," Du Bois coined a term "double consciousness" to refer to the psychological challenge of reconciling an African heritage with a European upbringing and education.

> It is a peculiar sensation, this double-consciousness, the sense of always looking at one's self through the eyes of others, measuring one's soul by the tape of a world that looks on in amused contempt and pity. One ever feels his two-ness—an American, a Negro; two souls, two thoughts, two unreconciled strivings; two warring ideals in one dark body, whose dogged strength alone keeps it from being torn asunder. (Du Bois 9)

Like Du Bois, the four authors effectively feature their "tragic" Eurasian characters who embody such double consciousness. Sui Sin Far emphasizes the difficulties she and her siblings had faced, "Leaves" is interspersed by scene after scene in which the Eurasian child is "inspected," "surveyed," and "scanned from head to foot," indicating the biracial subject's differentness, which Sui Sin Far represents as the fundamental condition of Eurasianness—being different from other children, being different from both whites and Chinese, being different from one's own father and mother. Unlike her sister Edith, Winnifred chooses to escape the harsh social and historical conditions for Eurasians by acting as an ethnic exile. Nonetheless, in her autobiography *Me*, Winnifred still expresses her sense of inferiority caused by other people's gaze at her dark Eurasian physical features, as well as her desire to embrace the white world. Like Du Bois who saw racism as the leading factor to African American people's low self-esteem, Winnifred in her Eurasian novels responds more directly to the issues of racial purity and nativism that affected the American encounter with immigrants in the early century. Although Diana Chang and Aimee Liu locate their Eurasian characters in war-time Shanghai and exotic Chinatown respectively, their portrayals of Eurasians' split consciousness are penetrating and profound. Because Eurasians are products of two races and cultures, their struggle for identity is circumscribed by forces quite beyond their control, and each translates a sense of racial displacement into feelings of worthlessness and illegitimacy. In Diana Chang's case, three Eurasian characters' problem of selfhood stems from their racial ambivalence. Their disintegration of self is reflected by Shanghai's dividedness and fragmentation. Living in a schizophrenic existence, the three Eurasian characters yearn for a coherent wholeness through different racial choices. In Aimee Liu's *Face*, the Eurasian character Maibelle entangles with her insider/outsider status to Chinatown. Not only this, her Eurasian identity directly results in a violent racial abuse on her in Chinatown. Maibelle's quest for identity is mapped by her struggle to remember and confront the incident of rape that she has erased from her memory. To sum up, as Robert Park describes in "Human Migration and the Marginal Man," mixed blood is the typical type of the marginal man, who lives between two distinctive groups, never being completely accepted by either. All Eurasian characters under each writer's pen experience such marginality. They are doomed to spiritual instability, intensified self-consciousness, restlessness, and homelessness. Of course, each writer in the texts offers her Eurasian characters ways out of the identity crisis although sometimes the resolution seems utopian and unrealistic. Generally speaking, they suggest a Eurasian identity which is improvisational, open, and fluid.

The rationale for choosing Sui Sin Far/Edith Eaton, Winnifred Eaton, Diana Chang, as well as Aimee Liu as research objects of this book lies in that all the four authors are Eurasian themselves, and are attempting to represent a Eurasian consciousness in their literary texts, on the one hand. They attempt to navigate the color line, overturning and undermining the fixed expectations of Eurasian identity, using self-representation as one way to contest their half-caste racial status. On the other hand, and more importantly, the corpus of texts discussed in this book functions as a record of differing psychological responses to shifting racist environments. As such, they also chart the history of Eurasians who negotiate their identities within constraints of American racial hierarchies that were shaped by white and nonwhite binary configurations throughout the twentieth century. From the turn of the century when Eurasians emerged as new ethnic subjects to the 1990s when Eurasians hold a big share in the U.S. population, Eurasians' feeling of inadequacy and inferiority is still there. Racism is highly durable, so a delineation of Eurasian writers' writing up to the present day continues to demonstrate both the potency of racist phenomena and the psychological effects of racism upon Eurasian subjects.

Chapter One examines the works of the turn-of-the-century Sui Sin Far/Edith Eaton, concentrating on her autobiography and short stories. Because Sui Sin Far is half-Chinese, critics tend to read her works as the author's complete identification with her Chinese heritage—a brave position to take on in a time when the Chinese in America were the targets of extreme racial hostility, especially on the West Coast. However, Sui Sin Far's self definition of her identity is complicated. Being sympathetic to Chinese Americans, she assumes the role of ethnic interpreter, positioning and repositioning herself around Chinese Americans, but decidedly outside Chinese America. In fact, Sui Sin Far never refers to herself as Chinese, only as (Chinese) Eurasian. Through analyzing Sui Sin Far's narration of her Eurasian experience in her autobiographical essay, as well as her changing stances in relation to Chinese in some short stories, this book tries to prove that Sui Sin Far's works can not only be read as championing the cause of the Chinese but as creating subtle disjuncture within and thereby deconstructing a totalized concept of Chinese American identity. Rather than asserting Chinese identity, she grapples with a complex racial sensibility of Eurasians. In terms of Eurasian identity, Sui Sin Far is much ahead of time. She presuposs a "raceless" ideal future for Eurasians, but in contrast to Mestiza writer Gloria Anzaldua, Sui Sin Far stops short of racelessness in one crucial respect. Although she does refuse the racial designations of her time and place, when she imagines a future in which such designations disappear, she falls into a vision of cultural homogeneity rather than a vision of mixed blood as "new" people.

Chapter Two offers a discussion of Winnifred Eaton who made her literary career by masquerading as a Japanese Eurasian, selling romance novels under the pen name Onoto Watanna. In fact, similar to her sister Edith Eaton, Winnifred resists complete absorption into any specific racial category by adopting several authorial personas throughout her writing career. From Onoto Watanna to Winnifred Mooney to Winnifred Babcock Reeve, to Winnifred Eaton Reeve, as well as Winnifred

Babcock Eaton, rather than positioning herself around a single ethnic focus, Winnifred continuously moves between them, thereby rendering the notion of biological racial purity meaningless. Factually, Winnifred Eaton's strategy of continuous claiming and then abandoning is a kind of expression of Eurasian consciousness or sensibility. Her continuous moves exhaust the authenticity and stability of ethnic categories. As such, she is as much as ethnic exile as cosmopolitan. Focusing on the anonymity of her autobiographical novel *Me* and the racial crossing in her Eurasian novel *The Heart of Hyacinth*, this book aims to reveal Winnifred Eaton's narrative strategy in creating Eurasian sensibility, especially racial crossing or passing. By the act of passing, she seeks to evoke a fluid and utopian Eurasian identity which can smoothly navigate the color line, although the social and historical conditions of passing were harsh.

Chapter Three focuses on Diana Chang and Aimee Liu. Although they write in different historical moments and geopolitical climates, their exploration of Eurasian identity have two points in common. On the one hand, both Diana Chang and Aimee Liu have a common feature in their writing career, that is, they both turn to write "white" (non-Asian American theme) novels in their later career. In particular, among Diana Chang's six novels, *The Frontiers of Love* is the only work focusing on ethnic American (Eurasian) experiences. Her other five novels basically are books about white protestant characters. Similarly, Aimee Liu attempts to suggest a new possibility for an ethnic author. Unlike Diana Chang who writes on obvious "white" characters, Liu believes Asian writers must not limit themselves to Asian themes. She seldom writes about the dominant-suppressed narratives to please the dominant culture, and always tries to eliminate chances for exotica from her narratives. Hence, this book regards all their writings on the whole as an articulation of their mixed Eurasian consciousness. On the other hand, both Diana Chang and Aimee Liu locate their Eurasian characters' searching for identity in a special landscape. This chapter employs Gloria Anzaldua's theory of borderlands to analyze Chang's *The Frontiers of Love* and Liu's *Face*, defining Diana Chang's setting Shanghai and Aimee Liu's Chinatown as borderlands, where Eurasian characters physically and emotionally experience the inadequate feeling as Americans and as Chinese—yearning for oneness as well as resistance to the tearing fragmentation. In term of Eurasian identity, both Chang and Liu imply that "constant improvisation" is the most reasonable resolution for identity dilemmas.

In *Questions of Cultural Identity*, Stuart Hall states that "the question, and the theorization of identity is a matter of considerable political significance, and it is only likely to be advanced when both the necessity and the 'impossibility' of identities, and the suturing of the psychic and the discursive in their constitution, are fully and unambiguously acknowledged" (Hall, 1996 1). In this sense, because of its racial ambivalence and "impossibility," Eurasian identity is a worthy question to be explored. While far from complete, it is hoped that this book could make contributions to the ongoing discussion of mixed race literature, and engage other scholars of ethnic American literature to take up the questions posed in these chapters, aware of the values and meanings of multiple authorial practices and literary strategies of mixed race writers.

Chapter One

Edith Eaton: "Planting a Few Eurasian Thoughts in Western Literature"

I have come from a race on my mother's side which is said to be the most stolid and insensible to feeling of all races, yet I look back over the years and see myself so keenly alive to every shade of sorrow and suffering that it is almost a pain to live.
———Sui Sin Far, "Leaves from the Mental Portfolio of an Eurasian"[1]

This chapter will examine the works of the turn-of-the-century short story writer Sui Sin Far/Edith Eaton.[2] Because Sui Sin Far is half-Chinese, critics read her works as the author's entirely embracing of her Chinese heritage—a brave position to take on in a time when the Chinese in America were the targets of extreme racial hostility, especially on the West Coast. However, Sui Sin Far's self-definition of her identity is complicated. Being sympathetic to Chinese Americans, she positions and repositions herself around Chinese American identity, but never "enters" it. In fact, Sui Sin Far never refers to herself as Chinese, only as (Chinese) Eurasian. Through analyzing Edith's narration of her Eurasian experience in the autobiographical essay, as well as her changing stances in relation to Chinese in some short stories, this chapter attempts to prove that Sui Sin Far's works can not only be read as championing the cause of

---

1 The epigraph is taken from Sui Sin Far's autobiographical essay "Leaves from the Mental Portfolio of an Eurasian" published originally in *The Independent*, Jan. 21, 1909, 132. References are hereafter cited in the text as "Leaves." For a new edition of Sui Sin Far's writing, see *Sui Sin Far: Mrs. Spring Fragrance and Other Writings*, eds. Amy Ling and Annette White-Parks (Urbana: University of Illinois Press, 1995). In my discussion all references to the work of Sui Sin Far are to this edition and are given in parentheses with page numbers.

2 Throughout this book, the author's name will be used as Sui Sin Far, Edith Eaton, and Edith Eaton/Sui Sin Far interchangeably, as Amy Ling does in her chapter on the Eaton sisters in *Between Worlds: Women Writers of Chinese Ancestry*. It will reflect this project's argument that Eaton assumed a variety of authorial positions in her works in order to avoid being centered with a single ethnicity. Sui Sin Far/Edith Eaton often signed her articles and stories with both names.

the Chinese but as creating subtle disjuncture within and thereby deconstructing a totalized concept of Chinese American identity.

I. Sui Sin Far/Edith Eaton Criticism and Her Eurasian Subjectivity

Edith Maude Eaton (1865-1914) is widely held to be the first Chinese American writer in North America.[1] But compared with most early Chinese American authors, Sui Sin Far's status is special, because she is Eurasian. As a daughter of an English entrepreneur and a very westernized Chinese woman, Edith Eaton was born in Macclesfield, England in 1865. Her father, Edward Eaton, from a wealthy family married her mother in Shanghai, where he was sent to further the family fortune. Her mother, Grace Trefusius was thought to be from Shanghai, taken to London as a child, and trained to be a missionary teacher in the colonial home.[2] At that time, such marriage between English and Chinese might have required a great deal of courage and encountered huge troubles, because China had not yet recovered from its defeat in the Opium War, and people resented the humiliation that Great Britain had brought to the "Celestial Empire."[3] Besides, England had long deemed China to be a "heathen country" in need of civilizing. It was because of the interracial marriage, which was frowned upon by the Eaton family as well as by the society, the Eaton family soon set off on what would turn out to be a long series of moves between England, the United States, and Canada, ever in search of a place to call home.[4] According to Annette

---

1   Regarding Edith Eaton's birth date, there were two versions. According to Sui Sin Far's *New York Times* obituary, her birth year was 1867, but Amy Ling and Annette White-Parks both argue with evidence that she was born in 1865. In this project, I choose to follow the latter version. See "Edith Eaton Dead: Author of Chinese Stories under the Name of Sui Sin Far," *New York Times*, April 9, 1914, 11; Amy Ling, *Between Worlds: Women Writers of Chinese Ancestry* (New York: Pergamon Press, 1990), 183; Annette White-Parks, *Sui Sin Far/Edith Maude Eaton: A Literary Biography* (Urbana: University of Illinois Press, 1995), 1-8.

2   Mrs. Eaton also used the name Lotus Blossom, which unfortunately signifies the orientalist stereotype of a submissive Asian woman. To avoid that connotation here, I use her other names as Grace Trefusius or Grace Trefusius Eaton. In Annette White-Parks' *Sui Sin Far/Edith Maude Eaton*, Mrs Eaton is shown in a Western dress. See Annette White-Parks, 11.

3   It was not until the turn of the century, especially after the Boxer Rebellion (i.e., after 1900), that the Chinese attitude toward the West began to change. For more, see Xiaohuang Yin, *Chinese American Literature since the 1850s* (Urbana and Chicago: University of Illinois Press, 2000), 87.

4   According to Sui, her father's pursuit of a career as a landscape painter rather than a businessman might also be one of the reasons that caused him to split with his family. S. E. Solberg,

White-Parks, to Sui Sin Far, "the home of her more permanent roots was in eastern Canada—Montreal, where her family had settled in 1873, where she was raised and lived as an adult until age thirty-two, where she returned intermittently between working and publishing in the United States, and where she died and is buried" (White-Parks, 1995 xiv). The family, with a total of fourteen children, was extremely poor. So Edith was sent out to work early, and by eighteen, she had found work as a typesetter, and then began a career as a stenographer and journalist, all the while struggling to publish short fictions.[1]

Yet, in addition to poverty and instability, the unique family background also made Eaton suffer much under the heavy burden of what she called the "cross of the Eurasian." In specific, although she and her siblings were "English breed with English ways and manners of dress," the prejudice against her mother's race also had strong impact on Sui's life. Growing up in a middle-class white neighborhood, she experienced various forms of bigotry against "Orientals" early in childhood.

> When I look back over the years I see myself, a little child of scarcely four years of age, walking in front of my nurse, in a green English lane, and listening to her tell another of her kind that my mother is Chinese. "Oh, lord!" exclaims the informed. She turns me around and scans me curiously from head to foot. Then the two women whisper together...
>
> I am at a children's party...there are quite a number of grown people present. One, a white haired old man, has his attention called to me by the hostess. He adjusts his eyeglasses and surveys me critically. "Ah, indeed!" he exclaims, "Who would have thought it at first glance. Yet now I see the difference between her and other children....Very interesting little creature!" (*MSF* 218)

Such curiosity, no matter how innocent it might have been, surely hurt little Edith's feelings. After their immigration to the United States in 1871, the "covert smiles and sneers" that little Sui encountered soon turned to be outright discrimination toward Chinese or Eurasians with Chinese blood. Therefore, since Edith embarked upon her literary career, she had sought to give expression to her grievances over Eurasians through writing. Beginning with her early article "Half-Chinese Children," Edith made many attempts to plant "a few Eurasian thoughts in Western literature." In this sense, Sui Sin Far was the first writer in North America to depict the ambiguous position of

---

"Sui, the Storyteller," *Turn Shadows into Light: Art and Culture of the Northwest's Early Asian Community*, eds. Mayumi Tsutakawa and Alan Chong Lau (Seattle: Young Pine Press, 1982), 86; Xiaohuang Yin, 87.

1   For more on her life, see Annette White-Parks, *Sui Sin Far/Edith Maude Eaton: A Literary Biography*, 1-8.

the Eurasian. To borrow Amy Ling's words, Sui Sin Far is a "spiritual foremother of a well-known contemporary Eurasian author" (*MSF* 11).

Between 1897 and 1913, Eaton published numerous short stories and articles in newspapers, regional magazines, and national periodicals such as the *Independent*, *Good Housekeeping*, *Century*, the *Westerner*, and *Land of Sunshine* and a book length collection of stories titled Mrs. Spring Fragrance (1912).[1] In her own days, Edith Eaton was read primarily by a white middle-class audience inspired by an Orientalist taste for the exotic. However, after her death in 1914, except several appreciative obituaries, Sui Sin Far was neglected by both readers and critics for more than half a century.[2]

Edith Eaton criticism began to flourish in 1974, when *Aiiieeeee*! recognized Sui Sin Far's role in founding an "authentic" tradition of Chinese American literature in contrast to the "white tradition of Chinese novelty literature" that prevailed in her era.[3] In 1976, S. E. Solberg delivered a paper on the Eaton sisters at an Asian American conference, which he subsequently published in 1981 under the title, "Sui Sin Far/ Edith Eaton: First Chinese-American Fictionist" which observed that Sui Sin Far's fiction sought "not to exploit, but rather to record, explain, and somehow give meaning to the experience of the Chinese in America" (Solberg, 1981 33). This paper presented pioneer work on Sui Sin Far and laid the foundation among contemporary critics for studies that followed. William Wu's 1982 book, *Yellow Peril: Chinese Americans in American Fiction,* 1850-1940, took note of Sui Sin Far's uncollected short story "A Chinese Ishmael" and her only published volume, *Mrs. Spring Fragrance*. Amy Ling's "Edith Eaton: Pioneer Chinamerican Writer and Feminist," published in 1983, noted that "no one before Sui Sin Far has written so sympathetically and extensively about the Chinese in America, and never before from this far inside" (Ling, 1983

---

1 Sui Sin Far provides a more complete list in her acknowledgements at the beginning of *Mrs. Spring Fragrance: the Independent, Out West, Hampton's, the Century, Delineator, Ladies' Home Journal, Designer, New Idea, Short Stories, Traveler, Good Housekeeping, Housekeeper, Gentlewoman, New York Evening Post, Holland's, Little Folks, American Motherhood, New England, Youth's Companion, Montreal Witness, Children's, Overland, Sunset,* and *Westerner.*

2 Annette White-Parks observed that during the sixty-one-year silence of Sui Sin Far criticism, there were two dissertations on Asian American literature with a brief discussion on Sui Sin Far and citations in two Canadian dictionaries. For details, see Annette White-Parks, *Sui Sin Far/Edith Maude Eaton,* 1-2.

3 Although English-born and raised in England and then Montreal, Quebec, Sui Sin Far was included in *Aiiieeeee* and later *The Big Aiiieeeee!* because of her strong identification with her Chinese heritage.

288). From the mid-1980s on, there has been a growth in Sui Sin Far scholarship, with the appearance in 1995 of the two most important works to date: Amy Ling and Annette White-Parks' critical edition of *Mrs. Spring Fragrance and Other Writings* and Annette White-Parks' *Sui Sin Far/Edith Eaton: A Literary Biography*. Recognized as a unique record of early resistance to racist discourses, her work was included in *The Big Aiiieeeee! An Anthology of Chinese American and Japanese American Literature* (1991) and the *Heath Anthology of American Literature* (1995) and is now being widely taught at American universities.[1]

Today, being a literary canon in Asian American literature, Sui Sin Far/Edith Eaton's works frequently appear in various research monographs and articles, examined from different research perspectives. For example, in *Edith and Winnifred Eaton: Chinatown Missions and Japanese Romances* (2002), Dominika Ferens adopted a cross-disciplinary approach that brought current theoretical concerns from anthropology into the reading of the Eaton sisters, viewing Sui Sin Far through the paradigm of ethnography. However, no matter how Sui Sin Far and her works were explored, the assessment of Sui Sin Far/Edith Eaton cannot escape the early mode, which highlighted Edith's commitment to the Chinese communities in North America, reading Edith as a precursor of Chinese American writers who "claimed America" on behalf of the disenfranchised Chinese minority. Patricia Chu, in *Assimilating Asians*, for example, lauded Sui Sin Far's "uncompromising moral character" and asserted that, though she wrote her own versions of "immigrant romance," Sui Sin Far's stories served more political agendas by allowing her to Americanize, and thereby humanize Asian characters in a stringently anti-Chinese turn-of-the-century social climate. By doing so, critics basically held the same idea that Edith Eaton as a writer totally embraced and ennobled her ethnic roots by serving as a champion of the Chinese Americans.

Yet, this idea failed to account for the author's evasiveness or ambiguity in terms of Chinese identity, and for the complexities of her own racial self-definition, even

---

1   Of all these early scholarships on Sui Sin Far, only Dong and Hom were negative in their assessment of Sui Sin Far's work. They hold that Sui Sin Far's late nineteenth-century characters and style cater to the late twentieth-century values of explicit and vociferous rejection of assimilation and stereotyping. But Amy Ling criticizes that their reading of Sui Sin Far's stories is in a literary fashion, missing the irony, the subtle nuances, and the humor and exaggerating the author's faults, is very one-sided and narrow-minded. See Lorraine Dong and Marlon K. Hom, "Defiance of Perpetuation: An Analysis of Characters in *Mrs. Spring Fragrance.*" *Chinese America: History and Perspectives*, 1987 (San Francisco: Chinese Historical Society of America, 1987),154; Amy Ling and Annette White-Parks, 12.

though some critics took notice of Edith Eaton's Eurasian background. For instance, Xiaohuang Yin, in his work *Chinese American Literature since the* 1850s devoted a chapter to Sui Sin Far. At the start of the chapter, Yin pointed out Sui Sin Far's particularity as the first Chinese American writer in North America—she "expressed both her feelings as a Eurasian and her keen desire to explain what kind of people Chinese Americans were" (Yin 85). Yin noticed Edith's Eurasian aspect, but drew little distinction between "Eurasian" and "Chinese American," stating that Sui Sin Far/Edith Eaton "emphatically identified with her Chinese mother's oppressed people, assumes a Chinese identity, despite the mental torment she experienced as the member of a despised race" (86). For Yin, the author's expression of her trouble stems not from her racial mixture, but from her link to the Chinese. However, Edith Eaton repeatedly demonstrates in her works that it is the fact of being Eurasian, or in other words, the in-betweeness of racial status that gives her "the sense of being differentiated from the ordinary" (*MSF* 290).

Symptomatically, Eaton's biographer, Annette White-Parks, mentioned the term Eurasian but failed to connect Eaton's "trickster" strategies to the question of Eurasian difference, although she noted that the author was "ingenuous at trickster stylistics, often masking her personal identity under various guises" (White-Parks, 1995 209). White-Parks regarded Sui Sin Far as a literary spokeswoman for her mother's people who came to identify with the Chinese. It is true that Sui Sin Far did champion the Chinese in America, but it is untrue to parallel her defense for the Chinese with her sense of being Chinese American. In one of the last statements before her death, Eaton again refers to the Chinese as her "mother's people," not as her own, and she dreams of "planting a few Eurasian thoughts in Western literature" by writing a book about "half-Chinese," thereby distinguishing herself from those who are full-Chinese.

Amy Ling, as well, stoped short of the fullest implications provided by Sui Sin Far's treatment of mixed race. Early in 1981, Ling divided "Chinamerican" writers into three categories, and devoted the last category to Eurasians, "whose numbers will undoubtedly increase with the increasing numbers of interracial marriages."[1] Ling did recognize the conflict inherent in being Eurasian. "Coexisting and unresolvable opposites are daily experiences for bicultural people and particularly for Eurasians. Which language, which nationality, which culture will dominate? By which race shall one be known?" (Ling, 1990 112). Amy Ling argued that Sui Sin Far chose to

---

1　"Chinamerican" is the earliest form of the definition of Chinese American. See Amy Ling, "A Perspective on Chinamerican Literature." *MELUS*, Vol. 8, No.2, *Ethnic Literature and Cultural Nationalism* (Summer 1981), 76-81.

champion the cause of the Chinese to assert her Chinese side over her white side. However, Sui Sin Far declares in her autobiographical essay, "I have no nationality, and I am not anxious to claim any" (*MSF* 230).

So far, only two critical essays have been published discussing the biracial Eurasian identity in Sui Sin Far's writings. Carol Roh-Spaulding's "Wavering Images: Mixed-Race Identity in the Stories of Edith Eaton/Sui Sin Far" explored Sui Sin Far's ambivalent assertions of her "mixed-race identity," and revealed "the insufficiency and instability of ethnic categorization," from the perspective of her personal Eurasian (Korean and white) background.[1] It is both an advantage and a disadvantage for Roh-Spaulding to take her own Eurasian background as part of evidence in her discussion, because a Eurasian background could provide her direct feelings as a biracial figure, but the problem is that her radical orientation for building a kind of Eurasianism is prone to make her research less objective and persuasive. The other essay is Vanessa Holford Diana's "Biracial/Bicultural Identity in the Writings of Sui Sin Far," published in 2001. Focusing on the role of genre manipulation in Sui Sin Far's literary and political innovations, the author argued that Sui Sin Far's specific focus on the position of biracial and bicultural individuals was a major strategy in her redefinition of "race" as a category in American thought. This paper concluded that Sui Sin Far "transformed the narrative forms and genres, short fiction and essay, realism and sentimental romance, into tools for artistic creation, subversion and cultural affirmation" (Diana 181).

Sui Sin Far's legacy is manifold. First and foremost, she objectively depicted the Chinese American life in a fair and sympathetic manner, which was an act of supreme courage in the face of rampant anti-Chinese hysteria in North America around the turn of the twentieth century.[2] To borrow Amy Ling's words, she "right/writes wrongs" and "uplifts the downtrodden" (Ling, 1990 40). But the one aspect that most concerns the present investigation is her Eurasian subjectivity which has not been fully appreciated by her critics. While some have understood that her mixed racial sensibility was greatly meaningful to her, they do not recognize the extent to which she resisted any

---

1   For detailed discussion, see Carol Roh-Spaulding, "Wavering Images: Mixed-Race Identity in the Stories of Edith Eaton/Sui Sin Far." *Ethnicity and the American Short Story*. Ed. Julic Brown (New York: Garland Publishing, 1997), 157-160.

2   For a historical account of the anti-Chinese hysteria, see Sucheng Chan, *Asian Americans: An Interpretive History* (Boston: Twayne Publishers, 1991), Chapter 5. For literary representations of the same, see William F. Wu, *The Yellow Peril: Chinese Americans in American Fiction, 1850-1940* (Hamden: Archon Books, 1982). Particularly Chapters Ⅰ, Ⅱ, and Ⅳ.

single ethnic categorization. First of all, some relevant history must be reviewed in order to better understand Edith Eaton's "supreme courage" for objectively portraying the lives, feelings, sentiments of Chinese American in the special era, as well as her acute sense of racial displacement.

II. Anti-miscegenation Discourses and the Eurasian Problem

In the United States, objections to intermarriage were generally framed in terms of the taboo nature of miscegenation, which was cast as a violation of natural or divine laws.[1] The taboo against interracial marriage ran deep in American culture. As Peggy Pascoe has demonstrated in her history of miscegenation law and the making of race in America, the notion that interracial marriage was "unnatural" became so taken for granted in the post-Civil War era that "between the 1860s and the 1960s, majority Americans saw their opposition to interracial marriage as a product of nature rather than a product of politics" (Pascoe 1).

On the West Coast, where Sui Sin Far lived and worked during her mature writing years, much of the well-established and virulent anti-miscegenation sentiment of the time specifically targeted the Chinese, from 1898 to 1912. One of the members of the California legislature wrote in 1878: "were the Chinese to amalgamate at all with our people, it would be the lowest, most vile and degraded of our race, and the result of the amalgamation would be a hybrid of the most despicable, a mongrel of the most detestable that has ever afflicted the earth" (Osumi 6). This legislator's statement proved effective, for that same year a revision of an amendment was made to the California constitution, stating that "the intermarriage of white persons with Chinese, negroes, mulattoes, or persons of mixed blood, descended from a Chinaman or negro from the third generation, inclusive, or their living together as man and wife in this State, is hereby prohibited" (6). The original amendment, directed solely against the intermarriage of negroes and whites, was revised to include the Chinese and those of mixed race, and became effective in April, 1880. It was not until 1967 that anti-miscegenation laws in the United States were ruled unconstitutional. Edith Eaton, who lived in San Francisco for many years, was a product of such kind of marriage.

Regarding Eurasians, two questions are noteworthy. For one thing, they are invisible from history. According to Emma Jinhua Teng, from the very first arrival

---

1　Miscegenation is a term coined by the Irish-born American journalist David Croly and used more commonly in Edith Eaton's time than it is now. See Xiaohuang Yin, 100.

of Chinese sailors on American shores, mixed families formed.[1] For instance, in New York, where Chinese began to arrive decades before the California Gold Rush, many married Irish and other European immigrant women.[2] By 1900, 60 percent of all marriages in New York's Chinatown were between Chinese men and European or Euro-American women.[3] Such partnering was not confined to New York, and mixed families existed across the nation, wherever Chinese settled, from Boston to Chicago, San Francisco, and Los Angeles. Indeed, because of the fact that Chinese female immigration to the United States was tightly restricted between 1875 and 1945, Chinese male immigrants who wished to form American families often had little choice but to look beyond their own ethnic group, especially during the early years. As a result, the first generation of children born into the emergent Chinese immigrant communities was largely mixed.[4]

Yet, these mixed race individuals have often been rendered invisible in the master narratives of history, whether national histories (Chinese, American) or ethnic histories (Chinese American). The reasons for this erasure are multifaceted. "First, Eurasians have always constituted a very small numerical minority…Second, Eurasians disrupt boundaries between white and nonwhite, rendering them problematic figures in accepted paradigms of nationalist and ethnic histories…Finally, the histories of mixed families have been obscured through shame and silencing" (Teng 8). Take Asian American historiography for example. Normative presumptions of monoracial identity have contributed to their invisibility. Such presumptions are evident in the authoritative textbook account of the development of a second generation of Asian Americans. "Though second generation Asian Americans date back to the early

---

1　In the United States, Sino-American mixed families mainly arose from two distinct phenomena: Chinese migration to the United States (predominantly male), and the return migration of American men who married Chinese or Eurasian women in Asia. American men who established interracial families overseas tended not to bring their Asian wives home, although some sent their children back to the United States. Different from Edith Eaton's case, in China Town, most Eurasians were born to Chinese fathers—sailors, laborers, merchants, students, teachers and others. See Emma Jinhua Teng, *Eurasian Mixed Identities in the United States, China, and Hong Kong, 1842-1943* (Berkeley and Los Angeles: University of California Press, 2013), 7.

2　For more, see John Kuo Wei Tchen, *New York Before Chinatown: Orientalism and the Shaping of American Culture,* 1776-1882 (Baltimore: Johns Hopkins University Press, 1999).

3　See Mary Ting Yi Lui, *The Chinatown Trunk Mystery: Murder, Miscegenation, and Other Dangerous Encounters in Turn-of-the-Century New York City* (Princeton, NJ: Princeton University Press, 2005), Chapter 3.

4　See, for example, Lisa See, *On Gold Mountain: The One-Hundred-Year Odyssey of My Chinese-American Family* (New York: Vintage, 1995).

1850s, they composed a very small subpopulation until the 1920s. Children were few in number because very few Asian women came" (Chan 103). The premise of this statement is that Asian American children are produced by Asian fathers and Asian mothers: the "normal" family is single race.

For the other, discourses around Eurasians are nearly negative and sensational. As early as 1858, a satirical cartoon on the cover of *Yankee Notions* magazine portrayed an Irish woman speaking with her Chinese husband and their three children in a mixed-up dialogue interspersed with pidgin—the "result" of immigration. What is implied is the corruption or mongrelization of American culture—a notion that was at once comic and threatening.[1] As the Chinese immigrant population expanded during the next few decades, the anxiety concerning the mixing of races became increasingly pronounced, generating much public discourse on the issue.

Drawing on prevailing fears concerning racial amalgamation, anti-Chinese agitators used the issue to mobilize support for the call to stem Chinese immigration. They linked the fear of economic competition to the notion of sexual threat posed by Chinese men to white women. Chinese cheap labor, the argument went, undermined the white men's ability to support their family, leaving white women and girls no choice but to prostitute themselves, or perhaps to cast their lot with the Chinese. The threat of miscegenation was also a threat to the imagined racial homogeneity of the nation. David Croly, who infamously coined the term "miscegenation" in an inflammatory pamphlet of 1863, warned that "the opening of California to the teeming millions of east Asia" would lead to the amalgamation of Chinese and Japanese into a "composite race" that would one day supplant the Anglo-Saxon majority.[2] Cautioning against racial amalgamation as a source of pollution, chaos, and degradation, anti-Chinese propagandists invoked the threat of miscegenation as a compelling reason to curtail Chinese immigration. William Wu has demonstrated, "a cluster of short stories and novels on this 'Yellow Peril' miscegenation theme were published between the 1880 and the 1910s" (Wu 10). Even scientific authorities like Herbert Spencer expressed approval for Chinese exclusion in light of the question of amalgamation. Spencer saw only two possible outcomes of Chinese immigration to the United

---

1　See "The Result of the Immigration from China," *Yankee Notions*, March 1858, quoted in Emma Teng, 91.

2　David G. Croly, *Miscegenation: The Theory of the Blending of the Race, Applied to the American White Man and Negro* (New York: H. Dexter, Hamilton & Co., 1864), 19. This pamphlet was originally written as a hoax during the election of 1864. See Sidney Kaplan, "The Miscegenation Issue in the Election of 1864." *Journal of Negro History*, 34.3 (July 1949): 274-343.

States— either the Chinese would "remain unmixed" and thereby constitute a separate and slave-like class, "or if they mix they must form a bad hybrid." Either scenario would be damaging for American national development.[1]

In accordance with the rise of anti-Chinese sentiment, Nevada had passed a law prohibiting miscegenation between the whites and Chinese as early as 1861, and by 1910, six other states in the west and south had followed suit.[2] In spite of this harsh anti-miscegenation environment, owing in large part to the strictures on the migration of Chinese women to the Unites States during this era, interracial marriage still remained the predominant marriage pattern for Chinese in New York City until 1925.[3] Therefore, the children of mixed families increasingly drew the attention of journalists and reformers. In 1890, a description of Chinese-Irish intermarriages raised questions of Eurasians. As evidenced by the sight of mixed-race children: "Around the gutters, playing on terms of equality with the other gamins, may be seen a few boys whose features betray their mingled blood." The writer pondered the fact that "it is only about 12 or 15 years since these marriages began, so that the children are all yet young. What kind of people the hybrids will prove to be is yet an unsolved problem."[4] When Harry Wilson reported on the "Children of Chinatown" for the *New York Times* in 1896, he similarly represented mixed children as a "problem." Such children, he wrote, present "a view that is at once bewildering—a problem for which there is no solution...they were the result of marriage between a Chinaman and an American

---

1   Letter of Herbert Spencer to Baron Kaneko Kentaro, August 26, 1892, published by the *London Times*, January 22, 1904. Quoted in Emma Teng, *Eurasian Mixed Identities in the United States, China, and Hong Kong, 1842-1943*, 97.

2   By 1910, anti-miscegenation statutes affecting Chinese had been passed in Arizona, California, Mississippi, Montana, Nevada, Oregon, and Utah. Between 1910 and 1950, Wyoming, South Dakota, Georgia, Idaho, Maryland, Missouri, Nebraska, and Virginia added such statutes. See Pascoe, *What Comes Naturally*, 88.

3   Based on figures from the U.S. Census, Julius Drachsler's study of New York intermarriage found ten cases of registered intermarriages involving Chinese between 1908 and 1912, with the wives virtually evenly distributed among German, British, Canadian, French, Irish, Norwegian, Russian, Scottish, and Spanish ancestry. Julius Drachsler, *Intermarriage in New York City: A Statistical Study of the Amalgamation of European Peoples* (New York: Nabu Press, 1921), 106. According to Shepard Schwartz, between 1908 and 1924 approximately 55 percent of Chinese in New York were in interracial marriages. Shepard Schwartz, "Mate Selection among New York City's Chinese Males, 1931-38," *American Journal of Sociology* 56.6 (May 1951): 562-568. See also Lui, *The Chinatown Trunk Mystery*, 155-157.

4   *Harper's Weekly*, November 22, 1890, quoted in Emma Teng, 97.

woman."[1]

In this context, as a "problem" without solution, Eurasians were despised and feared for blurring the color line. In nativist Americans' eyes, they radically destabilized the racial hierarchies of the era, threatening the social and political orders. Thus, like the better-known figure of the "tragic mulatto/a," the Eurasians were often depicted as tragic Eurasians in literature. "Physically, they were said to be weak, indolent, lacking vitality, short lived, infertile, and susceptible to disease. Mentally and morally they were purposely prone to alcoholism, promiscuity, criminality, hysteria, insanity, and suicide" (Teng 96). Especially in popular Anglo (white) cultural fictions, the Eurasians were often portrayed as out of place, stranded between two states of being. Elaine Kim notes that "the dilemma of the Eurasian in Anglo-American literature is unresolvable. He must either accept life as it is, with its injustices and inequalities, or he must die" (Kim 9).

Usually, Eurasians are portrayed as a "problem," portending racial extinction, the decline of civilization, or social unrest. For example, in Sui Sin Far's contemporary Jack London's short story, "Chun Ah Chun," published in the same year as *Mrs. Spring Fragrance*, the protagonist's Eurasian kids are ungrateful, who take advantage of their father's riches and allow their father to sail back to China with no sense of parental loss. According to Elaine Kim, most portrayals of Eurasians are by Anglo American writers, who "either romanticize the conflict of blood or invoke it as the explanation for cruel or stoic Oriental behavior or for valiant, superior Anglo behavior" (Kim 9). Kim points out that the characters' white side is usually valorized over the Chinese (or Japanese) side, and the unresolvable dilemma of mixed blood usually ends in death.

However, there is a difference between Anglo and Asian American portrayals of the Eurasians' situation. Anglo portrayals, as Kim notes, offer no possibility for coming to terms with one's mixed racial ancestry, "most of the stories about Eurasians end with the death of the protagonist. The only real victory possible…is mistaken identity" (Kim 9). This is in marked contrast to Asian American depictions, where even if the option of choosing to pass for one racial identity solely is available, it is rejected. Sui Sin Far is a good case in point. She did not choose to pass for a white although she looked not particularly Asian. For her, self-representation was possible, although it remained linked to feelings of inferiority. She attempted through her work to give shape and meaning to a mixed racial sensibility by challenging Anglo writers' negative preoccupation with (Chinese) Eurasians, thus manipulating her position for

---

1 *Harper's Weekly*, November 22, 1896, quoted in Emma Teng, 99.

her own gain. Through examining Sui Sin Far's autobiography, "Leaves from the Mental Portfolio of an Eurasian," the next part plans to explain how Sui Sin Far/Edith Eaton uses her personal anecdotes to describe her growing awareness of Eurasian identity and contest her half-caste racial status.

III. A Racial Pioneer: Sui Sin Far/ Edith Eaton and Her Autobiography

In 1895, Edith Eaton wrote a piece on "Half-Chinese Children: Those of American Mothers and Chinese Fathers" for the *Montreal Daily Star*, describing the lives of Eurasian children in the Chinatowns of New York and Boston.[1] Echoing Paul Spickard's contention that the monoracialist impulses of both the Euro-American majority and Asian American minority communities prior to the 1960s left those of mixed race "with no place to be,"[2] the article informed readers that "the white people with whom these children come in contact, that is, the lower-class, jibe and jeer at the poor little things continually, and their pure and unadulterated Chinese cousins look down upon them as being neither one thing nor the other—neither Chinese nor white" (*MSF* 187). But in a departure from the dominant representations of the time, Edith Eaton noted, "the sneers and taunting words which are their birthright... do not prevent these children from developing and becoming as fine a lot as a globe trotter could wish to see" (*MSF* 187-188). For Edith, these early publications represented a start toward realizing her childhood ambition of writing a book about the "half-Chinese," an ambition, she would later explain to *Boston Globe* readers that arose from her "sensitiveness to the remarks, criticisms and observations on the half Chinese which continually assailed her ears."[3]

If the early "half-Chinese children" has been a measured defense of the "new hybrid brood," driven to convey to the world "all that she felt, all that she was,"

---

1   New edition can be found in Amy Ling and Annette White-Parks, ed., *Mrs. Spring Fragrance and Other Writings* (Urbana: University of Illinois Press, 1995), 187-191.

2   In regard to Eurasian's racial category, Paul Spickard, a pioneering historian of Asian Americans and mixed marriages, has argued that prior to the 1960s conventions of hypodescent meant that "as far as whites were concerned, such (Asian-white mixed-race) people were consigned to the Asian group." But psychologically, they are rejected by Chinese as well as the whites. For more, see Paul Spickard, "Who Is an Asian? Who Is a Pacific Islander? Monoracialism, Multiracial People, and Asian American Communities," in *The Sum of Our Parts*. eds. Teresa Williams-Leon and Cynthia L. Nakashima (Philadelphia: Temple University Press, 2001).

3   See Sui Sin Far, "The Half Chinese Writer, Tells of Her Career," *Huston Globe*, May 5, 1912.

Eaton's autobiography goes much further by fully claiming her Eurasian status, speaking not from generalizations and sometimes biased observation but from personal experiences, thus justifying her kind in a world dominated by pathological images of the "half-caste." Amy Ling has stated that Edith Eaton "boldly assumed and asserted her Chinese identity" (Ling, 1990 55). But, in fact, in "Leaves from the Mental Portfolio of an Eurasian," her autobiographical essay, Eaton emphatically demonstrates her "wavering" self-image as neither white nor Chinese and her hope that her resistance to the notion of categorical purity will contribute positively to a mixed-race future.[1] Ranging from Eaton's early childhood in England to her young womanhood and adulthood experiences in the United States, Canada, and Jamaica, "Leaves" takes us to feel her lifelong sense of racial displacement, creating a composite picture of Eurasian experiences.

First of all, to emphasize the difficulties she and her siblings have faced in various English and Anglo-Canadian social settings as Chinese Eurasians, "Leaves" is interspersed by scene after scene in which the Eurasian child is "inspected," "surveyed," and "scanned from head to foot," indicating a biracial subject's differentness, which Edith Eaton represents as the fundamental condition of Eurasianness—being different from other children, being different from both the white and Chinese, being different from one's own father and mother. Sui Sin Far begins the narration of "Leaves" with a scene from early childhood. Recalling herself as a small child of four walking in an English lane, the little "Miss Sui" suddenly overhears her nurse tell another that her mother is Chinese. Then the informed turns her around and scans her curiously from head to foot. Sensing that she must be different from other children, the girl asks her mother about being "Chinese," whereupon her mother slaps her and her nurse brands her a "storyteller." Similarly, Edith Eaton expresses double consciousness through another scene in which the "merry romping child" is suddenly made aware of the veil separating her from the others. In this incident, a small girl (little Sui) plays happily at a party until she is suddenly called to be inspected by a

---

1　It should be noted that Sui Sin Far's autobiography "Leaves from the Mental Portfolio of an Eurasian" and short stories such as "In the Land of the Free," "One White Woman Who Married a Chinese," and "Her Chinese Husband," were first published in *The Independent*, a notable progressive journal that advocated fair treatment to immigrants, and committed to representing diverse ethnic and racial types. Sui Sin Far's writing suited perfectly the agenda of *The Independent*'s chief editor, Hamilton Holt, who undertook to promote a form of short autobiography for he believes such narratives would be of deep human interest and perhaps some sociological importance. See Hamilton Holt, *The Life Stories of Undistinguished Americans, as Told by Themselves* (New York: J. Pott & Company, 1906), vii.

gentleman who is greatly surprised to find the child's Chinese ancestry revealed upon close scrutiny. The man exclaims that "who would have thought it at first glance. Yet now I see the difference between her and other children. What a peculiar coloring! Her mother's eyes and hair and her father's features, I presume. Very interesting little creature!" (*MSF* 126). The child who was passing for the same is discovered to be different from the other children, given away by her "peculiar coloring," which is uniquely mixed.

In many respects, these scenes resemble an even more famous scene from Du Bois's essay on "double-consciousness," published in the *Atlantic* magazine in August 1897.[1] In this essay, Du Bois recalls a childhood experience in which it "dawned upon him with a certain suddenness that he was different from the others...in heart and life and longing, but shut us from their world by a vast veil" (Du Bois 9). Such experiences, one after another, lead him to perceive his double-consciousness as an African American.

> It is a peculiar sensation, this double-consciousness, the sense of always looking at one's self through the eyes of others, measuring one's soul by the tape of a world that looks on in amused contempt and pity. One ever feels his two-ness—an American, a Negro; two souls, two thoughts, two unreconciled strivings; two warring ideals in one dark body, whose dogged strength alone keeps it from being torn asunder. (9)

Like Du Bois, Edith Eaton represents the accumulation of such experiences as formative in her sense of identity as one who is "different," and hence imbued with double-consciousness, always looking at herself through the eyes of others.[2]

As little Sui grows older, double-consciousness is further generated when she and her siblings are publicly labeled as "Chinese," which conflicts with the Eaton family's own sense of their Englishness.[3] In Hudson City of New York, Edith and her

---

1   W. E. B. Du Bois is famous for his description of American black experience as a life behind a "veil" and for his statement that the problem of the twentieth century would be "the problem of the color line." He founded *The Crisis*, the monthly publication of the National Association for the Advanced of Colored People (NAACP) in 1910.

2   "Leaves" bears remarkable similarities to Du Bois' text in terms of narrative structure, wording, and theme, and it is not inconceivable that Eaton would have been influenced by Du Bois' work. Eaton's first book, *Mrs. Spring Fragrance* (1912) was published by the publisher of Du Bois' *The Souls of Black Folk* (1903), A.C. McClurg of Chicago.

3   According to Annette White-Parks, the Eaton family in Montreal "maintained a public image as English Canadian." Growing up with an Anglicized mother and with few opportunities to meet other Chinese until later in her life, Edith and her siblings were raised as British Presbyterians. For more, see Annette White-Parks, *Sui Sin Far/Edith Maude Eaton: A Literary Biography*, 70.

brother Edward Charles are taunted by a group of children chanting "Chinky, Chinky, Chinaman, yellow face, pit-tail, rat-eater" (*MSF* 219). When the family later arrives in Canada, they are surrounded by curious onlookers who peer at them murmuring, "Chinoise, Chinoise" about the girl's mother; and about the brood of children belonging to the "Chinoise" and the white man who are Edith's parents, they murmur, "Les pauvres enfants." Thus, Edith's girlhood lesson is that there is something very wrong about being part-Chinese which makes her complain.

> I have come from a race on my mother's side which is said to be the most stolid and insensible to feeling of all races, yet I look back over the years and see myself so keenly alive to every shade of sorrow and suffering that it is almost a pain to live... I feel like a criminal... Why are we what we are? I and my brothers and sisters. Why did God make us to be hooted and stared at? Papa is English, mama is Chinese. Why couldn't we have been either one thing or the other? Why is my mother's race despised? (*MSF* 221-222)

In this way, being simply taunted as "Chinese" as though its utterance alone is sufficient insult, Edith Eaton is distanced and despised by white children. However, factually, young Edith Eaton has trouble attaching meaning to the word Chinese, because the only Chinese person she has known is her Westernized mother. Edith grew up in a highly Westernized household, and never visited China. When she and Charlie first encounter a group of working-class Chinese in Hudson City, Edith recoils "with a sense of shock," asking her brother, "Are we like that?" (*MSF* 219). Furthermore, Edith notes that when she begins her work in the Chinese community, one drawback is that she is unacquainted with her mother tongue. Chineseness thus first becomes apparent as something external to herself, a word that is whispered, and a "mocking cry." Edith told the *Boston Globe* in 1912 that a turning point came when she accompanied her mother on a visit to a young Chinese woman who had just arrived in Montreal. "From that time," she wrote, "I began to go among my mother's people, and it did me a world of good to discover how akin I was to them" (Teng 180).

Ironically, despite her assertion of Chinese pride and enthusiastic defense of Chinese Americans, Sui Sin Far finds that having a Eurasian background prevented her from being fully accepted by the Chinese. Although she lauds that "how great and glorious and noble are the Chinese people!" (*MSF* 222), Edith finds that the Chinese merchants and people generally are inclined to regard her with suspicion, and the Americanized Chinamen actually laugh in her face when she tells them that she is of their race. Edith Eaton further writes how the Chinese subject her to racial scrutiny. Some Chinese women discover that she has Chinese hair, color of eyes and complexion, but they are very anxious to know whether she would marry a Chinaman, because "full-blooded Chinese people have a prejudice against half white" (*MSF* 223). Although Edith Eaton is ultimately embraced by these women, this experience once again reminds her of her outsider status. Some critics hold that Sui Sin Far describes Chinatown and Chinese people from an insider perspective,[1] but from the above examples, it can be concluded that Sui Sin Far could never acquire an insider position in her writing; at most, she is a "relative" who knows some aspects about Chinese which are rarely known by the people of her age. As the narrator of "Leaves" elsewhere represents herself as an outsider among Chinese, Edith Eaton's relationship to Chinese American communities is ambivalent. Moving across the country, Edith always lives in boarding houses in white neighborhoods and she does not speak Chinese. Her claims to Chineseness are tenuous at best.

Secondly, apart from the scenes of racial scrutiny and taunting, "Leaves" also includes scenes that elucidate the diverse ways in which Eurasians attempt to navigate the color line through strategies of passing. Edith Eaton gives an account of numerous incidents, many of which can be tied back to her own siblings. One sister, May, is believed to be the Eurasian described in "Leaves" in this fashion.[2]

> I meet a half Chinese, half white girl. Her face is plastered with a thick white coat of paint and her eyelids and eyebrows are blackened so that the shape of her eyes and the whole expression of her face is changed. She was born in the East, and at the age of eighteen came West in answer to an advertisement. Living for many years among the working class, she had heard little but abuse of the Chinese. It is not difficult in a land like California, for a half Chinese, half white girl to pass as one of Spanish or Mexican origin. This the poor child does, tho she lives in nervous dread of being discovered. (*MSF* 227)

From the perspective of the biracial subject, Edith Eaton states that it is not passing that is a source of anxiety, but conversely the fear of being discovered that leads the passer to live in "nervous dread." She further tells of other Eurasians who choose to pass as Japanese Eurasians (a clear reference to her sister Winnifred) because Japanese

---

1 For example, William Wu in *Yellow Peril: Chinese Americans in American Fiction,* 1850-1940 acknowledged the insider perspective of Sui Sin Far's sympathetic stories about Chinese Americans; Solberg, Amy Ling and Yin also consider Sui Sin Far as the first to deal with the Chinese North American experience as an insider.

2 According to Amy Ling, this is the hypothesis of L. Charles Laferriere, grandson of Edith and Winnifred's sister Anges. A photograph of May in his possession shows a young woman with heavily darkened eyelids, which would seem to corroborate Laferriere's theory. See Amy Ling, "Creating One's Self: The Eaton Sisters," in *Reading the Literature of Asian America.* eds. Shirley Geok-lin Lim and Amy Ling (Philadelphia: Temple University Press, 1992), 305-318.

are in those years held in higher esteem.[1]

> The Americans, having for many years manifested a much higher regard for the Japanese than for the Chinese, several half Chinese young men and women, thinking to advance themselves, both in social and business sense, pass as Japanese. They continue to be known as Eurasians; but a Japanese Eurasian does not appear in the same light as a Chinese Eurasian. (*MSF* 228)

After this, Edith turns to narrate passing as part of the "troubles and discomforts" thrusted upon Eurasians by a racist society, declaring, "Are not those who compel them to thus cringe more to be blamed than they?" (*MSF* 228). Annette White-Park has demonstrated that "on one level, Sui Sin Far announces to the public her Eurasian identity and protests what people in her position are being put through, on another, she announces to her own family that she will not "cringe" behind an English mask, as do they" (*MSF* 173-174).

Indeed, Edith Eaton herself was sharply critical of the act of passing, and she distanced herself from the phenomenon, which she deemed as a form of racial treachery and opportunism. Despite the differences in her siblings' specific choices— passing as Mexican, as English, as Japanese, Edith was the only one among the fourteen children choosing to be true to her Chinese heritage, to be "the unfortunate Chinese Eurasians!" (*MSF* 228).[2] In "Leaves," a Chinese Eurasian woman—no doubt Edith Eaton herself—breaks off her engagement when her fiancé asks: "Wouldn't it be just a little pleasanter for us if, after we are married, we allowed it to be presumed that you were—er—Japanese?" (*MSF* 229). Although Edith knows passing could make her life easier, she still vows that she will never attempt to pass for white, Mexican, or

---

1 Why the nineteenth-century American public had a more favorable impression of the Japanese than the Chinese is a complicated phenomenon. In addition to economic and political reasons, the fact that Japanese immigrants were relatively more Westernized seems to have been an important element in shaping that viewpoint. For a brief yet explicit summary of the issue, see Harry H. L. Kitano, "The Japanese," in *Harvard Encyclopedia of American Ethnic Groups*. Ed. Stephan Thernstrom (Cambridge: Harvard University Press, 1980), 561-571; Yin, 111.

2 As Winnifred's granddaughter, Diana Birchall, has written, "one by one during the 1890s, they married and became absorbed into the white community." Edward Charles cut off communication with his family after his marriage in 1888 to Isabella Maria Carter. He became a successful businessman and joined several white-only clubs. Grace married Walter Blackburn Harte in 1891 and moved to New York City, then Chicago. In 1912, she was admitted to the Illinois bar. May moved to San Francisco, where she passed for Mexican before eventually marrying a Euro-American man. She hid her Chinese origin even from her own grandchildren. Anges married a French Canadian, while Rose married a Frenchman. Sara moved to Boston and married artist Karl Bosse. Winnifred married Bertrand Babcock and then Frank Reeves. See Diana Birchall, *Onoto Watanna: The Story of Winnifred Eaton* (Chicago: University of Illinois Press, 2001), 19-21.

Japanese Eurasian, declaring, "I will not be that sort of half breed, and prefer to reflect honor upon those who are of mixed Asiatic and European nationality."[1]

Then, the third group of scenes is about Edith Eaton's varying responses to her experience of racial prejudice. In one of the most famous incidents, Edith recounts how she outs herself in a small midwestern town where she works as a stenographer. At a dinner party with her employer, "Mr. K," Edith finds that the conversation turn to a racist discussion of the "Chinaman." Mr. K shakes his rugged head and says that "I cannot reconcile myself to the thought that the Chinese are humans like ourselves. They may have immortal souls, but their faces seem to be so utterly devoid of expression that I cannot help but doubt" (*MSF* 224). Her companions' demeaning remarks about the Chinese make Edith feel very embarrassed. They mock that a Chinaman is "more repulsive than a nigger," who is always giving people "a creepy feeling" (*MSF* 224).[2] Edith Eaton portrays herself facing a difficult choice, in danger of losing her job and possibly worse, saying "a miserable, cowardly feeling keeps me silent. If I declare what I am, every person in the place would hear about it the next day" (*MSF* 224). Having passed as white up to that point, Edith chooses with great effort to courageously tell her employer, "the Chinese people may have no souls, no expression on their faces, be altogether beyond the pale of civilization, but whatever they are, I want you to understand that I am—I am a Chinese" (*MSF* 225). Although her employer immediately apologizes, she leaves town shortly thereafter. This is the only instance throughout her work in which Edith Eaton identifies herself as Chinese. Critics have interpreted such scene as example of Edith Eaton's great moral integrity and her choice to identify with the Chinese, despite their low status.

1   See Sui Sin Far, "The Persecution and Oppression of Me," *The Independent* 71 (August 24, 1911), 425. "The Persecution and Oppression of Me" is Edith Eaton's second lifelet, with condemnation of passing as its main theme, which differed in many respects from "Leaves." For example, whereas the focus of "Leaves" is on the Eurasian's experiences of being racialized as Chinese, as Other, "Persecution" conversely presents a series of scenes in which the narrator is mistaken for white, perceived as "same" rather than "different." It is only when her difference is revealed, Eaton contended, that she was subjected to "persecution and oppression."

2   The people at this luncheon table reflect the society in which they are living. It is the decade of the annexation of Hawaii, when America hovers on the verge of a war with the Philippines, a period during which, Ron Takaki observes, racism and expression and expansionism joined hands and climaxed in the Spanish-American War. Values to humans are not assigned by ethnicity, but by such physical features as eye shape, hair texture and skin color, and a religious background that Christian missionaries labeled as "heathen." For more, see Ronald T. Takaki, *Iron Cages: Race and Culture in 19th Century America* (Seattle: University of Washington P, 1979); White-Parks, "A Reversal of American Concepts of 'Other-ness' in the Fiction of Sui Sin Far," 19.

Patricia Chu argues that "although she says she no longer wishes to die at the stake for the sake of her mother's people, she clearly feels that the only moral choice for herself is to do just that, albeit not literally; to remain there, passing as white, would be to suffer indefinitely from the cowardly, shameful feeling that for her always accompanies silence" (Chu 101). However, this book considers that on the one hand, owing to American society's notion of the one-drop rule, which defines anyone who has one drop of black (non-white) blood is black (non-white), Edith's statement—"I am a Chinese" is an accurate expression. On the other hand, Edith Eaton's decision to declare "I am a Chinese" must be understood primarily as a rhetorical gesture of protest against the ignorant prejudice of the midwesterners who allege to hate the Chinese even as they have never met one, only by identifying herself as such can the party understand her protest. Therefore, in light of Sui Sin Far's self-positioning as one who stands between two communities, this book contends that her practices of self-outing are less an attempt to claim Chinese identity than an anti-racist gesture aimed at critiquing white prejudice—a gesture that fits perfectly with the *Independent*'s liberal agenda and its white, middle-class readers.

Actually, Sui Sin Far's responses to racial prejudice are varying. On the one hand, she counters white prejudice by claiming affinity with her Chinese side. "I'd rather be Chinese than anything else in the world," she screams to her childhood tormenters. She is always ready to do battle, with taunting children or bigoted adults. She fights alongside her siblings, taking part in "many pitched battles" and seldom leaving the house without being "armed for conflict" (*MSF* 220). She even fancies herself as a martyr who will acquire "glory in the idea of dying at the stake" for the "great and glorious and noble" Chinese people. On the other hand, the narrator knows in some other way that she cannot fully identify with the people for whom she defends so passionately. On one occasion, she feels defeated and gets serious illness. Nervous sickness resulting from her sense of racial aberrance leads her to a comparison with Jesus Christ's burden. She states pessimistically that "the cross of the Eurasian bore too heavily upon my childish shoulders" (*MSF* 221). She concludes the "Leaves" with the observation that, although prejudice seems to be diminishing, "My experience as an Eurasian never cease" (*MSF* 230). In short, Edith Eaton's varying responses are related to her own unfixed racial sense of self. Rather than asserting Chinese identity, she grapples with a complex racial sensibility. In Roh-Spaulding's words, "she consciously practiced what can be called a radical ethnic indeterminacy" (Roh-Spaulding, 1996 159).

Taken together, Sui Sin Far's "Leaves" expresses a particular Eurasian subjectivity that is simultaneously critical of both white and Chinese prejudice. Eaton's double-consciousness as a Eurasian is thus forged between the dominant society and the Chinese immigrant community. She defines herself as a Eurasian, because she cannot bear to be mistaken as the persecutor of her mother's people. Sui Sin Far insists on her doubleness, on her identity as a Eurasian, even when she could easily pass for white. Sui Sin Far declares herself to be a racial "pioneer," adding that "a pioneer should glory in suffering" (*MSF* 224). She consciously embraces a racial identity far more difficult than the default position of whiteness that is available to her.

In American racial discourse, Sui Sin Far/Edith Eaton's portrayal of her Eurasian's neither/nor plight is very much like Naomi Zack's analysis of American mixed race: "An American of mixed race is unlikely to fall into any of the traps of racial identity that involve imbuing the self with fixed, thing-like qualities. These traps need external recognition and a shared history, neither of which is available to Americans of mixed race"(163-164). Coincidentally, Sui Sin Far presupposes an ideal future for Eurasians, which probably comes closest to Naomi Zack's term of "racelessness." Zack states that "perhaps it is the very racelessness of being of mixed race in a biracial system that makes the possibility of such an identity valuable. It would have to be an identity that looks to the future rather than to the past, an identity founded on freedom and resistance to oppression rather than immanence and acceptance of tradition" (Zack, 1993 164).

Similarly, Sui Sin Far describes a life she opts for—"so I roam backward and forward across the continent. When I am East, my heart is West. When I am West, my heart is East" (*MSF* 230). However, she stops short of racelessness in one crucial respect. Although the narrator does refuse the racial designations of her time and place, when she imagines a future in which such designations disappear, she falls into a vision of cultural homogeneity rather than a vision of mixed blood as "new" people. In this sense, Mestiza writer Gloria Anzaldua went much further. In her book *Borderlands/La Frontera*, Anzaldua repeats the theme of *mestizaje*, in which the mixing of "bloods" and cultures will create a new consciousness, a "cosmic race." Gloria Anzaldua's "new mestiza" has also provided a framework to deconstruct binary either-or identities and to reconstruct a truly multiethnic self, transforming ambivalence into something positive. This new mestiza is one who "copes by developing a tolerance for contradictions, a tolerance for ambiguity…learns to juggle cultures… operates in a pluralistic mode—nothing is thrust out, the good, the bad, and the ugly, nothing rejected, nothing abandoned" (Xicay-Santos 28-30). Sui Sin Far/ Edith Eaton's narrator muses, "Only when the whole world becomes as one family will human beings be able to see clearly and hear distinctly" (*MSF* 230). This distinction is crucial because the idealized view of difference as insignificant ("we're all the same") never addresses the ways in which constructions of difference underscore an imbalance of power. Still, as a pioneer of mixed race, the Eurasian Sui Sin Far opts for the risks of a provisional identity living out on the symbolic frontier where "individuality is more than nationality." In her final statement, Sui Sin Far leaves us with the image of her own racial body as the locus of opposing forces. "I give my right hand to the Occidentals and my left to the Orientals, hoping that between them they will not utterly destroy the insignificant 'connecting link'" (*MSF* 230).

IV. "Wavering" Identity: Sui Sin Far's Short Stories

In a 1903 letter, Sui Sin Far wrote to the associate editor of *Century Magazine*, Robert Underwood Johnson, "I have read many clever and interesting Chinese stories written by American writers, but they all (the writers) seem to me stand far off from the Chinaman—in most cases treating him as a 'joke'."[1] Contrasted to the dominant turn-of-the-century Anglo writers who depicted the Chinese in the form of Yellow Peril stereotypes as "heathen, unassimilable, hatchet-waving rateaters and pipe-smoking opium addicts" (Kim 13), Sui Sin Far's short stories collected in *Mrs. Spring Fragrance* seek to reject the negative images and describe the Chinese as fully human.[2] When countering the negative stereotypes of Chinese, Sui Sin Far did not limit her portrayals of Chinese to single images. To use her own words, her Chinese characters are "both illuminating and obscuring." In other words, Sui Sin Far's portrayal of Chinese characters is a blending: part exotic, part familiar, sometimes sophisticated, sometimes lovable. As the publisher A. C. McClurg's 1912

1　For example, Frank Norris's "The Third Circle" and Olive Dibert's "The Chinese Lily" illustrate the Yellow Peril attitudes which popular writers of Sui Sin Far's era perpetuated.

2　According to White-parks, Sui Sin Far's language usage reflects the categorizations prevalent during her lifetime. These include: Chinaman, a generic slang term for Chinese in North America at the turn of the century; American, for residents of China, Chinese immigrants to North America, and people born in North America of Chinese ancestry (used interchangeably with "Chinese-Americans"); Eurasians, for people of Chinese and White parentage, the progeny of interracial marriages; and Americanization, for the adaption by Chinese or Chinese Americans of western manners and culture which, if it involves denying Chinese culture, becomes assimilation at its most negative, implying betrayal and loss of roots. See, White-Parks, "A Reversal of American Concepts of 'Other-Ness' in the Fiction of Sui Sin Far," 32.

advertisement for *Mrs. Spring Fragrance* described the book as part "local color," part exotica, featuring "quaint, lovable characters" in "unusual and exquisite stories of our Western Coast" (White-Parks, 1995 45), Sui Sin Far's stories did open an entirely new world of Chinese to many readers in those days. Why does Sui Sin Far create her Chinese or Chinese American characters in such a binary structure when championing the Chinese? In terms of Eurasian identity, what does Sui Sin Far want to express through the ambiguous portrayals? The following section will attempt to answer these questions by a close examination of Sui Sin Far's short pieces.

Although it has been stated that the author's name will be used as Sui Sin Far, Edith Eaton, Sui Sin Far/ Edith Eaton interchangeably in this book, how to understand the author's pen name Sui Sin Far is always an important thing. While contemporary criticism is indecisive over the use of name—Edith Eaton or Sui Sin Far or interchangeably, critics like Elizabeth Ammons insist on using Sui Sin Far because "that is the name she published under and that is how she refers to herself in her autobiographical essay" (Ammons 119). Moreover, Elizabeth Ammons recognizes the blending feature of the name, especially the English part "Sin Far," declaring "while these two words may be camouflaged for western readers to whom the whole name looks convincingly eastern, they can leap out at a person from China, to whom the name does not look very Chinese at all" (119). Indeed, from a Chinese perspective, this book disagrees with critics and readers at home and abroad who translate Sui Sin Far as *shuixianhua* or explain the name as "fragrant water lily" or "narcissus,"[1] for all these explanations fail to account for the pen name's mingling feature which makes readers (both the white and Chinese) feel both familiar and exotic. In fact, as a blending of Chinese sound and western words, the name Sui Sin Far is a very good utterance of Edith Eaton's unique Eurasian sensibility .

Before 1900, Edith Eaton signed her work "Sui Seen Far," an early spelling of Sui Sin Far.[2] Sui is really the name "little Sui's" mother called her as a girl in "Leaves." Roh-Spaulding explains that "sui" is pronounced like the first person singular form of "to be" in French, which was the language Eaton heard as a child during her family's

---

1   Sui Sin Far critics like Amy Ling, Annette White-Parks, Xiaohuang Yin share the same understanding of the name as "Fragrant Water Flower," or "Fragrant Water Lily," or Narcissus although the three kinds of flowers have different implications in Chinese culture. For more, see Amy Ling, *Between Worlds*, 41; Yin, 18.

2   According to Yin, Sui Sin Far signed her name as "Sui Seen Far" especially for work that appeared in *Land of Sunshine*, a popular magazine published in Los Angeles during the 1890s, for example, "The Chinese Woman in America." See Yin, 112.

visit in Quebec (Roh-Spaulding, 1996 111). According to Ammons, in Latin, "sui" means "of herself" (Ammons 120). If "Sui" is really the name given by her mother, it can be inferred that "Sui" is a Chinese element, because Edith Eaton's mother Grace is old enough when she leaves China to accept English Christian education. She already knows Chinese (Cantonese), as Sui Sin Far writes in "Leaves," "though a child when she left her native land, she remembers it well" (*MSF* 222). Along with Grace's pro-Chinese stance, she may give her children a Chinese given name. Whatever it is, Sui is definitely part of her name from her childhood. But "Sin Far" or "Seen Far" must be the author's word game when she invents a pen name. The earlier spelling, Seen Far, suggests "penetrating insight" (Patterson 140). Together with Roh-Spaulding's explanation of "Sui," Sui Seen Far means "I am" the one who has "seen far" into something. Here "something" can be Chinese culture, or more specifically, the situation of the Eurasian. The latter spelling, Sin Far, contains the English word "sin," disclosing the author's awareness that miscegenation indicates transgression of racial boundaries, as she laments in "Sweet Sin," "I am where the sin is!" (223). It is well known that Edith Eaton did not know Chinese, her Anglicized spellings of Chinese sounds were not standardized at the time when she wrote. She chose to spell her name Sin Far which has clear meanings in Western culture, rather than sing or xin or xing and fah or fa. To some extent, it reflects her double consciousness as a Eurasian. "The name demands that we read it, that we see in it simultaneous Chinese and English possibilities" (Ammons 120). The blending of American and Chinese elements as shown in her pseudonym suggests Edith Eaton's intention in creating a special Eurasian awareness, which foils the identification of the authentically Chinese and makes a special effect of the juxtaposition of the exotic and the familiar.

Sui Sin Far is remembered for a conscientious effort to create a more objective image of Chinese Americans. However, similar to her invention of the pseudonym, Sui Sin Far's portrayals of the Chinese also present a picture of mingling of various images. Simply to put it, on the one hand, contrasted to the popular fiction of the period which always presented the Chinese Americans as brutal, deceitful, stupid, superstitious, and mysterious, exhibiting all the worst traits of humanity,[1] Sui Sin Far's portrayal sought to emphasize the humane, civilized nature of their personalities. For her, like immigrants from any other country, the Chinese (Americans) are people of various virtues—they are kind, helpful, patriotic, selfless, and adventurous pioneers who contribute a lot to American development and Chinatown is a harmonious place

---

1 Portrayals of traditional Chinese in "Chinatown fiction" in popular American literature are examined ably and thoroughly in Wu, *The Yellow Peril*, 71-163.

with a democratic spirit. On the other hand, Sui's writing occasionally falls prey to the stereotypes of the day, and repeats the racial pattern established by mainstream writers. Her Chinese characters are sometimes Orientalized, depicted again as opium-addicted "murderous Chinese," or lack of passion and masculinity.

Her last published story, "Chinese Workmen in America"(1913), a plea for the acceptance of working-class Chinese in America, belongs to the former. In the story, Sui Sin Far embraces assimilationist rhetoric, yet it maintains her stance as an informed outsider who is beyond the scope of ethnic classification. Unlike her contemporaries, who were generally "China-oriented" and saw themselves as "cultural ambassadors," she was concerned with the lives of Chinese Americans.[1] Her focus was on "those who come to live in this land."

> In these days one reads and hears much about Chinese diplomats, Chinese persons of high rank, Chinese visitors of prominence, and others, who by reason of wealth and social standing are interesting to the American people. But of those Chinese who come to live in this land, to make their homes in America, if only for a while, we hear practically nothing at all. Yet these Chinese, Chinese-Americans, I call them, are not unworthy of a little notice. (*MSF* 231)[2]

According to Sui Sin Far, these immigrant Chinese work as laborers upon their arrival in the United States, but are hardly known. During their residence in America, they not only maintain a faithful and constant correspondence with their countrymen, but also contribute their hard-earned money to worthy charities. They help building schools and churches; their democracy is "pleasant to witness" for they will listen to laundrymen and lawyers alike; they are "stalwart, self-respecting countrymen from the district around Canton city and province," and most importantly, some of them are "American-born descendants of the pioneer Chinese who came to this coast long before our transcontinental railways were built, and helped the American to mind his ore, build his railways and cause the Pacific coast to blossom as the rose" (*MSF* 232). To complete this happy picture of assimilation, Sui Sin Far predicts that "the next generation will see many Americans whose ancestors were Chinese" (*MSF* 232) —a veiled reference to the mixing of races.

Sui Sin Far acts as a spokeswoman for her literary subjects. Given that her readers are middle-class whites, Sui Sin Far endeavors to create tolerance and awareness about Chinese Americans through her humanizing descriptions. But,

---

1 For example, Yan Phou Lee and his autobiography *When I Was a Boy in China*, published in 1887.

2 Xiaohuang Yin speculates that Sui Sin Far was likely the first writer to use the term Chinese-Americans to refer to Chinese immigrants and their American-born descendents. See Yin, 110.

"the more she praises their virtues, the more clearly she indicates that her laudatory power is authorized by her relatively more secure American status" (Roh-Spaulding, 1996 116). It should be noted that Sui Sin Far employs the pronouns "they," "their," and "them" to maintain a distance between her own identity and that of the Chinese Americans. Moreover, it is worth noting that sometimes Sui Sin Far writes with occasional cultural inaccuracies. "The Americanizing of Pau Tsu" depicts an old-fashioned woman Pau Tsu. As a newly arrived Chinese wife, Pau Tsu considers divorcing her Americanized husband as a means of keeping her Chinese identity. Such behavior would contradict her personality, because divorce was a great humiliation for a traditional Chinese woman. This example evidences that Sui Sin Far is a writer who champions the Chinese woman's individuality and sensibility. Meanwhile, it reveals her outsider status in relation to Chinese tradition or the Chinese American community.

In the distance she maintains between herself and her characters, Sui Sin Far/Edith Eaton creates a space in which she may both commit herself to the Chinese American cause and move out of reach of claiming her own Chinese American ethnicity. Similarly, Sui Sin Far also manipulates such a strategy in her autobiography. She states that when she feels alone in a strange place, "the appearance of even a humble laundryman" gives her "a sense of protection," and makes her feel "quite at home" (*MSF* 227). Evidently, her sense of kinship with laundrymen is exactly because of her distance from them. She just feels great sympathy and kindredness toward them instead of accepting them from her heart. In fact, Sui Sin Far gives her intimate relationship to her audience. No matter what the narrative tone or her Occidental appearance in the photograph is, what Sui Sin Far impresses them is more sameness than differentness for white readers. Therefore, Sui Sin Far/Edith Eaton's success in championing the Chinese American cause is obtained from her stance she maintains between white Caucasian and Chinese American. Nevertheless, it is the only stance the author could maintain if she expects to be taken seriously as a champion of their cause. Facts prove that her manipulation of authorial stance is right in subverting the stereotypes of Chinese and deepening understanding of Chinese Americans.

Sometimes, Sui Sin Far's portrayals of the Chinese fall into another category which fits directly into Chinatown stereotypes with the description of the opium-addicted "murderous Chinese." Edith Eaton's first published work "The Gamblers" (1896) is such a case. The story is similar to many Anglo white authors' depiction of the unscrupulous Chinese gamblers who finally turn to be murderers. Although Edith Eaton never again created such a purely stereotypical portrayal in her later writing career, Eaton's later works on the Chinese are always embedded with stereotypical elements. Her characterization of Chinese men seemingly echoes the stereotyped image in which Chinese men are devoid of passion and masculinity.[1] Under her pen, the lack of passion and masculinity of Chinese men contrasts sharply with the ruddy, stalwart image of white men and the "rough elegance" they possess. In "The Story of One White Woman Who Married a Chinese," to Minnie, her Chinese husband Lui Kanghi is the best man she has met and an ideal husband. This is not because he is attractive as a masculine or romantic figure, but because he is reliable and can provide the security that is vital for her survival in "a world which has been cruel to her" (*MSF* 72). Compared with her ex-husband James, who is "strong, tall and well built" possessing masculinity and physical strength, Lui's appeal lies in his spiritual or moral grandeur—he is not James's equal in terms of physique and sexual prowess.[2]

In addition to the occasional stereotypical characterization, Sui Sin Far occasionally employs an Orientalizing and exoticizing style. She frequently uses the adjective "quaint," writing "he was a quaint, serious little fellow" in "The Wisdom of the New" and "he was a picturesque little fellow with a quaint manner of speech" in "Its Wavering Image." Moreover, Sui Sin Far is prone to use "flowery, honorific language" to attempt to render for an English reader the flavor of translated Chinese such as "Have you eaten your rice?" in "The Chinese in America" as well as the Spring Fragrance's babies who were "transplanted into the spirit land before the completion of even one moon" (*MSF* 12-13). Amy Ling attributes such usages to the fact that Eaton was an outsider to Chinatown and the Chinese community and to her unfamiliarity with the Chinese language. Or she may attempt to fit into the genre of "Chinatown tales" such as Helen Clark's *The Lady of the Lily Feet and Other Tales of Chinatown*. Besides, it

---

1 Critics hold that once stereotypes are established and widely accepted, it is hard for anyone, no matter how broad-minded and strong-willed, to dismiss them completely. In spite of having adopted a new social perspective, Sui Sin Far was not entirely free from the influence of the popular stereotypical belief in her generation. See Solberg, "Sui Sin Far/Edith Eaton," 34; Dong and Hom, "Defiance of Perpetuation," 162-165.

2 According to Yin, this was a prevailing view in the West in Sui Sin Far's time. As Lynn Pan states, those white women in England who chose to marry Chinese during the early twentieth century did so mainly because they thought them more reliable in terms of providing financial support and sharing housework. Pan also reports that "marrying down" was a common phenomenon in cross-race relationships between Chinese men and white women in England. Although Chinese-Caucasian marriages were quite common in Great Britain at the time, in general most white women who married Chinese men were from blue-collar backgrounds. Lynn Pan, *Sons of the Yellow Emperor: A History of the Chinese Diaspora* (New York: Kodansha International, 1994), 91, 272; Yin, 116.

may be speculated that Sui Sin Far was clearly aware of her use of the flowery words. No matter what reason it is, Sui Sin Far did write such "stereotyping" or "exoticizing" plots in her stories, which, to a certain extent, indicate her ambivalent relation to Chinese Americans. By alternating and amalgamating stereotyping images of the Chinese along with full and sympathetic portrayals, Eaton's stories act to unsettle and resist any totalized version of the Chinese Americans. In terms of her ethnicity, Sui Sin Far consciously maintains a distance between her identity and Chinese American identity.

Sui Sin Far's stereotypical characterization can be regarded as a narrative strategy to defend Chinese Americans. In order to make her voice heard, Eaton's solution is to create more types of images which would complicate the popular stereotypes and "Chinatown tales" of her day. When depicting the more negative traditional Chinese, Sui Sin Far tends to portray differently from those of popular American fiction. Rather than being sinister villains incapable of assimilation, they are presented as having human emotions and often being the innocent victims of their environment. In "The Prize of China Baby," the traditional Chinese husband who wants to give his baby daughter away is not a cold-blooded villain or the perpetrator of a female infanticide. What he wants to do is to give the baby to a close friend, a childless doctor who wishes desperately for a child. Pau Lin poisons her son in "The Wisdom of the New" because she, suddenly brought from rural China to an American metropolis, is shocked by the cultural differences she has encountered. Driven mad by the American values her husband tries to impose upon her, she regards death as the only way of saving the baby from an American education that she believes will request her baby to deny his cultural heritage. In short, in both stories, Sui Sin Far attributes the inhuman side of the Chinese to the hostile environment.

This narrative strategy can throw light on the fact that Sui Sin Far/Edith Eaton insists on writing short stories and newspaper articles all through her writing career rather than a novel, "the most preferred category of modern western fiction," since her sister has published many sentimental novels with Japanese settings and earned a lot in wealth and popularity.[1] Regarding this question, many reasons have been summarized. One explanation for Sui Sin Far's concentration on the genre of short fiction was her

---

1   Sui Sin Far's opinion about pretending to be Japanese rather than Chinese may be contained in this strong statement by one of her characters in "A Chinese Ishmael," a story not collected in *Mrs. Spring Fragrance*: "This I do say: I am only a slave, but still a Chinese maiden. He is a man who, wishing to curry favor with the white people, wears American clothes, and when it suits his convenience passes for a Japanese." See *Overland Monthly* 34 (July 1899), 44.

physical limitation and economic necessity. Because she was sickly all her life and because she nearly always had to support herself by means other than writing, Eaton was unable to devote all her time and energy to complete a novel, although she had the ambition to write a novel. "Appetite must be gratified before ambition," she wrote to Charles Lummis in 1897, and four years later, in a fit of despair, wrote that she was "giving up story writing." But her jobs as stenographer and typist barely paid the bills. As late as 1911, she wrote to Lummis that she was still "trying to write a novel." Until Sui Sin Far's death in 1914, there was no novel coming out.[1]

Another explanation centers on Sui Sin Far's incapability of writing a novel represented by S. E. Solberg, who calls Sui Sin Far's stories "Chinatown Tales."

> Sui Sin Far was trapped by experience and inclination into working within a sub-genre of American prose; what, for lack of a better term, we might call Chinatown Tales. Such classification by subject matter (Chinatown, or more broadly, the Chinese in America) breaks down an established literary form, the novel, into sub-genres defined by content, not form or stylistic skill. Eaton, by choosing to identify with and write about the Chinese, found herself alone in an essentially formless field... She did manage to dip into...deeper currents beneath the surface color of Chinatown but no matter what she saw and understood, there was no acceptable form to shape it to. Had she been physically stronger and had a more sophisticated literary apprenticeship, she might have been able to create that new form. As it was, she was defeated... When she turned her hand to fiction the possible was limited by the acceptable.... She never acquired the control of style necessary to deal with her subjects in depth and length. What she wrote were chiefly sketches, vignettes... (Solberg, 1981 33)

Addressing the same issue fifteen years later, Elizabeth Ammons raises the question by pointing out two possibilities. One is that Sui Sin Far was forced to stick to short fiction because of the bigotry in the United States against Chinese at the turn of the century. In Ammons's words, "the reading public could be counted on to digest a story here and there about Chinese Americans but not a long novel."[2] The other possibility lies in that like Sarah Orne Jewett before her and Sherwood Anderson after her, Sui Sin Far manipulated to her advantage the tradition of regional and sketch fiction that she inherited primarily from women to offer not a long narrative about one individual but a multifaceted, collective narrative about a group of people and a network of issues. Annette White-Parks is an important critic who recognizes the connection

---

1   For more, see Annette White-Parks, *Sui Sin Far/Edith Maude Eaton,* 12.

2   According to Ammons, Sui Sin Far was severely limited as an artist by the market or the publisher's concept of it. For more, see Elizabeth Ammons, *Conflicting Stories: American Women Writers at the Turn into the Twentieth Century* (New York: Oxford University Press, 1992), 116-117.

between Sui Sin Far's short story writing and her sense of Eurasian mixedness. She argues that "what we see is Sui Sin Far conceiving 'that new form' in process, molding and shaping it word by word out of the tensions generated by her border position, in joint response to her determination to plant 'a few Eurasian thoughts in Western literature' to meet the demands on her as a writer marginalized by race, gender, class in the imperialistic marketplace of her era" (White-Parks, 1995 3).

Based on the critics' explanations, this book puts forward that on the one hand, Sui Sin Far's short stories result from the then hostile racism against Chinese Americans. In order to champion the Chinese American cause in the harsh racial environment, Sui Sin Far had to find a strategy. In this sense, short story is the best genre for her to convey her enthusiasm for Chinese Americans because short stories appear far more frequently in magazines and newspapers than they would have as novels, giving her many chances to make a voice for Chinese Americans. On the other hand, and more importantly, short stories enable Sui Sin Far to create various and competing depictions of Chinese Americans, some of which are in accordance with and some of which are resistant to the stereotypes current in her day. "Sui Sin Far found in the short story and sketch, and then in the collecting of those forms into *Mrs. Spring Fragrance*, a way of expressing a variety of Chinese American experiences and issues" (Ammons 117). It is difficult to judge what version of Chinese American identity Sui Sin Far means to affirm, or whether she means to affirm one at all. But, this difficulty is exactly the point. "The ambivalent stance of Sui Sin Far's art reflects the ambiguity of her identity" (White-Parks 3).

To sum up, Edith Eaton's stories represent a variety of ethnic stances in relation to Chinese American identity. By blending the "lovable" and the "quaint" characters, the sympathetic and stereotypical narrative styles, as well as creating a distance between her identity and Chinese American identity, Edith not only champions the cause of Chinese Americans by breaking Chinese stereotypes, but also deconstructs the single Chinese identity later critics assumed to impose upon her. To put it simply, Sui Sin Far/Edith Eaton assumes the role of ethnic interpreter, positioning herself as sympathetic to the Chinese Americans, but decidedly outside "Chinese America." It is hard to assert which Chinese American image Edith Eaton wants to affirm. In fact, Edith Eaton's project is neither to ennoble her ethnic roots nor to deepen her identification with the Chinese but to reveal the racial indeterminacy for those who are racially, ethnically, or culturally in-between. "The personal story of what life was like for the Chinese and Eurasians in America at the turn of the century is Sui Sin Far's special contribution to American letters" (Ling, 1990 40).

Sui Sin Far's Eurasian consciousness is not only reflected in her relations to the Chinese part, but also in her attitude toward interracial marriage and Eurasians. In the stories, these "wavering women" struggle between two sides of a conflicted identity, thereby literalizing the inevitable tensions arising from the historical encounter between Chinese emigrants and white Americans on the West Coast in the early part of the century.

Interracial marriage or "miscegenation" has long been a familiar phenomenon in American society. Because Edith Eaton herself was a product of interracial marriage, she was naturally interested in the subject. As discussed in the second part of this chapter, because of miscegenation's taboo nature in America, in the stories written by mainstream American authors of the time, few interracial relationships could end up with good results. "The forbidden love between young people of different races or religions is the American form of Romeo and Juliet, and only occasionally is there a happy ending... death is the only fair fate for these unmarriable victims" (Newman 15-16). In the same tone, Sui Sin Far's description of interracial romance usually ends with death, at least for the non white characters. "The Smuggling of Tie Co" is not an explicit portrayal of an interracial relationship but suggests that issue. It tells of a Chinese woman's unrequited love for a white American. Disguised as a man, Tie Co emigrates from China and works in a laundry in Canada. She then falls in love with Jack Fabian, a contrabander, known as the "boldest in deed, the cleverest in scheming, and the most successful in outwitting Government officers" (*MSF* 104).[1] When the story opens, Jack Fabian is found on his bad luck, he is unemployed and has difficulty in making a living. Tie Co, a frail lad of quick intelligence, becomes strongly attached to Fabian and decides to offer him a job—smuggling her into the United States. On their journey, Tie Co outpours her love to which Fabian makes no reaction, revealing that she is willing to go to New York, so that Fabian could make fifty dollars. Unfortunately, they are discovered by the police after crossing the border. In order to spare Jack Fabian from being caught with evidence, Tie Co jumps from a bridge, committing suicide. The next day's search for body produces "Tie Co's body, and yet not Tie Co...the body of a girl—a woman" (*MSF* 108). Facing this result, Jack shows little emotion, rather than being moved by her love and ultimate sacrifice, he only ponders "over the mystery of Tie Co's life—and death" (*MSF* 109). Jack's failure to recognize Tie Co's affection makes her self-sacrifice valueless and extremely

---

1   Carol Roh-Spaulding argues that, in the story, the white man's name, Jack Fabian is the amalgamation of Jack London's rough, dashing spirit and Fabian Socialism. See Roh-Spaulding, "Blue-Eyed Asians," 136.

foolish. According to Yin, the young woman's name Tie Co implies that she is a tragic figure, because translated literally, "Tie Co" may mean "very bitter" or "sorrowful" in Chinese (114). To some extent, this story fortifies the image of a self-sacrificing Chinese woman. What's more, employing the elements of masquerade, Edith Eaton aims to call into question the notion of "authentic" identity. Eaton creates a disjuncture between appearance and "authentic" identity, where the "authentic" is maintained only at the cost of individual human suffering, and in this case, death. Posing as a boy, Tie Co enjoys a certain degree of mobility and the companionship of Jack Fabian, but ultimately her crossing of nationality, gender, and racial boundaries in her love for a white man reveals that the border is a dangerous place to be.

Other noteworthy stories concerning interracial love include "The Story of One White Woman Who Married a Chinese" and its companion piece, "Her Chinese Husband," which are more complex than "The Smuggling of Tie Co" in many respects.[1] In the stories, Edith Eaton employs first person narration and describes from the perspective of a white woman who contrasts her experiences as the wife of a white American with those as the wife of a Chinese immigrant. Minnie, a "white working-class woman," begins by stating the question assumed to be foremost in the reader's minds: "Why did I marry Lui Kanghi, a Chinese?" Almost half of the story is used to explain her motivation for accepting "the lot of the American wife of a humble Chinamen in America." Unlike some white women who marry "Chinamen" only for money, Minnie expresses her real affection for her Chinese husband. But, she takes care to explain that she chooses Lui Kanghi only after being deserted by her white husband James Carson, "a very bright and well-informed" man who thinks her too ignorant to be his wife. It should be noted that Edith uses such a large space to explain the cause of this interracial marriage, suggesting that the act of miscegenation is highly unusual and difficult to justify except as an acceptance of defeat.[2] When

---

1 Amy Ling once pointed out the subtle internalized racism in the contrast between the straightforward language of "The Story of One White Woman Who Married a Chinese" and "Her Chinese Husband" which both assume a white woman's perspective, and the flowery, honorific language of the stories that attempt to render for an English reader the flavor of translated Chinese. See Amy Ling, *Mrs. Spring Fragrance*, 13.

2 Until *Loving v. Virginia*, 388 U.S. 1 (1967) nullified all laws forbidding interracial marriage, thirty-seven states had anti-miscegenation laws. Originally enacted to prohibit intermarriage between Caucasians and blacks, the laws were later extended to Asians in fifteen states. In California, marriages between whites and "Mongolians" were illegal after 1880. However, most of Sui Sin Far's stories on intermarriage cover the period before the 1880s, when Chinese-Caucasian marriages, although rare, were still possible. After 1880, some interracial couples in California would register their marriages in states that did not have laws against Asian-Caucasian marriage. For more information on interracial marriages between Asians and whites in the earlier years, see Paul R. Spickard, *Mixed Blood: Intermarriage and Ethnic Identity in Twentieth-Century America* (Madison: University of Wisconsin Press, 1989), 25-120; Betty Lee Sung, *Chinese American Intermarriage*

she feels "weary of working, struggling and fighting with the world" (*MSF* 71), and is about to drown herself and her infant child, Minnie is rescued at the last moment by Lui Kanghi, a Chinese businessman who later marries her.[1] Old-fashioned Minnie cannot reach the standards of the "New Woman" her husband admires, so she takes refuge within the Chinese community and Lui Kanghi's household. In sharp contrast to the callous and brutal James, Lui is a good man of tenderness and responsibility, who always treats Minnie with "reverence and respect," and does everything to help her recover from the traumatic experience of her past without causing her to feel indebted to him for his kindness. Lui Kanghi proves that "the virtues do not all belong to whites" (*MSF* 74). As Minnie asserts, their union means "happiness, health, and development" (*MSF* 79).

Nevertheless, no matter how perfect the marriage is, it runs counter to one of the deepest taboos in American society at the time. So, like popular American fiction's depiction of intermarriage, Minnie and Lui's happy marriage ends with the death of Lui. He is shot through the head by some Chinese who are opposed to all progress, and who "hate with a bitter hatred all who would enlighten or be enlightened" (*MSF* 83) This statement reveals that unlike the then-popular American fiction in which Chinese who love Caucasians are usually murdered by white mobs[2], Lui is killed by his own countrymen in this story. Thus the story's conclusion indicates that not only whites as represented by Minnie's ex-husband, but also the Chinese are in part responsible for the taboo against interracial marriage. "In Sui's time the bitterness and frustration felt by traditional Chinese made them sometimes assault their Americanized countrymen—those who had betrayed their ancestors" (Yin 102). The *Daily Alta California* reported in 1870, "It appears that hostile feelings exist on the part of some Celestials…against those…who have become so far Americanized as to have their queues cut off, and wear our dress."[3] According to the same report, in one

---

(New York: Center for Migration Studies, 1990), 1-19.

1   According to Yin, Lui Kanghi's given name, "Kanghi," implies that he is a "cultivated Chinese." He continues to argue that Sui intends to use the "sophisticated" name as a subtle indication to suggest why Lui is more individualistic than his peers and that he is different from tradition-oriented Chinese immigrants, most of whom are peasants from rural regions in South China. See Yin, 114.

2   For example, in Bret Harte's "Wan Lee, the Pagan," a Chinese man who is romantically involved with a white woman is killed by a mob. *The Writings of Bret Harte* (Boston: Houghton Mifflin, 1896), 2: 262-280.

3   *Daily Alta California*, May 12, 1851, 2, cited in Ronald Riddle, *Flying Dragons, Flowing Streams: Music in the Life of San Francisco's Chinese* (Westport: Greenwood Press, 1983), 39.

brutal fight alone, several Americanized Chinese in San Francisco's Chinatown were fatally wounded by their more traditional compatriots.

While the two stories are chiefly about intermarriage, they touch upon another familiar phenomenon of American society—children of mixed blood. In his vision of a mixed race future, Lui Kanghi demonstrates his optimism. At the end of the first story, Minnie feels less able to justify her marriage to a "Chinaman," because she worries about the future of her young son by her Chinese husband. "As he stands between his father and myself, like yet unlike us both, so will he stand in after years between his father's and his mother's people. And if there is no kindliness nor understanding between them, what will my boy's fate be?" (*MSF* 83). The speech apparently reflects one of Sui Sin Far's own concerns over the social dilemma imposed on Eurasians at the time as she did in "Leaves." As Werner Sollors points out, unlike the case of mulattoes, who hailed for many idealists a "New World synthesis," "Eurasian remained a challenge to the melting pot theory until as late as World War Ⅱ" (Sollors, 1989 269). Correspondingly, a Chinese Eurasian recalls: "This is the greatest loneliness—of not being totally accepted by any group, I guess it's like being a stranger at every banquet, but never being the host" (Yung 89). In contrast, Lui Kanghi feels more hopeful and progressive. When an old Jewish mulatto midwife who nurses Minnie declares the baby as a prophet coming into the world, Lui Kanghi adds to this messianic overtone: "What is there to weep about? The child is beautiful! The feeling heart, the understanding mind is his. And we will bring him up to be proud that he is of Chinese blood; he will fear none and after him, the name of half-breed will no longer be one of contempt." (*MSF* 82) This hopeful prediction echoes Sui Sin Far's own prediction in "Leaves," "My experiences as an Eurasian never cease; but people are not now as prejudiced as they have been" (*MSF* 230), and she adds, "I believe that some day a great part of the world will be Eurasian." (*MSF* 224) However, such hope is short-lived in "Her Chinese Husband." The hopeful resolution suggested by the birth of the Eurasian son is undercut when Lui Kanghi is shot through the head by his countrymen. The tragic ending suggests that neither the prejudiced whites nor the traditional Chinese are ready for a racially mixed America, so generally speaking, Eurasian's future is gloomy.

Under Sui Sin Far's pen, most of her Eurasian characters waver between the two conflicting halves, experiencing the mental torment caused by racial ambivalence. "Its Wavering Image," exploring a Chinese Eurasian woman's choice of racial identity, is such a good example. As a daughter of a Chinese man and a white woman, Pan "wavers" between a white and a Chinese sense of self and between the things these sides symbolize—romantic and sexual fulfillment on the one hand, family and community on the other. Like her name, the hybrid man-beast of the forest, Pan is caught between the conflicting forces of nature and culture. Her "wavering" seems so irresolvable and causes her so much anguish that the most meaningful aspect of her racial identity is not her choice of either side but the permanent disequilibrium between them. After her mother's death, Pan has always regarded herself as Chinese and led a tranquil and pleasant life in Chinatown with her father. At this stage, Pan's Chinese identity is partly formed on the basis of the unknown elements of her white side, and partly because of white people's racial scrutiny which makes her feel embarrassed and consciously want to ignore her white blood. As in her depiction of Little Sui's perception in "Leaves," Sui Sin Far also explores how the white gaze is used to construct racial barriers and unequal power relations. "She always turned from whites. With her father's people she was natural and at home; but in the presence of her mother's she felt strange and constrained, shrinking from their curious scrutiny as she would from the sharp edge of a sword" (*MSF* 61). Yet, although the Chinese treat her kindly, she often feels lonely when she realizes that she is not truly one of them.

Pan's tranquility is broken with the arrival of the opportunistic young white journalist, Mark Carson, with whom Pan later falls in love. After his arrival, Pan is forced to deal with the conflict inherent in her racial sense, "the mystery of her nature began to trouble her" (*MSF* 61). Without knowing he is a man who "would sell his soul for a story," Pan feels free to associate with Mark. Pan offers Mark Carson an insider's view of Chinese culture, religion and ritual. She serves as an ambassador, and the Chinese welcome him into private ceremonies and settings.

Compared with Pan's innocence and Chinese friendliness, Mark is depicted as a dastardly villain, who poses a double threat of sexual and cultural violation to Pan. At the beginning of the story, Mark scrutinizes Pan with the tactical eye of a hunter assessing his quarry, a clear implication of Mark treating Pan as a sexualized object. He even assumes Pan's frankness as a sexual freeness.[1] Judith Butler explains that, a mixed-race woman's "vacillation" between racial identities serves as an "erotic lure," because she represents "the specter of a racial ambiguity that must be conquered."[2]

---

1   The turn-of-the-century mainstream media and legal practice usually associate the Chinese women with sexual freeness. Immigrant laws in the late nineteenth century enabled California immigration officers to forbid entry to Chinese women if they were suspected of coming to the US to work as prostitutes. See Chan, 101.

2   For more, see Judith Butler, *Feminists Theorize the Political* (New York: Routledge, 1992), 172.

In this sense, to Mark, Pan represents a sexual object to be conquered. What's more, Pan's racial ambiguity is threatening to Mark because she disturbs the racial categorization on which the stability of his own identity relies. So, like delivering orders, he often urges Pan to leave Chinatown and be a white woman. Moreover, in the act of investigating and exposing the Chinese, Mark enacts Orientalism, which Said describes as something that "not only creates but also maintains… a certain will or intention to understand, in some cases of control, manipulate, even to incorporate, what is a manifestly different (or alternative and novel) world" (Said 12). Factually, Mark's interactions with Pan negotiate an uncomfortable tension between desire and fear of difference. He nearly convinces Pan that she "had lived her life alone" before meeting him (*MSF* 62), which implies that he does not wish to see her as a Chinese woman at all but rather a white woman abandoned among foreigners. In this cultural blindness, Mark dismisses Pan's Chinese family and community as well as her own Chinese identity as non-existent and therefore equal to isolation.

Pan is too young to comprehend that Mark's attraction to her may involve a great deal more than the ordinary romantic relationship. She begins to trust Mark fully. She leads Mark around Chinatown, initiating him into the simple mystery and history of many things. In one scene, after their walks, Pan and Mark climb to a high room open to the stars. At this stage, this once-Chinese girl begins to regard herself as white, experiencing an internal struggle. She feels "at times as if her white self must entirely dominate and trample under foot her Chinese" (*MSF* 62). In a sentimental romance, Pan would eventually marry Mark, choosing the race allied with her sexual maturity and leaving Chinatown and her father behind. But in reality, racial indeterminacy is not so easily resolved. The real internal conflict begins when Mark urges her to leave Chinatown with him, insisting, "You do not belong here… you are white—white" (*MSF* 63). Pan fails to recognize Mark's pride of racial purity and his Orientalist attitude toward Chinese. She even imagines the possibility that Mark will accept her in connection to Chinese culture and the Chinese community. Because Pan refuses, Mark finally demands of her, "Don't you see that you have got to decide what you will be—Chinese or white? You cannot be both"(*MSF* 63). Gina Marchetti explains men's need to force a choice and their conflating of women's racial, sexual and moral identity in *Romance and the Yellow Peril*. As representatives of "taboo sexuality," Marchetti states that Eurasian women pose an implicit threat to "racial boundaries and traditional morality" at the same time that they fascinate white men (Marchetti 71). Pan clearly will not be forced to give up her Chinese identity or community, despite her desire for Mark. Later, Pan's nearly broken heart by Mark's coercion is temporarily calmed by his love song about the wavering image of the moon. It is the love song that helps Mark win back Pan's trust, and then he seizes the opportunity to declare, "Oh, Pan! Pan! Those tears prove that you are white" (*MSF* 64).

In the end, Pan is betrayed by Mark's publication of what she has related to him in trust. Betrayed, she sits once more under the "wavering image" of the moon, this time alone. She swears that she would not be a white woman for all the world. The true "wavering image" here is Pan's own unstable image of herself. Pan's biracial identity positions her on the blurred border between Chinese and White cultures in a segregated America, where there is the chance for love at the cost of the love of her Chinese family and community. She fails to recognize that her split racial identity cannot be resolved through Mark, and for that mistake she becomes his victim. Moreover, Chinatown is depicted as allusively as Pan's wavering mind in this story. It implies that her seemingly happy life is not truly rooted in the Chinese community and that subconsciously she searches for belonging. In the last image of the story, the young Chinese child of a friend comforts Pan. She climbs into her lap, pressing her head against Pan's "sick bosom." The image calls forth both Pan's former uncomplicated Chinese self, and a glimpse into her future as a Chinese mother.

Sui Sin Far's Eurasians find that a wavering identity is too painful to sustain, yet intensifying either side of their identity is not a satisfactory answer. The strong presence of the wavering image throughout Eaton's stories of conflicted identity represents the possibility of a strategically conceived positioning. "My experiences as a Eurasian never cease," she relates, "so I roam backward and forward across the continent. When I am East, my heart is West. When I am West, my heart is East" (*MSF* 230). For Edith there is no happy amalgamation of races and cultures; there is only the continually shifting, wavering frontier between whites sand Asians, Asians and whites, where she positions herself as a "pioneer."

Taken together, the stories collected in *Mrs. Spring Fragrance* negotiate the tensions between competing and contradictory versions of an ethnic category characterized primarily by stereotypes in the minds of many of Eaton's turn-of-the-century readers. This disjuncture between fictional depiction and social description, documentation and stereotype, evokes the same sense of ethnic disequilibrium that lies at the heart of mixed-race experience. In a world that emphasizes nationalism, Sui Sin Far consciously practiced what can be called ethnic indeterminacy. She insists that she has no nationality and is "not anxious to claim any. Individuality is more important than any nationality" (*MSF* 230). Thus Edith Eaton reclaimed the Eurasian's neither/nor condition and transformed it into a claim for individualized prefiguring. Edith

Eaton dreamed of one day getting to China. As she told her readers, "As my life began in my father's country it may end in my mother's" (*MSF* 230). An early death in 1914 prevented her from realizing this hope, as it cut shorter her ambition of writing a book about the half-Chinese. It is fair to say, her assertion of cosmopolitanism and her envisioning of a time when "the whole world becomes one family" (*MSF* 223) reveals that Sui Sin Far is far ahead of her time. Although in reality she never feels at home in different nations, although the time she envisions has not yet come, Sui Sin Far's contribution to "plant a few Eurasian thoughts in Western literature" is important and everlasting.

Chapter Two

Winnifred Eaton: Constructing Fluid Eurasian Identity Through Racial Passing

I myself was dark and foreign looking, but the blond type I adored. In all my most fanciful imaginings and dreams, I had always been golden-haired and blue-eyed.
——Winnifred Eaton, *Me: A Book of Remembrance*[1]

Born in 1875, Montreal, Canada, Winnifred Eaton is Edith Eaton/Sui Sin Far's younger sister, who is the eighth of fourteen children.[2] While Edith Eaton adopted the Chinese pen name Sui Sin Far and championed the Chinese in North America, Winnifred made her literary career by masquerading as a Japanese Eurasian, selling romance novels under the pen name Onoto Watanna. She is a writer of sheer productivity. Between the late 1890s and the late 1920s, she published fifteen novels and hundreds of short stories and magazine articles; as a scenario editor in Hollywood during the 1920s, she also wrote dozens of scenarios and screenplays. But this American novelist of Chinese descent left no trace of herself in her works as a

---

1   The epigraph is taken from Winnifred Eaton's fictional autobiography *Me: A Book of Remembrance*, first anonymously published in 1915. See Winnifred Eaton, *Me: A Book of Remembrance* (Jackson: University of Mississippi Press, 1997), 41. All references about *Me* in this book are to this edition and are given in parentheses with page numbers.

About the author's name, (Lillie) Winnifred Eaton (Babcock) (Reeve), Lillie appears on her birth certificate as her first name with Winnifred as a middle name. However, she apparently never used Lillie. Her grandson, Paul Rooney, who lived with her, was surprised to learn of this first name when Winnifred's birth certificate was retrieved in the spring of 1990. Bertrand Whitcomb Babcock was Winnifred Eaton's first husband, from 1901-1917. The marriage ended in divorce. Her marriage to Francis Fournier Reeve lasted from 1917 until her death in 1954.

2   Winnifred Eaton was born and raised in Canada, but the majority of her works were published while she was living in the United States. In this sense, this book classifies Winnifred Eaton as an Asian American author rather than an Asian Canadian.

Chinese or Chinese American writer. Throughout her thirty-five-year career, Winnifred chose to remain silent about her Chinese ancestry, and her adoption of a Japanesque pseudonym, Onoto Watanna, and her public pose as the descendent of Japanese and English nobility have rendered many scholars disappointed because of her denial of true heritage.[1]

As a matter of fact, similar to her sister Edith Eaton, Winnifred resisted complete absorption into any specific racial category by adopting several literary personas throughout her writing career. She changed her ethnicity like clothes. Rather than positioning herself around a single ethnic focus, Winnifred continually moved between them, thereby rendering the notion of biological racial purity meaningless. Focusing on Winnifred Eaton's anonymity in her autobiographical novel *Me* and racial crossing or passing in *The Heart of Hyacinth*, this chapter argues that Winnifred's articulation of identity as fluid and improvisational can be read as the expression of a distinctly Eurasian sensibility. By the act of passing, she sought to evoke a fluid and utopian Eurasian identity which could smoothly navigate the color line, although the social and historical conditions of passing were harsh.

I. The Ethnic Exile: Winnifred Eaton Criticism and Her Eurasian Sensibility

Known best as Onoto Watanna, Winnifred Eaton[2] was very popular in her day for her romances of Japanese and Eurasian heroines, which even garnered favorable reviews from William Dean Howells among others. William Dean Howells praised *A Japanese Nightingale* in the *North American Review*, "There is a quite indescribable freshness like no other art except in the simplicity which is native to the best art everywhere."[3] But her reputation failed to outlive her. By her death in 1954, few

---

1 For example, Annette White-Parks expressed a strong statement on this issue. See Annette White-Parks, *Sui Sin Far/Edith Eaton*, 33-34.

2 Oddly, Winnifred Eaton is most often referred to by critics as Winnifred Eaton and not as Onoto Watanna, except in the case of Yuko Matsukawa, while Edith is usually called Sui Sin Far. However, librarians have agreed to catalogue Winnifred by her pseudonym, Onoto Watanna, just as her sister is catalogued as Sui Sin Far. This book uses Winnifred Eaton, too.

3 Quoted from Amy Ling, *Between Worlds*, 54. According to Ling, in contrast to Howells' actual words, Winnifred Eaton is quoted as remembering that Howells had called her "a star of the first magnitude in the literary heaven." For more, see Amy Ling, *Between Worlds*, 185; D. Howells, "A Psychological Counter-Current in Recent Fiction," *North American Review* 173 (1901): 881.

people knew who she was, and most of her books were out of print. Since then, for more than twenty years, both Winnifred Eaton and her sister Edith have been unknown to students of literature.

In the early 1980s, S. E. Solberg and Amy Ling brought them to the attention of scholars.[1] However, in the early criticism, critics, on ideological grounds, had tended to praise the "authentic" sister who wrote about her "own" heritage and to look down upon the "phony" sister who hid her Chinese heritage and invented instead a "fake" Japanese heritage that faced less intolerance and racial discrimination in the turn-of-the-century America for commercial success. Solberg contrasted Edith's "integrity" to Winnifred's "willing capitulation to market forces" (Solberg, 1981 27). In contrast to Edith Eaton/Sui Sin Far whose works were valued as Asian American literary canon, Winnifred's fiction attracted little attention, even though copies of her once popular novels are accessible. Amy Ling's groundbreaking work *Between Worlds: Women Writers of Chinese Ancestry* (1990) provided much basic bibliographic and biographic material on the Eaton sisters, but Ling's note that Winnifred's "personal integrity did not measure up to Edith's" (Ling, 1990 49), and her construction of Winnifred as an intriguing but lightweight novelist who failed to rise above the racist discourses of her day resulted in more scholarly interest in Edith rather than Winnifred. Besides, the editors of *The Big Aiiieeeee!* claimed that Edith alone wrote "from reality instead of prejudice" in her era (Chin et al., 1991 iii), neglecting to mention Winnifred. This conscious and complete omission of Winnifred from the pages of *The Big Aiiieeeee!* testifies to the editors' understanding of her place among the "real and fake." Recent critics have followed this "good sister—bad sister" paradigm, producing a significant body of work on Edith and largely ignoring Winnifred.[2] For instance, Xiaohuang Yin's book *Chinese American Literature since the 1850s* (2000) includs detailed analysis of

---

1   Solberg and Amy Ling were the first scholars to recover the works of the Eaton sisters. See S. E. Solberg, "The Eaton Sisters: Sui Sin Far and Onoto Watanna" (Paper presented at the Pacific Northwest Asian American Writer's Conference, Seattle, Washington, 16 April, 1976) and "Sui Sin Far/Edith Eaton: First Chinese-American Fictionist," 27-39; Amy Ling, "Winnifred Eaton: Ethnic Chameleon and Popular Success," 5-15; "Revelation and Mask: Autobiographies of the Eaton Sisters," 49.

2   The lack of scholarly interest in Winnifred is reflected in her absence from literature anthologies that include the work of Edith. Aside from *The Big Aiiieeeee!*, Edith's work also appears in the *Growing Up Asian American* (1993) and the most recent edition of *The Heath Anthology of American Literature*. Winnifred, however, has received only glancing attention from anthologists. For example, one recent anthology that includes her work is Blackwell Publishing's *Nineteenth Century Women Writers: An Anthology*, by Karen Kilcup (1997).

Edith Eaton's writings but makes a cursory mention of Winnifred, merely noting she is a "best-selling writer" who "traded her birthright for recognition and popularity" (Yin 89).

In addition to her denial of true heritage, there is another reason for the lack of scholarship on Winnifred's novels, that is, romance. In her introduction to a 1999 edition of *Miss Nume of Japan*, Eve Oishi explained that "the lack of scholarship existing on Watanna's novel is a problem of genre" (Oishi xix). Winnifred chose to write romantic fiction, a mode viewed as unrelated to conflicts with ethnic studies projects of combating cultural hegemony. That is why scholars like Patricia Chu lauded Sui Sin Far for writing her own version of "immigrant romance" in a hostile social climate, without discussing Winnifred and her romance writing.

With the growing interest in literary "tricksterism," the performativity of race and gender, and Mikhail Bakhtin's theories of "heteroglossia" and the "carnivalesque" in popular culture, a door has been opened for the recovery of Winnifred's works. In a reversal of earlier trends, some criticism sprang from these theoretical breakthroughs. Lisa Botshon's analysis of Winnifred's autobiographical novel *Me: A Book of Remembrance* used Edith as a negative foil for the more adventurous Winnifred, who, according to Botshon, refused to be tied down by essentialist notions of race. Currently, the discourse of fluid cultural identity and heterogeneity has generated some bold interpretations of Winnifred's works. Hence, Winnifred is enjoying a sort of critical renaissance: her novels are being reprinted, and scholars are publishing articles and writing dissertations about her works.[1] Yuko Matsukawa's 1994 essay "Cross-Dressing and Cross-Naming: Decoding Onoto Watanna" marked a change in the scholarly attitudes toward Winnifred from a guarded curiosity to an almost unqualified enthusiasm for her subversive strategies. Noreen Grover Lape set out to recuperate Winnifred from the status of Edith's errant younger sister by pointing to Winnifred's successful representations of the "fluidity of cultural identity" (Lape 252). For Carol Roh-Spaulding, Winnifred was an inspiring example of radical racial indeterminacy and a creator of characters who eluded all efforts at racial

---

1   So far, many of Winnifred's novels have been reissued. In 1997, Linda Trinh Moser edited a reprint of Winnifred's *Me*, offering a sensitive analysis in the afterword. Besides *Miss Nume of Japan* (1899), introduced by Eve Oishi, was reprinted in 1999. Diana Birchall, Winnifred Eaton's granddaughter has published an eminently readable biography, and Dominika Ferens' book is the first book-length work on both sisters without valuing one over the other. Noreen Groover Lape, Samina Najmi, and Carol Vivian Spaulding, in their dissertations, devoted a chapter to Winnifred and some also to Edith. These and other critical works are listed in the Works Cited.

categorization. Likewise, introducing her discussion of Wininfred's *Heart of Hyacinth*, Samina Najmi suggested that "Onoto Watanna is far ahead of her time in breaking free of the notion of biological race to show how a fluid identity can empower women" (Najmi 129). Pat Shea credited Winnifred for having developed successful strategies of self-empowerment and discussing such taboo subjects as miscegenation in ways acceptable to a broad reading public. Till now, Jean Lee Cole is the only critic who deftly reconstructed Winnifred's position in the contemporary publishing marketplace and in the film industry, concerning the material and discursive conditions in which her fiction was produced.

This book of Winnifred, in terms of her biracial subjectivity, departs from the "good sister-bad sister" paradigm. Winnifred is treated as strategically as Edith Eaton in deconstructing a fixed ethnicity. Indeed, for critics of Asian American literature, Winnifred Eaton is something of a sticky wicket. Half-English, half-Chinese, Canadian-raised Winnifred is best remembered as the "Japanese" author of romance novels, Onoto Watanna. Certainly, no evidence suggests Winnifred identified with her mother's people. She refused to assert the Chinese identity. At least, she simply did not regard herself as Chinese in her professional life. Therefore, critical claiming of Winnifred Eaton as a Chinese American is unreasonable.

In fact, Winnifred's works are extensive and varied. Onoto Watanna is only one of her several personas in authorial positions. For her first seven novels, she assumed the Japanese persona, set her books in Japan, and romantically entangled Japanese or Eurasian women with English or American men.[1] But, in 1907, tired of Japanese themes, she took up an Irish-American persona, writing *The Diary of Delia, Being a Veracious Account of the Kitchen with Some Side-Lights on the Parlour*, the diary of an Irish immigrant cook.[2] In *The Diary of Delia*, in order to underline Delia's Irishness, Winnifred even wrote in an Irish accent, which, according to Amy Ling, is superior to her manipulation of Japanese English in her novels.[3] She then produced

---

1   The seven novels are *Miss Nume of Japan, A Japanese Nightingale, The Wooing of Wistaria, The Heart of Hyacinth, The Daughters of Nijo, The Love of Azalea, A Japanese Blossom*.

2   Originally, Winnifred submitted the novel to the *Saturday Evening Post* under the name Winnifred Mooney. But the *Post* accepted it promptly and published under her better known name Onoto Watanna.

3   For example, Winnifred writes, "Indade, ses I. Then I'll set here till the 24th, but civil a bit of work will I be doing" and "It's an onest gurl I am…and its ashamed I'd be to mix meseilf in any such mess at that." For more examples, see Onoto Watanna, *The Diary of Delia, Being a Veracious Account of the Kitchen with Some Side-Lights on the Parlour* (New York: Doubleday, Page & Co., 1907), 6-7, 10.

two of her better Japanese romances *Tama* (1910) and *The Honorable Miss Moonlight* (1912) followed by a delightful autobiography *Me* (1915) published anonymously and *Marion* (1916), the story of an artist's model based on her sister Sara's life. *Sunny San* (1922) was her last Japanese novel and a departure from the others by being set in the United States. With her last two novels, *Cattles* and *His Royal Nibs*, Winnifred Eaton abandoned her Japanese pseudonym and set the novels in the Bow valley of the Canadian province of Alberta, where she and her second husband, Francis Fournier Reeve, had a cattle ranch.

In short, Winnifred Eaton had created various ethnic identities and authorial personas throughout her career, from the role of Japanese noblewoman, to working-class Irish American, and to Albert a rancher's wife. Rather than trade on what Werner Sollors has termed "biological insiderism" of her Chinese background, Winnifred, on the one hand, dissimulated her ancestry, playing the game according to the rules of the literary marketplace. By appealing to the seemingly more benevolent stereotypes of the Japanese as exotic yet civilized, she disassociated herself from stereotypes of the Chinese as debased and inassimilable. On the other hand, she refuses to limit her auothorial persona merely to a fixed one. She moved between all personas she can manipulate, and "was never tied down by essentialist notions of race" (Botshon 55). At her most admiring assessment, Amy Ling describes Winnifred Eaton as an "ethnic chameleon," attests to her "ingenuity, her daring and cleverness" in taking on various ethnic personas, and lauds her "universal appeal" and her phenomenal literary success as the result of her "understanding of the human condition" (Ling, 1984 13). This book argues, however, Winnifred's strategy of continuous claiming and then abandoning is a kind of expression of Eurasian sensibility. Her continuous moves exhaust the authenticity and stability of ethnic categories. In this sense, it is appropriate to define her as an ethnic exile.

Undoubtedly, her Japanese persona was the predominant one in the life and writing career of Winnifred Eaton. Regarding why Winnifred built her career on her Japanese persona, Amy Ling's speculation is worth consulting.

> We can imagine the young Winnifred, setting out from the family nest having followed Edith's development from typist/secretary to journalist/story writer, thinking to herself: First of all, Edith is already going the Chinese route and I don't want merely to hang onto her skirts. Second, the Japanese are much more highly regarded in this society than the Chinese. Third, most people can't tell the two nationalities apart. Therefore, I'll give myself a Japanese identity, research whatever basic information I need, rely on my imagination for the rest, and no one will know the

difference. And she was right. (Ling, 1990 63)[1]

Through writing, Winnifred persuaded her audience that she was from a land across the waters. She even fabricated falsifying documents relating to her personal and family history, claiming Nagasaki as her birthplace and a Japanese noblewoman for her mother.[2] Especially, in the frontispiece of her third novel, *The Wooing of Wistaria*, Winnifred had herself photographed in a kimono with hair piled in Japanese fashion, standing before a screen painted with wisteria and iris. As it turns out, Winnifred had succeeded remarkably in assuming an ethnic persona that has no relation to her true biological or cultural background.[3] Amy Ling made a most generous assessment, "We have in Winnifred Eaton not a challenger or protestor, not a word-warrior, but a woman with her finger squarely on the pulse of her time" (55).

However, what is the pulse of her time? According to Ling, the pulse should be American public's positive perceptions of Japanese. But this explanation is just one side of a coin. In the 1870s and 1880s, Japan was still an insignificant player in the international arena. Its name connoted little of the glamour that it would acquire in the subsequent years. However, in the year preceding Winnifred's arrival in the United States, the Sino-Japanese War, which had long been making headlines in the Western press, ended with Japan's victory and unofficial annexation of Korea. China's defeat and the deprecation of Chinese things, then, were directly correlated in the North American media with the valorization of Japan and Japonica. According to the art historians Julia Meech and Gabriel Weisberg, sparked by the Japanese exhibits at the Philadelphia Centennial Exhibition, Japonisme (craze for all Japanese things) reached its high point in America in the 1890s with the installation of the popular Japanese pavilion at the World Exposition in Chicago.[4] European and American art dealers

---

1   This inference was testified in a late interview in which Eaton explained that she had chosen to write about the Japanese because her sister, Sui Sin Far, had already claimed the Chinese as the subject of her own writing. See James Doyle, "Sui Sin Far and Onoto Watanna: Two Early Chinese-Canadian Authors." *Canadian Literature* 140 (Spring 1994), 54.

2   According to Ling, Winnifred's grandson, Paul Rooney, considers that the invention of Nagasaki as Winnifred's birthplace and a Japanese noblewoman for their mother was the work of Bertrand Babcock, Winnifred's first husband and literary agent. See Ling, *Between Worlds*, 183-184.

3   Her books were so successful that "in many cases she received as much as $ 15,000 advance royalty before publication, with 50% over-riding royalty after publication." In New York city, she moved in a distinguished circle including such luminaries as Edith Wharton, Anita Loos, Jean Webster, David Belasco, Mark Twain, and Lew Wallace. For more, see Amy Ling, *Between Worlds*, 29.

4   The craze for "things Japanese" was inspired in Europe in the mid-nineteenth century,

worked aggressively to educate mainstream Americans in the new aesthetic and promote the artifacts that entered the United States in ever-increasing quantities. Japan itself took advantage of the favorable climate by sending lavish art and architecture exhibits to American world's fairs.[1] In literature, Japanese influences resonated as strongly as in art. Most Americans could get to "buying Japan" and indulge in the numerous magazines and books treating Japanese subjects published in the 1880s and 1890s. The most popular were works by William Elliott Griffis (*The Mikado's Empire*, 1880), Basil Hall Chamberlain (*Things Japanese*, 1890), Lafcadio Hearn (*Glimpses of Unfamiliar Japan*, 1894) and John Luther Long (*Madame Butterfly*, 1898). Winnifred Eaton, as an apprenticed writer, in "The Half Caste" (1898), indicated that she knew the works of Arnold and Hearn and was particularly interested in them as Westerners who had married Japanese women.

Therefore, Winnifred Eaton's romantic novels under the name Onoto Watanna nicely catered for the Japonisme.[2] In particular, her books were highly decorative like the porcelain and lacquers that became more and more common in American homes by the turn of the century. "Floral designs were stamped with colorful foils on the covers, the edges of the pages were gilded, even the interior pages were specially printed with scenes reminiscent of Japanese screens" (Cole 25). Reviewers even combined the physical form of the book with its contents, commenting on *A Japanese Nightingale* as a story of "the fragrant flower" which mirrors the pink cherry blossoms that cascade down the front cover of the book.[3] For a while Winnifred

---

following Commodore Matthew Perry's visit there in 1848. Although Perry's visit opened the country to American trade, Japonisme did not flower on American shores for several decades, due to the turmoil of the Civil War and Reconstruction. For more, see Jean Lee Cole, *The Literary Voices of Winnifred Eaton: Redefining Ethnicity and Authenticity* (New Brunswick: Rutgers University Press, 2002), 24; Gabriel P. Weisberg, "Japonisme: The Commercialization of an Opportunity." Ed. Julia Meech and Gabriel P. Weisberg. *Japonisme Comes to America: The Japanese Impact on American Graphic Arts,* 1876-1925 (New York: Harry Abrams, 1990), 16.

1   Various essays in Meech and Weisberg address the influence of Japanese arts on American painting, architecture, and home furnishings. Also see the volume edited by Holly Edwards, *Noble Dreams, Wicked Pleasures: Orientalism in America* 1870-1930 (New Jersey: Princeton University Press, 2000); N. Harris, 24-54; Meech and Weisberg, 26-34.

2   In her book, Birchall emphasizes the massive influence of *Japonisme*, which is certainly a North American phenomenon to which the Eaton family was not an exception. She presents a 1890s family photo with the three Eaton sisters posed in Japanese costumes to exemplify Montreal youth's fascination with Japanese things. See Birchall, 18.

3   For more details, see Jean Lee Cole, *The Literary Voices of Winnifred Eaton*, 20. It provides a picture of the cover of *A Japanese Nightingale* with elaborate stamping, gilt lettering, and pink

Eaton and Harpers did everything in their power to guard Winnifred's reputation as an authentic Japanese writer. Winnifred Eaton used her pen name for all publicity while insisting upon a Japanese heritage in her interviews. James Doyle notes that in "these interviews, her ethnic origins tended to shift: her father was sometimes Japanese and sometimes English; her mother was usually Japanese, but occasionally part Japanese and part Chinese" (Doyle 55).

Yet, there existed the other side of the coin—the fascination with Japan would prove short-lived. The turn of the century gave birth to much more ambivalence about Japan. In 1905, Japan's victory in the Russo-Japanese War marked the first time that an Asian nation had defeated a European nation in modern warfare. First the Californians and then most Americans began to perceive Japan's military prowess as menacing. Meanwhile, the Japanese immigrants, whose number increased from 24 326 in 1900 to 111 010 in 1920, began to be perceived as an economic and cultural threat in the first decade of the century. As early as 1907, the California legislature began hearings on a series of bills designed to prohibit ownership by Japanese immigrants. In the same year, the Asiatic Exclusion League was formed in San Francisco on the belief that Asiatic races (by the end of its tenure, grew to include Koreans and Filipinos as well as the Chinese and Japanese) were "unassimilable." Magazines like the *San Francisco Chronicle* and several nationalist organizations had boosted what Ronald Takaki called their "exclusionist clamor" against the Japanese.[1] Winnifred Eaton who would have known the racial tension in California (later in the whole nation) since it had attracted national attention, wrote most of her novels about the supposedly more admired Japanese while living in New York.

In general, the turn-of-the-century "Japanophilia" and "Japanophobia" are really two sides of the same coin: both are ideas about Japan based on a fantasy built by a century-long accumulation of Orientalia. So it is hard to tell which pulse Winnifred squarely puts her fingers on. But in this ambivalent social context, Winnifred still made a big success. Jean Lee Cole argued that Winnifred's American readers were quite clear in the distinction between Japanese art and the Japanese race. "The former was fashionable, collectable, and readily assimilable to American culture, the latter was not" (Cole 24). Although evidently the novels were written by a mixed-race

---

cherry blossoms.

1 For more information on anti-Japanese sentiments, see Roger Daniels, *The Politics of Prejudice: The Anti-Japanese Movement in California and the Struggle for Japanese Exclusion* (New York: Atheneum, 1968); Ronald Takaki, *Strangers from a Different Shore: A History of Asian Americans* (Boston: Little Brown, 1989).

person, a part-Asian woman who would have been condemned by the majority of the American populace as a "mongrel," a "yellow Jap"—a despicable half-caste, they still could find a source of appeal, that is, the author's deft demonstration of Japanese culture. Clearly unaware that Winnifred Eaton was born in Montreal, a reviewer for the *Literary Digest* lauded that the "fascination of Japan… could not be in better hands than those of Onoto Watanna, a native by birth" (1912, 795). Winnifred is very skillful in creating Japanese atmosphere, using sentimental language to depict fantastically transnational, beautiful, and strong-willed heroines. As Japanese scholars Thomas E. Swann and Katsuhiko Takeda have pointed out, in Onoto Watanna's works, "Japanese customs and manners were properly introduced to the west," while they conceded that "her novels reflect the feelings and sentiments of a visitor to Japan."[1]

Another explanation for Winnifred Eaton's literary success lies in her portrayal of Japanese and Eurasian heroines. All of them are very beautiful, feminine and vulnerable young maidens. As Eve Oishi notes, Watanna's heroines "match, in many ways, the popular stereotypes of Asian femininity—childlike, naive, and charmingly exotic" (xix). At the same time, they have a strong sense of finery, and are appealingly high-spirited and independent-minded, if sometimes a little naive. In other words, they are a satisfying mixture of the stereotypical qualities of "Oriental" women and the incentive traits of the progressive New Women. Such characters would hardly be associated with the "yellow peril" or "despicable half-caste" by popular Anglo writers. One more reason, according to Carol Roh-Spaulding, is that Winnifred's depiction of Japan partly satisfied escapists' yearnings for a purer, pre-industrial way of life. In her novels, "Japan is often portrayed in remote regions, retaining feudal values, very fit for the urban and educated readers' taste" (Roh-Spaulding, 1996 173). One *New York Times* review described *Tama* as "charmingly Japanese in form as well as in atmosphere…it holds the very spirit of Japan" (Ling, 1990 54). William Dean Howells praised *A Japanese Nightingale* for its "quite indescribable freshness" and "simplicity which is native to the best art everywhere" (Ling 54).

Whatever the rationale is, Winnifred was not a political novelist. Facing the day-

---

1 Although Winnifred immersed herself in a fantasy world she called "my mother's land," as a writer, she never visited Japan, and even after her Japanese novels had made her famous, she did not visit Japan. With respect to Winnifred's excellent portrayal of Japan and Japanese, Dominika Ferens notes that Winnifred not only relied on booklore, but also made friends with Japanese immigrant poet Yone Noguchi in the late 1890s, and she later employed several Japanese students in her home. These "native informants" may well have supplemented her secondary sources. See Ferens, 6; Ling, *Between Worlds*, 54.

to-day abuse of a person of Chinese descent, she chose to construct a Japanese persona in order to avoid the material and psychological cost of claiming Chinese descent (as represented by her sister Edith Eaton). As Dominika Ferens points out, "passing for Japanese was a logical career move for Winnifred at the turn of the century" (Ferens 117). On a personal level, her strategy of passing accomplished what Teresa Kay Williams described as a shift "from one 'minority' status to the 'more' acceptable minority status—in order to raise one's prestige and advance one's chances for a qualitatively improved life" (Williams 62). By becoming Onoto Watanna, Winnifred enacted mainstream orientalist fantasies, exploiting the discourse that feminized and aestheticized Japan. She not only supported her four children as a single mother, but also earned herself a position in the white-male dominant marketplace. Of course, her gender became a major selling point in the publishing marketplace. By the time she began writing, the subject of Japan had long been occupied by white males, yet there was ample space, particularly in the women's magazines, for a "half-blood Japanese who…is a clever writer of stories and speaks and writes English fluently" (Cole 121).

Nevertheless, passing for Japanese was not a single act, but a main part of expressing her mixed sensibility. At various points in her career, Winnifred wrote under the pen names Onoto Watanna, Winnifred Mooney, Winnifred Babcock Reeve, and Winnifred Eaton Reeve, as well as her given name, which has appeared as Winnifred and Winifred, and as Winnifred Eaton and Winnifred Babcock Eaton. Through these pen names Winnifred created various literary characters such as a working-class Irish American woman, an Englishwoman in the Canadian west, and of course, the first and foremost famous Japanese Eurasian woman.

Factually, most of these personas bear relevance to her biographical facts. First of all, her mother Grace Trefusius is an important figure. On the one hand, Grace was abducted as a young child by Chinese circus performers and later raised by an English missionary couple. Her mother's real-life romantic background and the particularity of her own real family heritage are factors which could have led to Winnifred's fascination with the romance genre and to her fabricated background. On the other hand, Grace always warned her children before their departure from home "not to tell anyone they were Chinese because she feared they might be sold into 'coolee labor.'"[1] So Winnifred exploited the romance, and made Onoto Watanna her main authorial persona. However, according to Winnifred's grandson, Paul Rooney, the invention of

---

1 This evidence is given by Eileen Lewis, Florence (one of Winnifred's sister)'s granddaughter, in a telephone interview. Quoted in Annette White-Parks' *Sui Sin Far/Edith Eaton*, 57.

Nagasaki as Winnifred's birthplace and a Japanese noblewoman for their mother was the work of Bertrand Babcock, Winnifred's first husband and literary agent.[1] So after her 1916 divorce from Bertrand Babcock, Winnifred remarried and went with her second husband, Frank Reeve, to Alberta, Canada. She tended to downplay her racial heritage in interviews. Then, working in Hollywood in the late 1920s and early 1930s, she occasionally referred to it again, finally dissociating herself entirely from Japan during World War II.[2] Her Irish persona may have been inspired by the birthplace of her paternal grandmother, or by the family life with her first husband, Bertrand Babcock.[3] Life on a cattle ranch in Calgary, Alberta from 1917 to 1925 doubtless inspired the persona of Winnifred Eaton Reeve. Anyhow, for Winnifred Eaton, simply passing for white and being done with it would have been an easier way to avoid her Chinese ancestry than so much circuitous self-fashioning.

In the act of passing as English or Irish or Japanese, Winnifred was also passing through these ethnic categories. As far as her Japanese pen name is concerned, linguistically, Onoto Watanna is not a Japanese name at all.[4] According to Matsukawa's explanation that considers "Watanna" as "to pass," "to cross," or "to go abroad" (Matsukawa 107), it can be concluded that Onoto Watanna is Winnifred's intentional fabrication. Winnifred Eaton's desire to pass for Japanese would be betrayed by her Japanese looking and Japanese-sounding name, Onoto Watanna. Factually, Winnifred Eaton understood this self-betrayed name during her writing career. She just resisted complete absorption into any specific literary persona. In this respect, Winnifred Eaton's literary practice was much closer to her sister's. Edith Eaton examined through her writing her relationship with the dominant ethnicity in her life by moving between literary genres and authorial stances that orbited around

---

1   Paul Rooney, grandson of Winnifred Eaton Babcock Reeve, interview, Toronto, Ontario, November 1989. Quoted in *Ferens' Edith and Winnifred Eaton*, 140.

2   In Naomi Lang's "Albert Women Who Make News," Winnifred was quoted as saying, "I'm ashamed of having written about the Japanese, I hate them so." For the first time, she publicly presented herself as "partly Chinese on her mother's side and very proud of the fact." Publicity photos of the older Winnifred show a very ordinary white woman, usually dressed in a modest hat and fur collar. See Ferens, 140.

3   Ibid. Regarding Winnifred's writing of an Irish maid, Dominka Ferens considers that through drawing attention to her distant Irish ancestry, Winnifred may again have been playing on ideas of heredity to authorize herself.

4   In terms of the pen name Onoto Watanna, the author of this book consulted several graduates of Japanese language and literature, none of them could recognize Onoto Watanna as a Japanese name, and no accurate Japanese words can equate with it.

the classification "Chinese" but allowed her to resist being pulled into its center of gravity. This identity she defines as Eurasian. Winnifred Eaton's career had similar patterns, although on a grander scale. Her frequent choices of foreign settings, and her continual claiming and then abandoning of the identity are the expression of herself as an ethnic exile. The next section will continue to discuss Winnifred's mixed Eurasian consciousness by analyzing her autobiographical novel *Me* which critics usually hold as Winnifred's protection of her Japanese persona.

II. "Peculiar Heredity": Autobiographical Novel *Me: A Book of Remembrance*

In 1915, *Century Magazine* serialized the anonymously authored *Me: A Book of Remembrance*, and soon the story and its author were caught in great interest. The *Toronto Star* reported that "while shocking the sensibilities of many of the old subscribers", the book's racy subject matter "increased *Century*'s circulation considerably"; publicity also fueled sales as New York City subway advertisements and billboards asked, "Who is the author of *Me*?"[1] Reviewers responded to both *Me*'s sensational content and to the question of the author's identity, "if all is true therein, the orthodox will find comfort in that the book ends with the heroine at prayer" (*Toronto Star* 1915), and "the author of *Me* is probably much more clever and fascinating than during the impulsive maidenhood of which she writes" (*New York Times* 1915). The speculation ended when a *New York Times Book Review* article "Is Onoto Watanna Author of the Anonymous Novel *Me*?" deduced the author's nationality, and ultimately her identity, from various clues, including an important detail featuring the heroine kissing a man's sleeve, which the writer claimed as a Japanese custom (Birchall 116).[2]

The mystery was satisfactorily resolved for readers. In 1914, in the four weeks between Thanksgiving and New Year, Winnifred Eaton completed the story that "is

---

1   According to Birchall, Winnifred Eaton's granddaughter, the original source of information on *Me*'s New York City publicity campaign is Doris Rooney's article, "Souvenir from the Past." *Field, Horse and Rodeo* (June 1963): 45-47. For more, see Diana Birchall, *Onoto Watanna: The Story of Winnifred Eaton*, 116.

2   Birchall provides a very thorough and amusing discussion of the article itself and speculates that the anonymous writer most likely knew Eaton, though it is not clear whether the author knew that "Onoto Watanna" was a fabricated persona.

frankly of herself" while in the hospital, recovering from an operation.

> It seems to me as though these two weeks I have just passed in the hospital have been the first
> time in which I have had a chance to think in thirteen years. As I lay on my back and looked at
> the ceiling, the events of my girlhood came before me, rushed back with such overwhelming
> vividness that I picked up a pencil and began to write. (*ME* 4)

In her introduction to *Me*, Jean Webster (Mark Twain's niece) wrote, *Me* is "pure reporting, the author has not branched out into any byways of style, but has merely told in the simplest language possible what she actually remembered" (*ME* i). Moreover, Jean Webster assured "I have known the author for a number of years, and I know that the main outline of everything she says is true, though the names of people and places have necessarily been changed in order to hide their identity" (i). Then, what were the circumstances of the time which inspired Winnifred to recollect the events of her girlhood and set them to paper?

Thirteen years earlier, a novel titled *A Japanese Nightingale* (1901) had brought fame to a writer named Onoto Watanna, who was none other than Winnifred Eaton.[1] Like her older sister Edith Eaton/Sui Sin Far, Winnifred Eaton was a Chinese Eurasian, the daughter of a Chinese mother and an English father, but she adopted a Japanese-sounding pseudonym in order to "pass" as a writer of authentic Japanese tales. As Onoto Watanna, Winnifred published many Japanese tales at the rate of one book per year, which proved to be commercially successful by satisfying the literary marketplace eager to consume stories of an exotic Japan. Since Winnifred had accumulated a high reputation in the literary marketplace as Onoto Watanna, why did she choose to publish *Me* anonymously rather than continue to use Onoto Watanna to attract the reading public, especially when writing such a truth-uncovering work? Before 1915, Winnifred Eaton has already published ten novels. As Winnifred advanced in her career, however, she became disgruntled with her writing. Objectively speaking, at the age of thirty-nine, Winnifred Eaton was by no means a writer at the close of her career, but she spoke as though she no longer had the desire to write—at least the kind of material with which she had become famous. "You perceive I had an excellent opinion of my ability at this time. I wish I had it now. It was more a conviction then—a conviction that I was destined to do something worthwhile as a writer" (*ME* 115). Therefore, like Winnifred's alter ego in *Me*, Nora frowns on her

---

1　Since its publication in 1901, *A Japanese Nightingale* was translated into many European languages including German, Swedish, and Hungarian. Moreover, it was adapted as a play and performed on Broadway in 1903 to compete with Giacomo Puccini's long-running *Madame Butterfly*.

own success that was founded upon "a cheap and popular device." The cheap device Winnifred refers to is nothing other than the genre of historical romance.[1] She declares, "I had sold my birthright for a mess of potage" (*ME* 153). Later, a series of public events—growing distrust of Japan and the Japanese as well as personal events—did move Winnifred to despair over her masquerade, precipitating a state of depression that coincided with her stay in the hospital.[2] Therefore, as her convalescence was to heal her body, Winnifred Eaton decided to write her autobiography to be part of her self-recovery. In order to convince readers of the authenticity of the text, the narration of the protagonist's life is told in the first-person singular form, the autobiographical fashion.

However, Winnifred was in an awkward predicament to narrate her real self. As a significant departure from Onoto Watanna, Winnifred Eaton promises in the opening chapter that "this story is frankly of myself," but scholars have been disappointed by how little Winnifred actually reveals about herself in the text, especially, how little she writes about her ethnicity. Annette White-Parks is clearly disgusted with Eaton's presumed reticence regarding her ethnicity when she describes *Me* as a "denial of racism" (White-Parks, 1995 34). Other criticism mainly centers on blaming Winnifred Eaton's fabrications and dissimulations—her decision to publish her autobiography anonymously, her decision to give her heroine a distinctly "white" name, Nora Ascough, as well as her refusal to pinpoint Nora's identity as half-Chinese.[3]

---

1   As a genre, romance came to its wane after the immense popularity as early as 1900. For example, as he decried the public's infatuation with the genre, William Dean Howells went on to suggest that "there are clear signs that its immense favor is abating; there are sullen whispers in the Trade that her historical romance, as a seller has had its day." See William Dean Howells, "The New Historical Romance," *North American Review* (1900) 171: 935-948.

2   On the one hand, Japan's emergence as a world-class military and imperial power made many Americans feel uneasy. Especially, after the Gentlemen's Agreement of 1908, relations between Japan and America noticeably cooled, growing into a mutual distrust that would explode most dramatically thirty years later at Pearl Harber. Besides, by the turn of the century, as more and more Japanese laborers arrived to take the place of the excluded Chinese, white American nativist and working-class groups began to lobby for similar checks against all Asians. On the other hand, Eaton's personal and professional lives in 1914 were remarkably affected by a series of events. Her older sibling Edward Charles and Edith had both passed away within the past few years. Moreover, she was on the path to divorcing her abusive husband, Bertrand Babcock.

3   For criticism attributing Winnifred Eaton's reticence to reveal her true ethnic identity to her need to preserve her audience's belief in her pseudonymous persona, see Amy Ling's "Revelation and Mask" and also see Matsukawa's "Cross-Dressing and Cross-Naming: Decoding Onoto Watanna."

Apparently, although Winnifred has the intention to reveal and recuperate a "true" self that had been eclipsed by the figure of Onoto Watanna through her autobiographical act, yet, if she had revealed the truth about herself, she would have undermined the validity of her biography that she had created and on which she based her literary success.[1]

To a large extent, critics' disappointment with Winnifred's *Me* resulted from their comparison with Edith Eaton's autobiographical text. Edith Eaton's autobiographical essay "Leaves from the Mental Portfolio of an Eurasian" published several years before *Me* focuses exactly on the very aspects of life which are seemingly omitted by Winnifred.

> I look back over the years and see myself so keenly alive to every shade of sorrow and suffering that it is almost a pain to live… the question of nationality perplexes my little brain. Why are we what we are? I and my brothers and sisters. Why did God make us to be hooted and stared at?… Why? Why? (*MSF* 221-222)

Such anguished depiction of being the ethnic other can not find direct expressions in *Me*. Ironically, in Winnifred's next novel, *Marion: The Story of an Artist's Model* (1916), critics can fulfill their expectations to some degree. Although this story did not center on Winnifred but her sister Sara, named Marion, Winnifred did describe in detail how she and her siblings were treated by their Montreal neighbors and how the Eaton children's Chinese ancestry becomes a factor in their relationship with each other, their parents, and potential romantic partners. Early in the novel, Marion overhears a gossip at the corner store, shocked and humiliated. "I felt ashamed and humiliated to hear our family thus discussed. Why should we always be pointed out in this way and made to feel conspicuous and freaky? It was horrid that the size of our family and my mother's nationality should be told to everyone" (*MA* 1-2). This text, in contrast to *Me*, gave literary critics what they wanted: anguished depictions of cultural differences, incidents of accommodation and resistance, experiences of discrimination. But *Me*, as Winnifred's autobiography, was never so frank.

Indeed, Winnifred downplays the fact of her own interracial background in *Me*, merely alluding to her "peculiar heredity" and stating rather darkly that her mother is a "creature" from a "foreign land" (*ME* 41). What *Me* primarily concerns is the protagonist, Nora Ascough's growth from a naive girl with childish dreams of love and fame into an experienced and somewhat more thoughtful young woman.

---

1   The biography mentions that Winnifred Eaton characterized Onoto Watanna as the daughter of an English merchant (descended from English nobility) and the daughter of a samurai warrior, she was stated born in Nagasaki but had spent most of her life in the United States.

Nora, an embellished version of Winnifred, leaves home to work as a journalist and stenographer in Jamaica. Being traumatized by a marriage proposal from a black Jamaican, she moves from Jamaica to Chicago, where she works briefly as a reporter. Then, after suffering the trials and humiliations of being a working girl in Chicago, Nora moves to Richmond. Finally she moves to New York to pursue her writing after her hopes of love are smashed. Generally speaking, as critics have interrogated, it is a little far-fetched to define *Me* as an autobiography of an ethnic woman. However, Linda Trinh Moser in the afterword to the 1998 reprint of *Me* noted that "textual silence regarding Winnifred Eaton's Chinese ancestry makes it difficult to read *Me* as an autobiography, let alone an ethnic one…but it is not impossible to do so" (*ME* 358). In the same tune, this book argues that in *Me*, Winnifred had a new project that was her new identity. Without apparently identifying her own Chinese heritage, or returning to her fabricated Japanese identity, Winnifred began to consider her identity seriously, although in a vague way, aimed to convey a sense of new self—her "peculiar heredity."

By 1912, Winnifred Eaton had published ten novels as Onoto Watanna and continued to claim the biography she had invented for her alter ego as her own. Not long afterward, however, her commitment began to show signs of wavering. Published in the April of *New York Times* two days after her death in 1914, Edith Eaton's obituary is unsigned. But Amy Ling attributes it to Winnifred, who was then living in New York and the one most likely responsible for its peculiar emphasis. The article is entitled "Edith Eaton Dead" with the subtitle "Author of Chinese Stories under the Name of Sui Sin Far."[1] In the roughly eight square inches of space, Winnifred took the opportunity to touch upon her current ethnic version of herself, despite the fact that doing so might result in falsifying her family history. As she did in *Me*, Winnifred willingly revealed her father's ethnicity. Of forty odd lines, only nine directly related to Edith. Most of the obituary was devoted to an account of the life of her father, Edward Eaton, including his family background, his travels to the East, his fluctuating fortune as well as his romantic history. Most particularly, in the obituary, Winnifred repeated and further fabricated her parents' biography. She wrote that her father was "fascinated with the East," without specifying a country. There he met according to the obituary, a "Japanese noblewoman who had been adopted by Sir Hugh Matheson

---

1 Winnifred begins the obituary by stating that Edith Eaton was known as Sui Sin Far "in the East." This statement is of much ambiguity, because we do not know if Winnifred is referring to Asia, where Sui Sin Far can have been little known because her work was never translated, or to the East of North America.

as a child and educated in England," but in reality, it was Shanghai-raised Grace Trefusius.

With respect to Edith and her work, Winnifred just wrote that "her short stories attracted favorable comments" and that her "best known work is *Mrs. Spring Fragrance*." It was in the ending lines of the obituary that Winnifred incongruously wrote that "One of Miss Eaton's sisters, Mrs. Bertrand W. Babcock, is an author, writing under the pen name of Onoto Watanna." Some may read the lines as Winnifred's consistent legitimating of her Japanese persona at the cost of her sister's literary reputation. Amy Ling contended that Winnifred felt compelled to do so, because the latest edition of *Who Was Who In America* listed her birthplace as Nagasaki, Japan. In other words, to tell the truths about herself on the occasion of her sister's death might cut short her career as Onoto Watanna and expose her as a liar. However, from the other angle, although Winnifred was not ready to admit her Chinese heritage, she went so far as to reveal, on a very public occasion, that Onoto Watanna was nothing more than a pseudonym. Factually, the year of Edith's death marked Winnifred's departure from her Japanese pseudonym and Japanese novels for good. In an unpublished document entitled "You Can't Run Away from Yourself," Winnifred describes her need for change.

> I dreamed of the day when I could escape from the treadmill of writing about a subject I did not love... Vogues are transient things and my readers probably were as tired of reading about little Japanese women as I was of writing about them... Came a day when publishers no longer made me tempting offers of large advance royalties; when editors ceased to solicit stories by me. I said to myself: "I can write another type of story. This is my opportunity to get away from Japanese tales." So I wrote three anonymous stories. (Birchall 140)

An understanding of the exploitative nature of the historical romance inspired Winnifred Eaton to abandon her pseudonym and write her autobiography with the hope that she was at least free to practice her craft independent of generic conventions.[1] From then on, she has seemingly taken a break from writing her Japanese romances. In 1914, she coauthored a cookbook, *Chinese-Japanese*

---

1 As David Shih points out, as a tacitly pro-imperial and white-supremacist discourse, the historical romance reflected and reinforced the idea of race as a biological phenomenon with social and cultural consequences. The cumulative effect of these romances on Winnifred Eaton was the graduation of "Onoto Watanna" from pseudonym to alternate self. The persona that she and her publishers protected and cultivated ultimately extended beyond the text to govern her life and the lives of her family. See David Shih, "The Self and Generic Convention," *Recovered Legacies: Authority and Identity in Early Asian American Literature*. eds. Keith Lawrence and Floyd Cheung (Philadelphia: Temple University Press, 2005), 43.

Cook Book, with her sister, Sara Bosse. She went on to publish *Me* and *Marion* anonymously, *Sunny San* (1922)[1] another Japanese novel in America, and two English-Canadian novels, *Cattles* (1923) and *His Royal Nibs* (1925). Therefore, as her first work after Edith's death, *Me* functions importantly as a transition—discarding an unwanted self and reinventing another more worthwhile one.

As *Me* reveals, it is about how the young author begins writing. But there is no mention of her interest in Japanese themes or how she came to choose her pseudonym. The only reference to any Japanese occurs on a page where Winnifred lists, a bit disingenuously, all the suitors who have proposed to her. One of them, a Japanese magnate, had served as her father's courier in Japan. Carol Vivian Spaulding points out that "Eaton's avoidance of the influence of Japan is absurd if *Me* is an attempt to reflect accurately on her career; but if accuracy were her aim, she would not have hidden her identity and called her narrator Nora Ascough" (Roh-Spaulding, 1996 182). Winnifred Eaton's omissions and evasions suggest that she promotes varying levels of "truth" about herself and her background in order to keep her audience's reading fluid and open. Because the "truth" of her personal history does not spring from any "authentic" ethnic source, Winnifred seemed almost to make it up as she went along. This improvisational technique can be traced to her fictionalized narrative in the text. In addition to depicting the romantic relationship between Nora and Mr. Hamilton, *Me* details the crucial year in which the seventeen-year-old Nora leaves her familial Canadian home to pursue a writing career and charts her travels to Jamaica, Chicago, Richmond and New York. Although the plot trajectory basically follows the events of Winnifred Eaton's life, many other details are fictionalized. There are two temporal alterations. First, the plot compresses the five years between her stay in Jamaica and her arrival in New York into one year. According to Birchall, Winnifred Eaton probably journeyed to Jamaica in February 1896, where she served as a reporter for the Canadian-run *Gall's News Letter* for five months, and she did not reach Chicago until May 1897.[2] Another temporally related discrepancy is the protagonist's age. Winnifred Eaton was actually twenty, not seventeen, when she left for Jamaica.

---

1   Regarding why Eaton returned to the formulaic romance with *Sunny San* in 1922, according to Birchall, it is perhaps spurred on by the financial problems of her second husband, Frank Reeve. Winnifred Eaton was ready to change the course of her life but not at the expense of her livelihood. See Birchall, 136.

2   Although the exact nature of her movements is unknown, Birchall speculates from *Me* and from the many profiles that featured the young Onoto Watanna that she may have stayed in "Boston, the South, Cincinnati, or New York," or a combination of these places. See Birchall, 30, 42.

Although this difference in age is marginal, Winnifed readily promoted it for the rest of her life. Birchall suggests that this gesture was common among American women writers (including Willa Cather), and that by making herself younger, Winnifred could seem even more "precocious;" she may also have altered her age in order to evade scrutiny into her past and her childhood, thereby protecting her Onoto Watanna persona.[1] In fact, Winnifred Eaton's obituary in a Calgary newspaper clipping in the Reeve Collection lists her year of birth as 1879 instead of 1875 (the actual year she was born), and the Reeve Collection itself lists 1879 as her birth date.[2]

The examples of conflating fact and fiction listed above are the tip of the iceberg. In fact, many clues in the text are very prone to make readers question the authenticity of *Me* as an autobiography, such as its combination of various literary genres, including the bildungsroman and the romance novel. Winnifred's dependence upon other genres and predilection for melodramatic phrasing such as "fate was a black, monstrous thing, a thief in the dark that hid to entrap me" (*ME* 12), often propel the autobiography into implausibility, although she denied the entrance of imagination or fiction into her autobiographical enterprise by claiming that irrepressible memory had structured the narrative. "As I lay on my back and looked at the ceiling, the events of my girlhood came before me, rushed back with such overwhelming vividness that I picked up a pencil and began to write" (*ME* i). In this respect, Roy Pascal has made an important observation in *Design and Truth in Autobiography* that autobiography actually has more relevance to the present situation of the writer than the events of the past. The nature of autobiography is not in its faithful reconstruction of historical experience, adds Paul John Eakin, but in the play "of the autobiographical act itself, in which the materials of the past are shaped by memory and imagination to serve the needs of present consciousness" (Eakin 5). Therefore, it is less useful to measure Eaton's level of authenticity and authority in *Me*. The text is not read as "pure reporting" but as a biographical moment that is important in the definition of the self. For Winnifred Eaton, the choice of seventeen-year-old Nora Ascough as the protagonist of *Me* signals not only a tacit rejection of Onoto Watanna but also a desire to reclaim some part of that earlier sense of self for the present.[3] In other

---

1　Amy Ling indicates that Winnifred changed her birthdate in order to appear younger than her second husband, Francis F. Reeve. See Ling, *Between Worlds*, 183.

2　According to Birchall, Eaton never told her children about her actual age, and the birth year engraved on her tombstone is 1879; more incredibly, she made her children unwitting accomplices by taking two years off their ages as well, a fact they did not discover until well into adulthood.

3　Birchall points out that Eaton may have named her protagonist after Hannah Ayscough, the

words, Winnifred turned to the autobiographical act as the first step toward faithfully representing herself. For her, "Anonymity" like Onoto Watanna, Winnifred Mooney and Winnifred Babcock Reeve is simply part of her repertoire.

The most important factor leading to critics' disappointment with *Me* is Winnifred's omission about the issue of race. In fact, however, Linda Trinh Moser has pointed out, "Eaton's clear concern with matters of class and sexuality should not be read as dismissal of race" (*ME* 363). In other words, Winnifred's understanding of race is interlocked with class and gender. In *Me*, any mention of sexuality and class inevitably leads us back to race. The central plot of *Me* revolves around Nora Ascough's relationship with an older man, a multimillionaire by the name of Roger Hamilton. As a member of cultural elite and "one of the greatest families in America" (*ME* 183), Hamilton never admits his love for Nora, maintaining that he is merely "interested" in her as his "discovery" (*ME* 241). Discouraged by his offers to keep but not marry her, Nora accuses him of being interested in her only as a "sort of curiosity," an understanding that finally makes her "sick at heart" (*ME* 241). Nora apprehends that her appeal to others is not derived from any inherent uniqueness, but from the idea of Asian women as "curiosity"—objects to be enjoyed and forgotten but not taken seriously. In order to affirm her own sense of integrity, Winnifred Eaton fashioned an Emersonian self-reliant Nora.

> Now, although poor and working, I was a free woman. What I had, I honestly earned. I was no doll or parasite who needed to be carried by others. No! To retain my belief in my own powers, I must prove that...I had the youthful conviction that I was one of the exceptional souls of the world, and could carry myself. (*ME* 244)

In this instance, Winnifred Eaton not only condemned mainstream prejudice against Asian (colored) women, but also put forward the values that were very fit for the New Woman standard.[1]

Another evident example to support Winnifred's involvement in the racial problem is Nora's unabashed and undisguised racism toward blacks. Before her arrival in Jamaica, Nora claims to be oblivious to racial hierarchies, and declares that "she had never even heard the expression 'race prejudice' before" (*ME* 41). However, when she arrives, her feeling is dominated by the demeaning reaction to people of color.

---

mother of Sir Issac Newton, to whom Eaton claimed relation. In this way, Eaton departs from Onoto Watanna by embracing a more credible genealogy. See Birchall, 7.

1   According to Carroll Smith-Rosenberg, the New Woman is a well-educated professional woman with independent economic income, endorsing free marriage and rejecting the Victorian stereotype on gender roles. For more, see Carroll Smith-Rosenberg, *Disorderly Conduct: Visions of Gender in Victorian America* (New York: A. Knopf, 1985).

> A crowd seemed to be swarming on the wharves, awaiting our boat. As we came nearer, I was amazed to find that this crowd was made up almost entirely of negroes. We have very few negroes in Canada, and I had only seen one all my life. I remember an older sister had shown him to me in church—he was pure black—and told me he was the "Bogy man," and that he'd probably come around to see me that night… It was, therefore, with a genuine thrill of excitement and fear that I looked down upon that vast sea of upturned black and brown faces. (*ME* 19-20)

Her deep prejudice comes clear in her relation to Burbank, a part-Hebrew black Parliament member with material wealth, who is in love with her but from whom she feels "a sudden panic of almost instinctive fear" (*ME* 40). Her reaction to Burbank's kiss and proposal is irrational. Physically sickened, Nora decides to flee Jamaica. Actually, compared with the treacherous Manning, a married white, who tries to force Nora into a sexual relationship, Burbank is always polite, speaking with an "odd mixture of embarrassment and assurance" (*ME* 54). But in Nora's eyes, Burbank's race acts as a sign of his depraved sexuality, despite his high social status and economic ability in Jamaica. By refusing Burbank, Nora clearly demonstrates that basic racial equality does not come with material wealth.

Moreover, as discussed before, Winnifred Eaton had a project in *Me*, that is, to explore her true birthright. Before *Me*, she never asserted her Chinese ancestry in public. Therefore, this book considers it to be her first and cautious attempt to reckon with her Chinese heritage. In this sense, *Me* takes on new significance. In *Me*, Winnifred alludes to Edith Eaton's death with a purpose. "The eldest, a girl with more real talent than I—who had been a pitiful invalid all her days. She is dead now, that dear big sister of mine, and a monument marks her grave in commemoration of work she did for my mother's country" (*ME* 194).[1] It should be noted that, although Winnifred Eaton continues to be vague about her mother's race, her tone suggests new appreciation for the importance of community—familial and racial. Indeed, Nora regrets that it "seemed a great pity that I was not, after all, to be the savior of the family, and that my dreams of the fame and fortune that not alone should lift me up, but all my people, were built upon a substance as shifting as sand and as shadowy as mist" (*ME* 194). Thus, it can be seen that Winnifred Eaton not only touches upon the race issue, but also at the final part of *Me*, improves herself through Nora's mature self who is hopeful of standing alongside her "people."

More blatant expressions of Nora's racial background exist. Elaborating on the

---

1　The monument to which Winnifred alludes is a gravestone placed in gratitude by the Chinese community of Montreal and Boston and inscribed with Chinese characters that read, "The righteous one who never forgets China."

introduction's reference to her "peculiar heredity," Nora states, "I mention these few facts about my parents' ethnic backgrounds merely in the possibility of their proving of some psychological interest later" (*ME* 4). In other words, the importance of her parents' different backgrounds is significant to the development of her identity and dictates her relation to the world. After devoting attention to describing the father's British ancestors, the refusal to disclose her mother's racial background creates a narrative gap. *Me*'s reviewers caught the scent of Winnifred's evasive tactics. Linda Trinh Moser points out, both the *Chicago Tribute* (21 August 1915) and the *New York Times Book Review* (22 August 1915) guessed the author was Eurasian. In fact, through Nora, Winnifred extensively explores the psychological anguish of being Eurasian, but in a very indirect way. "I myself was dark and foreign looking, but the blond type I adored. In all my most fanciful imaginings and dreams, I had always been golden-haired and blue-eyed" (*ME* 41). Similar to the little Sui in "Leaves," Nora attempts to deflect the racializing gaze of those "interested" in her or those "puzzled" by her nationality. "People stared at me... but in a different sort of way, as if I interested them or they were puzzled to know my nationality" (*ME* 166). But in contrast to Sui Sin Far's racial integrity to battle with the prejudice, Winnifred Eaton always expresses her preference of blondeness. Even later, she declares insistently, "I would have given anything to look less foreign. My darkness marked and crushed me, I who loved blondness like the sun." (*ME* 166) Her internalized rejection of her own dark hair and eyes is in contrast to her insistence that she knows nothing of prejudice. "What would I know of race prejudice? ... We do not encounter the problem of race. One color there is as good as another" (*ME* 41). On one level, Winnifred expresses her acute sense of racial inferiority. On the other, she deliberately depicts a utopian state for all races that could live harmoniously without limitations of race. Furthermore, in terms of her double ancestries, Winnifred Eaton places her whiteness over her raced side. Different from Edith Eaton's narrator of "Leaves" who relates to her mother's culture, never being tired of listening to her mother's story, *Me*'s narrator consistently elevates her father's status and relates to her English heritage. "My father's an Oxford man, and a descendant of the family of Sir Isaac Newton...the greatness of my father's people had been a sort of fairy story with us all..." (*ME* 26, 94). Besides, Winnifred gives *Me* a white narrator, and the narrative is set in North America as opposed to a foreign setting, suggesting that Winnifred Eaton consciously depicts the Other when writing as Onoto Watanna, but feels more at home as an author of white characters.

The *Literary Digest* lauded *Me* as the account of an unusual woman of "compelling charm" raised by unusual parents and argued that the unconventional way Nora "went to meet her thrilling experiences" could be true "only of a girl with such a heritage" (Roh-Spaulding, 1996 194). Indeed, in order to express her sense of such peculiar heritage, Winnifred highlights many important biographical moments and makes up obscured truths about herself and her family history. Winnifred moves between various ethnic personas, none of whom has any relation to her Chinese background, thereby deconstructing a fixed ethnic identity. This pattern indicates not the failure to place herself within an identity, but the fruition of a Eurasian sensibility.

III. Ideal of Fluid Eurasian Identity in *The Heart of Hyacinth*

Over the course of her career, Winnifred Eaton proved herself to be a successful author of popular romance. American readers were largely attracted by the "exotic" Japan and Japanese figures under her pen. However, more importantly, her novels also weave a complex narrative of identity in which she negotiates with orientalist binary constructions of the East and the West and explores through the Eurasian figures the promise and perils of boundary crossings. As a Eurasian author, Winnifred's creation of Eurasian characters is much more significant than her African counterparts or Anglo writers who depict mixed-blood characters' tragic fate as abjection or self-destruction. In her psychological book, *The Powers of Horror: An Essay on Abjection*, Julia Kristeva describes the abject as "…what disturbs identity, system, order. What does not respect borders, positions, rules. The in-between, the ambiguous, the composite" (Kristeva 4). This is a particularly proper description of certain mixed-blood characters, especially who inspire fear, repulsion, or awe. The characters such as Boddo in Walt Whitman's "The Half-Breed," William Faulkner's tragic mulatto Joe Christmas in *Light in August* as well as Toni Morrison's mixed-blood Elihue Whitcomb in *The Bluest Eye*, inspire dread not because of what they do but because of what they are. Their bodies are read as signs of their power to disrupt racial and social order. Their mere existence is itself the sign of degeneracy or danger, for they have proven themselves to be beyond classification. Hence, the ultimate fate for the mixed blood is usually death.

Publishing during a socially volatile era, the Eurasian Winnifred Eaton would thus have had the personal interest in expanding social awareness of Eurasians by portraying positive but non-threatening Eurasian characters. Different from the paradigmatic mixed-blood figure, Winnifred's Eurasians are also outcasts because of the absolute racial distinctions, but they are not ruined. They can choose a way out of their conflict by finding a way out of their culture. The tragic fates that predominate in tales of the mulatto/a never occur in Winnifred's novels. Generally speaking, with their biracial-bicultural characters, Winnifred's Eurasian novels respond more directly than her Japanese novels to the issues of racial purity.[1] Like their author, Winnifred's characters hover just out of the reach of ethnic classification. Their self-concept have been formed with little or no relation to social designations. They are often fleeing from something that would label or name them—from their family or their men or from confining social mores. In particular, Winnifred's Eurasian heroines, to some extent, subvert the generalizations of mixed-race woman by Gina Marchetti who argues that since a mixed-race woman is the product of racial and sexual transgression, she represents "a sexuality that cannot be contained" and poses a sexual and racial threat in her capacity to "reproduce" the transgression of her parents. Unlike the tragic mulattos in literature who commonly conceal their identity from their lovers or husbands until they are found out, Winnifred's Eurasian heroines never meet their doom. Their resistance to racial classification and sexual containment becomes a form of agency and a source of strength. *The Heart of Hyacinth* is a good case in point.

Published in the early fall of 1903, like other romances by Onoto Watanna, *The Heart of Hyacinth* was advertised by the publisher as a holiday giftbook, enchanting readers with its "exquisite" Japanese design and its "delicate," "charming" tale of Japan. A review emphasizes, "We have a childish pleasure for us in a story of Japanese life written by a native" (1903, *Republican*). Similarly, another review introduces the author as "Onoto Watanna, the dainty little gentlewoman from Japan, who writes so delightfully of her native country" (1903, *Nashville Banner*).[2] It is evident that Winnifred's Japanese writing persona still continued to allow her to dissimulate as an authentic ethnographer of Japan. Besides, because the plot of the novel is improbable and its setting idyllic, reviewers and critics have rarely gone beyond commenting on

---

1 At the turn of the century, the Reconstruction era had recently come to an end. Large numbers of immigrants from southern Europe and Asia were entering the country, and white supremacists were becoming increasingly alarmed at the prospect of sexual intermingling among the races. Many scientific and anthropological works were produced to support the anti-miscegenation discourses, such as Alfred Schultz's 1908 study *Race or Mongrel: A Theory That the Fall of Nations Is Due to Intermarriage with Alien Stock: A Demonstration That A Nation's Strength Is Due to Racial Purity*.

2 For more examples of the review of *The Heart of Hyacinth*, see Huining Ouyang, "Ambivalent Passages: Racial and Cultural Crossings in Onoto Watanna's *The Heart of Hyacinth*," *MELUS*. Vol. 34, No.1, (Spring, 2009): 211-229.

its fairy-tale-like quality. Therefore, the early readers failed to see the novel as a story that denaturalizes race, even though some reviewers easily read hereditarian theories into the text.

> The hereditary influences are not always known to persons subject to them, and out of this grow mysteries, grief, and surprises, which the author has treated with considerable appreciation. It is the conflict of inherent and acquired traits that gives *The Heart of Hyacinth* its particular importance. (1903, *Public Ledger*).

In short, the early reviews classify the novel into orientalist or hereditarian paradigms. Although the later paradigm notices Winnifred's experiment with "racial combinations and admixtures," the issue of mixed race has not got as much attention as it deserves.

It is only recently that the novel has begun to draw critical attention. Reading from the perspective of feminism, Samina Najmi's "White Woman in Asia" provides a discussion of Hyacinth's, the protagonist, sense of racial plasticity in order to defy white and Asian patriarchal expectations. "Through *Hyacinth* Watanna challenges prevailing notions of the 'naturalness' of blood ties and racio-cultural identity as immutable and inherited rather than acquired" (Najmi 142). Najmi suggested that "Onoto Watanna is far ahead of her time in breaking free of the notion of biological race to show how a fluid identity can empower women" (142). On the basis of Najmi's argument about Hyacinth's racial plasticity, this book continues to argue that *The Heart of Hyacinth* has both the subversive and constructive qualities in terms of the biracial Eurasian subject. What it subverts is the paradigmatic fate imposed upon Eurasians. Besides, it breaks the traditional white-supremacist view which places white (Western) culture over the raced or ethnic (Eastern) counterparts. Meanwhile, it explicitly constructs a fluid Eurasian identity represented by the characters Hyacinth and Komazawa (called Koma). On the one hand, through Koma's free and easy crossings between the East and the West, physically and culturally, Winnifred Eaton prophesies a fluid hybrid Eurasian subjectivity that counters the dominant paradigm of the tragic Eurasian and that of Eurasian as the unassimilable racial and cultural other.[1] On the other hand, through Hyacinth's negotiations of her cultural Japaneseness and biological American descent, Winnifred Eaton provides an even more liberating kind of boundary passing/crossing beyond limitations of racial category. At the end of the novel, rather than capitulate to racial designations, Koma and Hyacinth escape from

---

1   For portrayals of the tragic Eurasian, see Clive Holland's *Mousme: A Story of the West and East* (1901), John Luther Long's short story "Purple Eyes" (1898) and his novella *Madame Butterfly* (1898), also see W. Carlton Dawe's "Yellow and White" (1895), Jeanette Dailey's "Sweet Burning Incense" (1921), and Steve Fisher's "Shanghai Butterfly" (1933).

them and, in the form of self exile, achieve their ideal state of identity.

As a woman of half-Chinese and half-English descent, Winnifred Eaton dealt with Japaneseness through her Japanese romances and Japanese authorial persona, which links her with the practice of passing, or crossing of identity boundaries by those on the racial and cultural margins. The way Elaine K. Ginsberg defined "passing" is of much help.

> Passing associates with the discourse of racial difference and especially with the assumption of a fraudulent "white" identity by an individual culturally and legally defined as "Negro" or black by virtue of a percentage of African ancestry. As the term metaphorically implies, such an individual crossed or passed through a racial line or boundary—indeed trespassed—to assume a new identity, escaping the subordination and oppression accompanying one identity and accessing the privileges and status of the other. Enabled by a physical appearance emphasizing "white" features, this metaphysical passing necessarily involved geographical movement as well; the individual had to leave an environment where his or her "true identity"—that is, parentage, legal status, and the like—was known to find a place where it was unknown. (Ginsberg 2)[1]

Regardless of her racial integrity, by writing the Japanese romance and adopting the exotic Japanese name, Winnifred Eaton not only escaped the intense anti-Chinese sentiment, but also achieved authorship in the white-male-dominant literary marketplace. Similarly, in *The Heart of Hyacinth*, as an important narrative strategy, passing or crossing is closely related to two protagonists when they live between East and West.[2]

Set in Sendai, Japan, the story begins with a depiction of a quiet coastal village where "foreign devils" have long been a presence, in the form of first Catholic and then Presbyterian missionaries. Later, with the expansion of trade between Europe and Japan, the seacoast village has become something of a tourist spot. The citizens are uneasy about a "barbarian" invasion; white visitors are regarded as less fascinating. However, as it narrates, in this mythical village, cultural clash is coupled with interracial love: an English missionary falls in love with and marries Aoi, a young Japanese woman, and settles in his "adopted land," a sanctuary of "unbounded,"

---

1   Elaine Ginsberg continues to state that the meaning of passing or crossing through a racial line or boundary has been discursively extended to refer to "disguises of other elements of an individual's presumed "natural" or "essential" identity, including class, ethnicity, and sexuality, as well as gender. Here, the term means the crossings of established racial, ethnic, and cultural boundaries. For more information on the term passing, see Elaine K. Ginsberg, "The Politics of Passing." Introduction. *Passing and the Fictions of Identity*. Ed. Elaine Ginsberg (Durham: Duke UP, 1996): 1-18.

2   For more discussion of Winnifred Eaton and her passing strategy, see Ferens, 118-120.

"peace, rest and love" (*HH* 5).

Focusing on the protagonist, Hyacinth, the main plot covers seventeen years from the day of Hyacinth's birth to her marriage. Early in the narrative, Hyacinth is born in Madame Aoi's house to a very ill white woman who seeks a refuge from her faithless white husband, Richard Lorrimer. In fits of pain, the woman makes mysterious reference to her situation, but bears her daughter and dies without further explanation. After her death, the English missionaries make a meager attempt to contact the woman's family but eventually they decide to let Aoi become the infant's foster mother. Hyacinth grows up without knowing her real parentage; the community in Sendai also assumes that Hyacinth is Aoi's biracial daughter with her late English husband. In *The Half-Blood: A Cultural Symbol in 19th-Century American Fiction*, William J. Scheick discusses the trope of the "figurative half-blood." He states that "a pure white who evinces the virtues of both the noble savage and civilization…is usually compared to, thought to be, or described as if he were an actual half-blood" (Scheick 58). In this sense, Hyacinth is such a metaphorical or figurative Eurasian, who passes as a Japanese Eurasian in reality.[1] In her Japanese fiancé's eyes, Hyacinth has the enchanting half-English beauty. "Her eyes did not slant in shape, and yet which had a trick of closing half-way and then glancing out sideways. It was as if Hyacinth, with her wide eyes, had unconsciously fallen into the habit of copying nature, where all eyes about her were narrow and seemingly half closed" (*HH* 109).

Hyacinth's development is paralleled by that of Koma, eight years her senior, Madame Aoi's biologial Eurasian son with her late husband. Madame Aoi has converted to Christianity, and English is spoken in her home, though she retains Japanese dress. She keeps her son away from Japanese children to raise him as his father's heir. So Koma's life is extremely lonesome before Hyacinth's birth. Young Koma and Hyacinth pass idyllic childhood together. On one occasion, sixteen-year-old Koma and his adoptive younger sister return home in a small raft after a summer outing in the mountains. They smile to each other with their laughter and song ringing across the bay and floating back to them from the echoing hills. It is worth noting that Koma can easily turn to sing Japanese songs when speaking to Hyacinth in idiomatic

---

1   In fact, many examples of symbolic mixed-race characters can be found in the early twentieth-century white portrayals of Asian-white contacts in which "Eurasian" characters who combine the virtue of Chinese filial piety and white independent individuality turn out to be a pure white, without any stain of Asian blood, such as Rex Beach's *Son of the God* (1928) and Frank L. Packard's *The Dragon's Jaws* (1937). For detailed discussion, see Elaine Kim, *Asian American Literature*, 9-10.

English. This scene is significant because it not only signifies Koma and Hyacinth's golden childhood but also implies Koma's ability to navigate his bicultural identity smoothly.

When Koma comes of age, the missionaries advise Aoi to send Koma to England, in accordance with his father's will. Thus begin the painful conflicts that Koma and Hyacinth endure as children of East and West. During his four years away, Hyacinth enters school, where she is inspected with curiosity and contempt by her classmates because of the golden sheen in her dark hair and her "blue-glass" eyes. Even her teacher takes her aside on the first day and examines her "with the curiosity he would have bestowed upon some small animal" (*HH* 64). But Hyacinth's ebullient nature soon wins them over, and for a while she is regarded as—and regards herself as—fully Japanese. "In heart and nature she is all Japanese" (*HH* 78). Hyacinth integrates herself in the Japanese community, while the whites—her biological members are strange, unnatural, belonging to "monsters" or "savages and barbarians" in her eyes. Four years later, when Koma returns from England, she is "frightened into speechless," until Koma changes out of his "strange and unpleasant looking clothes" into a kimono. Hyacinth so thoroughly identifies with the Japanese that she even challenges the white sense of superiority. When the white missionaries appear, Hyacinth would call them foreigners, shouting strange names, "Foreign debbil! Clistian!" (*HH* 66). During her Japanese school years, she stops speaking English and refuses to go to church. What's more, she regards the Shinto teacher with respect and awe. For her, Shinto "gods were bright, beauteous beings, whose temples were glittering gold, whose priest kept them fragrant with incense and beaming lights by night" (*HH* 67). In sharp contrast, "the mission-house was empty, ugly, dark, and damp." Missionaries are considered as an "odious man, with terrible, long hairs falling from his chin, shouted and gesticulated to a congregation which often wept and groaned in unison" (*HH* 67). It is evident that the western beauty standard and white Christian norms are totally subverted by Hyacinth. Traditional Orientalist "concept of otherness," to use Annette White-Park's words, is also subverted. Hyacinth's passing into Japanese culture once again underlines that the true self, the biological race, does not necessarily cohere with one's ethnic and cultural identity.

Among Winnifred's novels, *The Heart of Hyacinth* is the most special one that works hardest against Western assumptions of cultural superiority. With the exception of Hyacinth and her mother, most of the white characters in the novel are satirized. Hyacinth not only makes clear the distinction between ugly Americans and the finer sensibilities of the Japanese, but also expresses her resentment of her father's proprietorship in her antagonism to all Western things and to white men in particular, whom she associates with control. She loathes the "sacrilegious beasts" who bring knives with which to chip off pieces of tombs and temples; and the women who "went about in hideous garments, with what appeared to be heavy flower-baskets upon their heads" (*HH* 169). They put on airs, have dreadful manners, and otherwise make nuisances of themselves. By doing so, Winnifred decenters the Western notion of beauty and civilization.

However, it is Koma who claims his English roots without any impediments that forces Hyacinth to acknowledge her difference. In a striking scene of self-discovery, Hyacinth asks Koma what the "barbarians" he has lived among are like. In reply, he simply hands her a mirror. In order to comply with the traditional custom discouraging female vanity and to abide by the wishes of her foster mother who does not want her to be aware of her "peculiar physical misfortunes," Hyacinth has never looked into a mirror. This point responds to one earlier scene in which Hyacinth looks at her own reflection in the well. Hyacinth shouts in surprise, "See, there's big cherry tree in well, and little girl under it also" (*HH* 48). As a child deliberately raised without mirrors, Hyacinth does not even recognize herself at the bottom of the well. Therebore, once she is at last forced to see herself in the mirror, she is horrified at first, at her blue eyes, light hair, and fair skin—features she considers hideous when she runs into the missionaries or white tourists. But Koma assures her that she is beautiful, and when he returns to England to finish his education Koma instructs her to keep the handmirror. Koma insists that through the mirror, Hyacinth can see her own image and learn much which the Japanese teacher cannot teach her. Nevertheless, although Hyacinth learns from Koma that she herself is white, the knowledge does not affect her love for Aoi and for Japan. She wears the kimono as camouflage and is not interested in trying her mother's American dress that Aoi has kept as an heirloom.

Of course, at times, Hyacinth is not entirely resistant to her white side. Sometimes Hyacinth even begins to privilege the Western cultural perspective. When she is alone, studying her face in the mirror, she begins to show her preference for white feminine beauty even though she is "distressed" by her face, by her "undoubtedly gray-blue" eyes which are "strange," and "unnatural" (*HH* 95). But she is pleased by the whiteness of her skin and other attractive features.

> What girl of her acquaintance would not be glad of such a complexion? She had small use for the powder-pot, into which her friends must dip so freely. Her mouth was rosy, the teeth within white and sparkling. Her chin was dimpled at the side and tipped with the same rose that dwelt in her rounded cheeks. The little nose was thin and delicate, piquant in shape and expression.

> Why should such a face have distressed her? She would not admit to herself that she was
> homely... what did their judgment amount to? They were rude, uncouth even to have hinted at
> her 'deformities.' They were one-eyed, seeing but one type of beauty. There must be another
> kind, for she was surely, surely beautiful. (*HH* 96)

Regarding Hyacinth's pride in her Caucasian-style beauty, Najmi considers that, by challenging her friends' ethnocentric judgment of her appearance, Hyacinth highlights her ability to use a sense of racial fluidity to empower herself (Najmi 88). Najmi states one side, and the other side—her preference for white beauty is further underscored in the following lines: "Then she fell into a reverie in which she speculated upon the possible existence of another people whose maidens' hair and eyes were not like the night, but reflected the day" (*HH* 96). In addition, in response to her Japanese fiancé Yoshida's suggestion that she stand in the sun so that "the goddess might darken her skin and eyes," Hyacinth refuses to believe it will work because missionaries insists that there is no sun-goddess. Hyacinth no longer holds a resistant attitude toward white missionaries. In other words, Hyacinth begins to vaguely admit her white side.

Despite these details that slightly indicate Hyacinth's favor to the Western cultural perspective, Hyacinth's passing as a Japanese Eurasian is insistent on the whole. At seventeen, she accepts a proposal from a strictly traditional Japanese family. During the engagement, however, the matter of Hyacinth's parentage is brought to light. Scandalized by the thought of a woman with white blood marrying a Japanese man, missionaries reattempt to contact Hyacinth's biological father after seventeen years. [1] Invoking his authority as "a parent" to his parishioners, Mr. Blount first tries to force Aoi to uncover the truth of Hyacinth's origins. When he fails, he warns various Western consuls in Japan.

> There is a white child in Sendai, the adopted daughter of a Japanese woman, concerning whose
> parentage there appears to be some mystery. The child has been brought up entirely as a
> Japanese girl and does not know as yet of her true nationality. She is soon to be married to a
> Japanese youth, a Buddhist by religion. (*HH* 132-133)

1　It should be noted that Mr. Blount is the exact representative of white patriarchy over its women. In the nineteenth century, when Winnifred Eaton was born, the idealized white woman was consigned to the "cult of true womanhood," an ideology which heralded her as the pious "mother of civilization whose task was to guard the national soul and strengthen the moral fiber of America." With this role, white women are forbidden to marry out. This is one of the major reasons for anti-miscegenation between an Asian man and a white woman. Indeed, the motivation behind most anti-miscegenation laws was not to limit the sexual selections of white men, but to "protect" white women and ensure the racial homogeneity of their children. For more, see Giddings, 35-39; Ryan, 145; Pat Shea, 21-22.

As the conflict of the novel intensifies, Hyacinth, in several key scenes, shows her resistance to white colonialist claims and her allegiance to her Japanese mother and homeland, reaffirming her Japanese identity. When she is confronted with Knowles, Lorrimer (Hyacinth's father)'s attorney, and Saunders, the young American attaché, Hyacinth further challenges white paternal legitimacy and masculine authority. She defiantly states that she will not leave Japan with her father even if she is forced to do so. When Knowles insists that she does not belong to Japan, "it is some fatal and horrible miscarriage of fate that has cast your destiny among this alien people" (*HH* 145), Hyacinth fiercely refutes that Japanese are her people. Shocked by Hyacinth's impassioned defense of her Japanese heritage, the two American men exclaim "grotesques, impossible, horrible," and conclude that "she is more Japanese than anything else" (*HH* 145).

In the same way, when Saunders intrudes into her house in order to "become acquainted with" her, Hyacinth undermines his racial assumptions and white male privilege by satirizing Saunders "coming like a thief." Despite that Saunders begs her pardon for his intrusion of romantic interest, Hyacinth clearly declares her contempt for his rudeness. "I understand but I despise it...I am a Japanese; we are not so uncouth and rude in our intercourse with strangers" (*HH* 162). Even though later Saunders insists to Aoi that he never considers Hyacinth as Japanese, Hyacinth's assertion of her Japanese identity makes his intrusion fruitless ultimately. To undermine white patriarchal power, Hyacinth asserts her Japanese identity with rebellious belligerence. Taking control of her own life, she first seeks the help of the Yamashiros, asking Yoshida's formidable father to hasten her marriage to his son so that her husband's claim on her may override her father's and she can stay in Japan. Responding to his disapproval of her white heritage, she exclaims to Yoshida, "It is not my fault I am English. I am Japanese here at heart...If you will marry me... I will be Japanese together" (*HH* 175). Faced with the futility of seeking Japanese patriarchal protection against the claims of another patriarchal system, she instead looks for solace in Japanese gods. She prays to god that, "she was a Japanese girl... Japanese in thought, in feeling, in heart, in soul. How could she leave her beloved home and people to go away with these cold, white ones, whom she could never, never learn to know or understand" (*HH* 172).

At last, Richard Lorrimer, Hyacinth's American father comes to Japan to claim his daughter. Koma's return from England coincides with Lorrimer's journey to Japan. They meet in passage, and Koma brings him home in hope of settling the matter. But the news of her father's arrival from America makes Hyacinth run to the hills.

She flees to one of her old childhood haunts in the thickly covered mountains around Sendai. Koma, who knows the mountains as well as Hyacinth does, goes out to find her although he is as reluctant as she is to deliver her to her father. When she finally has to face her father, she once again acts the role of a demure Japanese maiden to subvert Western colonialist claims.

> With drooping head, Hyacinth softly entered the room. At first glance she seemed no different from any other Japanese girl, save that she was somewhat taller. She was dressed in kimono and obi, her hair freshly arranged and shining in its smooth butterfly mode. Her face was bent to the floor, so that they could scarcely see more than its outline. She hesitated a moment before them; then, as though unaware of the impetuous motion towards her of the man who she knew was her father, she subsided to the mats and bowed her head at his feet. (*HH* 232)

Hyacinth's Japanese dress and manner of greeting shock the American couple. With her first glance at the tall but very Japanese-looking Caucasian girl, Mrs. Lorrimer, Hyacinth's stepmother who persuaded Mr. Lorrimer to abandon his first wife seventeen years ago, shudders, "It is unnatural—horrible" (*HH* 233). Hyacinth refuses to acknowledge this American woman as her mother, and cries to Aoi in Japanese that Aoi is her only mother, she will never have another. Mrs. Lorrimer complains to her husband, "We can't be expected to understand a girl—like that...she is different from us, so utterly alien. Just look at her. Would anyone believe she was your daughter?" (*HH* 235). But later she brightens at the thought of having a pretty doll-child around. Meanwhile, Lorrimer, whose conscience has never been easy over his abandonment of his former wife and child, agrees to let Hyacinth and Koma have one month together before they depart for America.

Different from Hyacinth's insistence on Japanese heritage, Koma, the real Eurasian, embodies Eaton's ideals of fluid crossings for Eurasians. Compared with Hyacinth, Koma can relatively traverse the two heritages he has inherited with ease. On the whole, we can see a change on Koma because of cultural influence. From his birth to his first departure for England, Koma lives in Sendai but is raised as an Englishman by his mother Aoi following his late father's will. During this period, Koma understands his special biracial status. He admits he is a son of English, at the same time, treating his Japanese side with deep love. With regard to Mr. Blount's Orientalist view that isolates Koma from the despised Japanese blood, Koma promptly puts forward his counterview. Mr. Blount believes Eurasian belongs to the West, declaring Koma is "in fact, one of us."

> He has the physical appearance, somewhat of the training, and let us hope, the natural instincts of the Caucasian. It would be not only ludicrous but wicked for him to continue here in this

isolated spot, where he is, may we say, an alien, and particularly when it is his duty to follow the wishes of his father as regards his English estate. Certainly this is not where Komazawa belongs. (*HH* 57)

Blount's distinction between East and West, white and nonwhite, further underlines whites' sense of superiority which was prevailing in the turn-of-the-century North America.[1] But Koma retorts that though he is English, Japan is also his honorable and dear home, he can not deny his other blood. However, in "Signs Taken for Wonders," Homi K. Bhabha has suggested that white colonialist claim is momentary. Colonialist power or colonial authority demands that "the space it occupies be unbounded," "its discourse nondialogic," "its enunciation unitary" and "unmarked by the trace of difference" (Bhabha 157-158). Its "unitary voice of command" will be definitely interrupted by ambivalence and resistance. Similarly, while Blount on the one hand claims Koma is one of the white, he also treats Koma as an alien who does not own full membership on the other, as reflected in his statement about Koma speaking English with an accent: "No and Yes. You have been brought up to speak the language. It is intelligible, but queer—wrong, somehow. You speak your father's language like a foreigner" (*HH* 59).

Koma is the embodiment of Winnifred's idealized Eurasian who asserts his Japanese heritage and his love for homeland without denying his English inheritance. Koma's capacity to navigate two identities is best presented in his twice crossings of the ocean between Japan and England, physically and culturally. When he first returns from England to Japan after four years' study, Koma appears to be an English gentleman. He speaks refined English, wears English clothes, and eats with forks. However, when he understands his Englishman appearance and behavior make him a "stranger, a fearful intruder" to Hyacinth, he discards the heavy, dark, mysterious clothes and appears like any other Japanese youth. For Koma, identity is fluid and situational, and he can complete his identity crossing like dress crossing. Similarly, during his second return to Japan, he again changes into Japanese clothing to reunite with his adoptive sister. At the end of his fifth year in England, Koma inherits his father's estate and reunites with his father's family, becoming a real Englishman. Therefore, through Koma, Winnifred Eaton depicts a utopian state of Eurasian who can free from displacement and alienation, and achieve a hybrid identity without difficulties. Certainly, passing is an uneven process of accommodation and resistance.

---

1   About dominant racial theory, see Robert Young's *Colonial Desire: Hybridity in Theory, Culture and Race* and Reginald Horsman's *Race and Manifest Destiny: The Origins of American Racial Anglo-Saxonism.*

Four years' education not only endows Koma with his British father's financial and cultural inheritance, but also assimilates him into colonialist racial ideology, which Koma once decidedly rejected before his passage to England. He is not only critical of Japanese customs, but also like Blount, begins to consider one's identity is determined by one's "natural parts," and reinforces Hyacinth to discover her real self.

Elaine K. Ginsberg explains "passing" as a kind of "trespassing"—a way to assume a new identity and access the privileges of another, and argues that "passing" creates the space for agency, including the opportunity to "construct new identities" (16). But the social environment for passing is harsh. For Hyacinth, at every turn, her desire to retain her Japanese identity is complicated by both Japanese and Western influences. To the Japanese would-be in-laws, some of the Christian missionaries, her American father and stepmother, and some of her girlfriends, she is disfigured, unenlightened, even pre-civilized. Like all of the white characters who believe that true identity is racially defined, Hyacinth is white, so she belongs to America with her father. Because she is not racially Japanese, the people of Sendai are just as unwilling as the whites to regard her as a real Japanese.

In fact, neither Koma nor Hyacinth can face the difficulties of being cultural and racial misfits. They want only to be together and to have the right to call themselves Japanese. In the penultimate scene of the book, Koma and Hyacinth drift aimlessly in a rowboat far out on the water, dreading what is to be their final separation. The image of the boy and the girl floating out beyond their troubles, which also means, beyond civilization and home, is a telling one in light of their solution. When Hyacinth complains that she is afraid to leave Japan and go out into the unknown, Koma persuades her to steal away with him at night, into self-imposed exile. Like Winnifred Eaton's other romances, the novel ends with a romantic marriage of Koma and Hyacinth. Paradoxically, instead of returning to Lorrimer, the white Hyacinth asserts her Japaneseness by breaking the Japanese tradition of filial piety and acting in defiance of her white father. The biracial Koma, in turn, chooses to remain in Japan to marry Hyacinth and thus places love for his family over the allure of life in the West. They arrange a bicultural marriage. At first, they go to pray at the Buddhist temple first and then go to the mission house, where a Reverend is waiting to marry them.

As a passing narrative, *The Heart of Hyacinth* suggests an important significance at the turn of the century for Eurasians. Compared with the turn-of-the-century representations of mixed-race characters which maintain racial separation and hierarchy, Watanna's construction of Eurasian identity as fluid not only challenges the traditional colonialist binary discourse, but also affirms what Ginsberg has called "the positive potential of passing," that is, passing enables "self-determination and agency" and creates "the opportunity to construct new identities, to experiment with multiple subject positions, and to cross social and economic boundaries that exclude or oppress" (Ginsberg 16). As far as the romantic ending is concerned, especially, the scene of the bridging of the East (Buddhist temple) and the West (mission house) signifies Winnifred Eaton's ideal of fluid Eurasian identities and harmonious racial and cultural hybridity. In this sense, Winnifred expresses the same aspiration as her older sister Edith Eaton/Sui Sin Far. In her autobiographical essay "Leaves from the Mental Portofolio of an Eurasian," Sui Sin Far also affirms such integrative and fluid identity by demonstrating her desire of bridging the East and the West. "I give my right hand to the Occidentals and my left to the Orientals, hoping that between them they will not utterly destroy the insignificant 'connecting link'" (*MSF* 230). In fact, this ideal of fluid identity is a common aspiration for those situated at the crossroads of cultures. In *The Souls of Black Folk*, Du Bois expresses his hope of having a fluid identity.

> The history of the American Negro is the history of this strife—this longing to attain self-conscious manhood, to merge his double self into a better and truer self. In this merging he wishes neither of the older selves to be lost. He would not Africanize America, for America has much to teach the world and Africa. He would not bleach his Negro soul in a flood of white Americanism, for he knows that Negro blood has a message for the world. He simply wishes to make it possible for a man to be both a Negro and an American, without being cursed and spit upon by his fellows, without having the doors of Opportunity closed roughly in his face. (Du Bois 9)

However, what makes Winnifred Eaton differ from Sui Sin Far is her attitude. While Sui Sin Far stands out to battle, Winnifred Eaton chooses to escape, or to borrow Carol Roh-Spaulding's word, secession.[1] Pauline T. Newton emphasizes that contemporary hybrids have their own ambivalence about racial/cultural border crossing and fluidity.[2]

---

1 Carol Roh-Spaulding coined the word secession to describe the portrayal of mixed race characters who achieve a kind of symbolic exile. See, "The Go-Between People: Representations of Mixed Race in Twentieth-Century American Literature," *American Mixed Race*, ed. Naomi Zack (Boston: Rowman & Littlefield Publishers, Inc, 1995), 103.

2 Pauline T. Newton suggests, in their attempts to construct an identity that negotiates contesting or shifting racial and cultural boundaries, diasporic women writers recognize fluid crossings as "a dream or an ideal that must be attained." While some of these writers "remain more upbeat and confident of their abilities to cross and recross boundaries," others "express caution about riddled complicities that arise as they cross multiple cultures, seeking transculturality." See Huining Ouyang, "Ambivanlent Passages," 225; Pauline T. Newton, *Transcultural Women of Late-Twentieth-*

Winnifred, aware of Eurasian vulnerability in a racially divided world and the problems of passing, outpours the utopian nature of the fluid identity. Hyacinth defines her beauty by standards that are neither fully Caucasian nor fully Japanese, so does she behave in the matter of love. She belongs neither to the Japanese boy, to whom she was betrothed, nor to her father and stepmother or, by extension, to an eventual American mate. By marrying Koma, whom she truly loves, and whose identity has also been made ambiguous, contested by forces beyond control—another Eurasian, Hyacinth resists becoming the embodiment of the tensions resulting from increased intersection between Japan and the West.

This solution is significant. Through the marriage of two people whose identities have been made ambiguous and troublesome by cultural forces beyond their control, Winnifred Eaton presupposes an idealized future for mixed people. Furthermore, the incestuous overtone suggests that the racial hybrid is a kind of exotic species that can only reproduce among its own kind, ironically echoing the horrible belief in sterility of the mulatto in the nineteenth century. In terms of their exile, Koma and Hyacinth can be regarded as edenic figures, the progenitors of "new people," to borrow Joel Williamson's term for mixed bloods. Rather than capitulate to racial designations, Koma and Hyacinth escape from them—a diaspora of two. Pragmatically and prophetically, Koma and Hyacinth's voluntary exile is a creative act of survival. It suggests the possibility of reinterpreting racial designations through the racially "mixed" offspring to come. Genetically, their offspring will be more "pure" than their parents, thus their miscegenous union mocks the idea of racial purity. This solution is also similar to Homi Bhabha's concept of the "Third Space," an alien territory that makes possible an alternative identity beyond the concept of margin and center and beyond the concept of pure or essential racial types.[1] To conclude, Winnifred Eaton is a Eurasian literary foremother who is far ahead of time in demonstrating a utopian ideal condition for Eurasians. Her contribution is great to those who find themselves racially, culturally, and nationally in-between.

Century U.S. American Literature, 7.

1   Bhabha's concept of the Third Space does not directly address the concept of mixed race, but much of his work on cultural hybridity—especially in the sense that the site of mixing is within—is applicable to the study of mixed race in literature. See Homi K. Bhabha, "Third Space," *Identity: Community, Culture, Difference*. ed. Jonathan Rutherford (London: Lawrence and Wishart 1990), 209-211

Chapter Three

Diana Chang and Aimee Liu: Searching for Eurasian Identity in Borderlands

To be Chinese was not enough; it did not define one's beliefs any more.
—— Diana Chang, *The Frontiers of Love*[1]
I cannot present a more Chinese self because it may be expected of me; that would be jumping through ethnic hoops held up by majority, Caucasian or Chinese, conceptions and assumptions leading directly to a stereotyping that we all know, nor can I not reveal a self who, though complex and very confusing often, is the self that I am.
—— Diana Chang, *The 1980 Interview with Amy Ling*
A person's geography is both inward and outward.
—— Aimee Liu, *Face*

Contemporary autobiographies and novels by Eurasian writers continue to demonstrate debates over the conflicting identity caused by biraciality. Eurasian identity and the crisis of self are the very subject of Diana Chang's 1956 autobiographical novel *The Frontiers of Love* and Aimee Liu's 1994 novel *Face*. *The Frontiers of Love* tells the story of three young Eurasians' search for identity and love in Shanghai at the end of the Second World War. *Face* tells the story of Maibelle Chung's searching for identity in New York's Chinatown through her struggle to recollect a suppressed traumatic past. Both of the texts are good examples which locate characters' quest for identity in a special landscape. The former is in the war time hybrid city Shanghai, and the latter in the exotic Chinatown. According

---

1 This epigraph is taken from Diana Chang's autobiographical novel *The Frontiers of Love*, first published in 1956. (repr., Seattle & London: University of Washington Press, 1994). All references about *The Frontiers of Love* in this book are to the 1994 edition and are given in parentheses with page numbers.

to Gloria Anzaldua, the borderlands geographically refer to "wherever two or more cultures edge each other, where people of different cultures occupy the same territory, where under, lower, middle and upper classes touch, where the space between two individuals shrinks with intimacy" (Anzaldua 19). In this chapter, "Shanghai" and "Chinatown" are defined as borderlands. Thus, the Eurasian characters in both texts are the subjects of borderlands, who, in Anzaldua's words, usually "straddle multiple cultures and negotiate contradictory identities" and experience "the sense of helplessness." Because of this perspective on the interaction of place and identity, this chapter will examine how the Eurasian characters construct their identity in their relation to the special landscape.

I. Criticism of Diana Chang and Aimee Liu and Their Eurasian Consciousness

Both Diana Chang and Aimee Liu have a common feature in their writing career—they both turn to write "white" (non-Asian American theme) novels in their later career. Diana Chang, author of six novels, in *The Frontiers of Love* deals with the identity struggle among young Eurasians in Shanghai at the end of World War II; however, her other novels are basically about white Protestant characters. Similarly, Aimee Liu makes such attempts to suggest a new possibility for an ethnic author. Unlike Diana Chang who writes on obvious "white" characters, Liu believes Asian writers should not limit themselves to Asian themes. She seldom writes about the dominant-suppressed narratives to please the dominant culture, and always tries to eliminate chances for exotica from her narratives. For instance, in *Solitaire*, Liu presents an autobiography duplex of an anorexic teenager who questions her selfhood, not an autobiography duplex of a bicultural woman on the threshold between China and the West. This is why Diana Chang and Aimee Liu are not so important in Asian American criticism as Maxine Hong Kingston. Their works, except those concerning Asian American themes, are seldom reprinted. However, considering their biracial background, this book regards all their writings as an articulation of their mixed Eurasian consciousness.

As her dust jacket for the University of Washington Press edition of *The Frontiers of Love* shows, Diana Chang is quite open about her own Eurasian identity. Her photograph clearly proves the fact, and the accompanying biography includes details of her mixed ancestry and her childhood spent in China. Born in New York to an American-educated Chinese father, an architect, and an American Eurasian mother (whose mother was Irish), Chang was taken to China at the age of eight months, and spent her early childhood in China, including Beijing, Nanjing, and Shanghai where she attended American schools. She returned to New York where she attended high school and then Barnard College, and has lived there since, with a brief period in France. In her 1976 talk, Diana Chang confessed frankly the "twoness" of her identity.

> I have to confess tentatively, not sure what I'm really saying, that I don't really feel like a minority here. Am I turned around? In China, I know I'd be considered foreign and lost to the tribe. And they'd be right because I'm not translating myself into English. I express myself in English. I've imagined from within the points of view of white Protestant characters, as well as Chinese personae. Am I an American who sometimes writes about the Chinese in her? My imagination, based here since high school, doesn't belong to me. I belong to my imagination. It has its way with me. It's closer to lilacs blooming in doorways than to moon gates and lotus ponds. I have not experienced the new China. Yet, I find myself saying, "we Chinese" quite often, which is very Chinese of me. Nice liberal Americans have no grasp of the Chauvinism of the Chinese they embrace.[1]

Relatively speaking, Diana Chang is a prolific writer. She is the author of six novels, three volumes of poetry as well as many short stories.[2] Chang's career began in 1956 with the publication of *The Frontiers of Love*, her best-known and critically acclaimed novel about three Eurasian figures' choice of identity in Shanghai in the summer of 1945. By 1963, she had produced three more novels *A Woman of Thirty* (1959), *A Passion for Life* (1961), *The Only Game in Town* (1963) before "Asian American Literature" formed an established field of study.[3] Her last two novels *Eye to Eye* (1974) and *A Perfect Love* (1978) appeared in the 1970s during the advent of Asian American studies.[4] After the 1980s, Diana Chang began to express her concern

---

1 See Diana Chang's talk, "A Hyphenated Condition," given at the MLA Convention, New York, December 1976, quoted in Amy Ling's "Diana Chang: The Hyphenated Condition."

2 Chang's short stories were mainly published in numerous magazines such as *The Virginia Quarterly Review*, *The Nation*, *The American Scholar*, *The New York Quarterly* and *New Letters*.

3 *A Woman of Thirty* is a fiction about witty, intelligent, resilient Emily Merrick who develops self-reliance after an unhappy marriage, a divorce, and an affair with a married man. *A Passion for Life* is about Barbara and Geoffrey Owens who decide to keep her baby, the result of rape after much anguish. See Diana Chang, *A Woman of Thirty* (New York: Random House, 1959); *A Passion for Life* (New York: Random House, 1961).

4 *Eye to Eye* tells a story of artist George Safford, a husband and father, who falls blindly and hopelessly in love with a Jewish writer, sees a psychiatrist about his problems, and makes a surprising discovery. *A Perfect Love* is about Alice Mayhew, frustrated in her marriage, having a passionate

about identity and selfness through the form of poetry. Till now, Chang has published three volumes of poetry, *The Horizon If Definitely Speaking* (1982), *What Matisse If After* (1984), and *Earth Water Light* (1991).

Although Diana Chang is ethnically classified as an Asian (Chinese) American writer, it is difficult to connect Diana Chang's ethnic identity with her literary productions, because except *The Frontiers of Love,* her other five novels are all about people of white Anglo-Saxon Protestants with an occasional Jew,[1] containing no Chinese or Chinese Americans at all. This is why critics exclusively focus on *The Frontiers of Love*, which was reprinted in 1994 with an introduction by Shirley Geok-lin Lim. Her other novels, which I call white novels, have been virtually marginalized by critics. Diana Chang herself, thus, was censured by certain critics.

Frank Chin, whose nationalist and masculine definitions of Asian America constitute an "authentic" Asian American sensibility, denounced some of his contemporaries including the most famous Maxine Hong Kingston. Diana Chang, owing to her writing of white characters in most of her novels, became one of Chin's objects of criticism.

> Now let me recommend someone to you whose work I respect and find fucked up as a thinker, a Eurasian, a Chinese-American, a mind and person, fucked up. Diana Chang. She just had another poem published in the *New York Quarterly* in which she fails to come to grips with her Chinese-American identity, but does repeat the clichés and racist stereotype with a certain style and an occasional nice line... She takes a stand with **white supremacy** as unconsciously and unwittingly and as sincerely as any of your writers and brings it off in a tour de force of writing flash and style. She manages to have her own voice and take that white racist rhetoric about universal of art and **being an individual instead of white or yellow**, and **mixing the best of East and West**... the whole stinking mess... and show us accurately, how she's made it work, how she believes it... All that she's trained herself to ignore, the enormity of her deafness, her forced ignorance shows through absences in her work... brilliantly. And what she writes consciously is pretty good too. (Chin, 1972 32 emphasis added)

By 1972, Frank Chin would have had the occasion to read three of Chang's

---

affair with a charming but married younger man. See Diana Chang, *Eye to Eye* (New York: Harper and Row, 1974); *A Perfect Love* (New York: Jove Books, 1978).

1 Novels including Jewish characters are *A Passion for Life* and *Eye to Eye*. With regard to Diana Chang's writing of white novels with occasional Jewish characters, if viewed from present research trends, she is far ahead of time in writing from an interethnic angle. Caroline Rody announced that in the last quarter of the twentieth century, literature is immersed in ethnic interconnection: an interethnic literature. See Caroline Rody, *The Interethnic Imagination: Roots and Passages in Contemporary Asian American Fiction* (New York: Oxford University Press, 2009).

white novels—*A Woman of Thirty* (1959), *A Passion for Life* (1961), and *The Only Game in Town* (1963).[1] For Chin, Chang does not have the "authentic Asian American sensibility"; instead, she has become "accomplices to white racism." Another point attributing to Chin's criticism is Chang's desire of "being an individual instead of white or yellow" and "mixing the best of East and West" which are exactly what Diana Chang strives to express about her mixed Eurasian sense. In Chin's eyes, there is no distinction between Eurasian and racially pure Chinese American. In other words, Chang's Eurasian voice is a kind of traitorism to Chinese American identity.

Similarly, Amy Ling, one of the most important scholars for the reception of Diana Chang in the Asian American field, keeps the same idea that the distinction between "Chinese" and "Eurasian" is insignificant. In her 1976 talk Chang says "as long as I'm not blonde, leggy, and of Massachusetts, I choose to be myself, with this elusive, confused identity known as Chinese-American, in this country" (Ling, 1980 69). Thus, Chang concludes that for her there is no choice but the complex hyphenated condition. But in *Between Worlds*, Amy Ling discussed the "hyphenated condition" of several Chinese American women writers with a little hint of Eurasian's biracial particularity. Especially, Ling disclosed her dissatisfaction with Chang's reply for her later white Caucasian characters which underscores Ling's assumption about Chang that she has betrayed her Chinese heritage in the service of a white, mainstream readership.[2] When asked why she no longer writes of Chinese or Chinese American characters, Chang replied that "I feel I'm an American writer whose background is Chinese. The source of my first and fourth novels was Chinese but *exoticism* can stand in the way of the *universal* that I strive for in my themes" (Ling, 1980 75). Therefore, Chang "often subsumed aspects of her background in the interests of other truths."[3] When asked why a Chinese or Chinese American cannot also be "universal," she responded that "we are living in the United States and here every man is white."[4] Admittedly, we have to say that Chang's reply is not accurate. It may be that she herself at that time did not have a clear idea about the distinction

---

1 This book classifies *The Only Game in Town* as a white novel, because factually the Chinese dancer in the novel has nothing to do with ethnicity, if judging from Frank Chin's criteria.

2 Certainly, Amy Ling's criticism is much milder than Fran Chin's. Ling even defends Chang's explanation as the result of the special historical era, namely, during the McCarthy era, all Americans, including Chinese Americans, had to disavow any relations to Communist China. See Ling, *Between Worlds*, 119.

3 See Diana Chang's conversation with Amy Ling, October 1979. Quoted from Leo Hamalian, "A *MELUS* Interview: Diana Chang," *MELUS*, 20: 4 (1995), 29.

4 Ibid.

between Eurasian and Chinese American owing to the persistent influence of the one-drop rule especially in the face of the vigorous Asian American movement. Anyhow, Chang should not have been accused if she wants to write and has written about the other side of her blood. As a person of double racial ancestry, must she write about the Chinese side and deny or ignore her white side? Of course, in her 1995 *MELUS* interview, Chang changed her way of saying by defending her writing of white novels as "inventing something." She said, "I don't think invention is a form of dishonesty. Novels are imagined, invented lies which can be more truthful than actual life itself" (Hamalian 35)[1]. Therefore, the problem of biracial and bicultural Eurasian is much more complicated than bicultural but racially pure Chinese American.

However, restricted by historical and social factors, Amy Ling shows her dissatisfaction with Chang's reply—"ethnicity does not or should not preclude universality" (Ling, 1980 75). In order to do so, Ling even cites Ralph Ellison's discussion of the relationship between "minority" and "universal" themes to criticize Chang's abandonment of ethnicity for "universality." According to Ellison, "all novels are about certain minorities: the individual is a minority. The universal in the novel—and isn't that what we're all clamoring for these days?—is reached only through the depiction of the specific man in a specific circumstance" (Ling, 1980 75). In terms of Chang's biracial background, Ling presumes that the Chinese identity is "closer" to her. Hence, Ling states that it is "a difficult stand to defend" her "prolonged avoidance of that which is closest to one's self when self-hood is one's major theme" (Ling, 1990 119). However, Ling's presumption that Chinese identity is closer to her is incorrect. Indeed, Chang's facial features are more Chinese as shown in her photograph and indicated by her poem "An Appearance of Being Chinese,[2]" but as is well known, one's identity largely depends on cultural affiliation or growing experiences. Though Diana Chang grew up in China, at her home, Western ways predominated due to her American mother, let alone she spent her formative years in New York and led a Western-

---

1 In fact, Diana Chang made a number of responses to the criticism of her deviation from Asian American ideology later. For example, she said, "Supposing they had restricted themselves to Asian American themes and characters… what a loss it would have been. We all live in the world, an increasingly global village. Why not write about others? Why should anyone disfranchise him or herself from any human history or experience? Is anything human alien?" For more, see Leo Hamalian, 38-40.

2 See Diana Chang, "An Appearance of Being Chinese," The *New York Quarterly*, No. 17 (1975), 67.

style life in America.[1]

For Chang, "to be Chinese was not enough" (*FL* 245). Although Liyi Chen, Sylvia Chen's father in *The Frontiers of Love*, admits that no geopolitical or cultural affiliation (including Eurasian) is sufficient to define the self, he also believes that "the bravest thing he had done" was to marry a white woman and "bring two Eurasians into the world" (*FL* 245). He hopes they will "be free from any narrow chauvinism," and be the "new citizens for an expanding century" (*FL* 245). Given this understanding, Eurasian should be distinguished from Chinese. The latter owns a specific ethnic or racial category, while the former splits it open. Therefore, Chang's resistance to categorization and desire to be an individual for herself are none other than the expression of her Eurasian consciousness.

Shirley Geok-lin Lim, as well, considers dual or multiple consciousness is the characteristic of all nonwhite Americans. So in her view, the difference between bicultural Chinese and those of mixed Chinese-Anglo ancestry might be viewed as insignificant (Lim and Ling 22). Nevertheless, Shirley Geok-lin Lim's contribution to Diana Chang's reception in the Asian American field is very important, especially her reading of the influence of existentialist philosophy on Chang's work. Lim holds that in Chang's novels, "the question of stereotypes, ethnicity, and of forging a new identity fall under a larger existentialist theme" (Lim, 1990 73).[2] In her introduction to the Washington University Press edition *The Frontiers of Love*, Lim argues that the novel illuminates a small cosmos in which the crossing of geographical, political, cultural and racial boundaries is an unavoidable and settling fact of existence. In such a space, "Life was not to be resolved, but to be lived—a constant improvisation" (*FL* 245). Finally, Lim affirms that the improvisation of self in its encounters with the world, a brave existentialist affirmation to the question of identity, is Chang's special contribution to Asian American literature.

Wei-hsiung Kitty Wu has also discussed the influence of existentialism on

---

1　In *Between Worlds*, Amy Ling has stated that the mother determines the cultural orientation in a home. Ling says, "Though the geographical location of the family and the father's strength of character have some bearing upon the answers, generally the mother sets the tone in a home and establishes its traditions. As a rule, hers is the initial care for the children; she determines their language orientation; she prepares the family food and the holiday celebration." See Amy Ling, *Between Worlds*, 112.

2　In a talk at Westchester Community College (March 19, 1982), Chang said she read the Existentialist philosophers at college and was particularly affected by Kirkegaard's *Fear and Trembling*. See Shirley Geok-Lin Lim, "Twelve Asian American Writers: In Search of Self-Definition," *MELUS* 13: 1/2 (1986), 76.

Chang's work. In her examination of Chang's later novels, Wu focuses on the motif of the fragmented and displaced subject. But Wu's criticism does not appropriately connect the thread of existentialism with the author's racial identity, concluding it is the author's "preferred cultural mode instead of ethnic identity that bears most significantly on her aesthetic choices" (Wu 1). Indeed, existentialism helped Chang's articulation of her Eurasian consciousness. According to existentialism, identity is an "ongoing struggle," as Sylvia's searching for identity is always "in process" and "improvisational." However, both Lim and Wu's critical discussions of existentialism subsumed racial consciousness under a larger project. In other words, although they discussed Chang's split consciousness and search for identity, they sacrificed Chang's racial identity for the service of philosophy or aesthetics. With the growing academic interest in transnationalism, diaspora and hybridity, Chang has achieved more critical attention, especially her "white" novels which critics have marginalized. Carol Roh-Spaulding is pivotal in her discussion of Diana Chang, who similarly goes beyond Chang's *The Frontiers of Love*, by examining the "raced" whiteness in Chang's white novels. Roh-Spaulding makes important criticism about Chang's split double consciousness, and reads all Chang's novels as a whole for expressing "Eurasianism."[1]

In Chang's Eurasian sense, race mixture possesses a salient distinction from cultural mixture: the physical embodiment of a Chinese-Caucasian mix—a blurring of phenotypes—forces a reading of race mixture as more definitively neither/nor than that experienced by an individual who is bicultural but racially pure. In *The Frontiers of Love* and several of her poems, Chang directly expresses her preoccupation with biracial identity. In the poem entitled "Second Nature," Chang explicitly explores the split consciousness resulted from a biracial background.[2] In "Saying Yes," Chang similarly tackles her peculiar emotion of "strange" longing to be "at home here." Like the Eurasian protagonist Sylvia Chen in *The Frontiers of Love*, Chang "was both as American as her own mother, and as Chinese as her father. She could not deny her own ambivalence" (*FL* 19). Meanwhile, as all the Eurasian characters experienced in the novel, physically and emotionally, the inadequate feeling as an American

---

1　See Carol Roh-Spaulding, "Diana Chang (1934-)," ed. Nelson, Emmanuel S. *Asian American Novelists: A Bio-Bibliographical Critical Sourcebook* (Westport, CT: Greenwood, 2000):38-43.

2　In the poem, Chang writes: Sometimes I dream in Chinese/I dream my father's dreams./ I wake, grown up/And someone else/I am the thin edge I sit on./I begin to gray—white and black and in between./My hair is America/New England moonlights in me.../I shuttle passportless within myself,/My eyes slant around both hemispheres,/Gaze through walls/And long still to be/ Accustomed,/At home here,/Strange to say.

and as a Chinese—the yearning for oneness as well as the resistance to the tearing fragmentation reflect the painful duality as a Eurasian.

Compared with Diana Chang, criticism about Aimee Liu is relatively less, or in a manner of speaking, very rare. A daughter of an American woman and a high-ranking Eurasian bureaucrat of the United States, Aimee E. Liu was born in 1953 in Connecticut. Blessed with affluence and the best Western education, she grew up in a predominantly white neighborhood. Although she defines herself as "an American who grew up in a very Caucasian setting," she also addresses the issue of growing up with mixed ancestry as feeling like an "oddball who couldn't fit in."[1] Before starting her career as a writer, Liu attended Yale University, and has worked as a fashion model, flight attendant and associate producer of NBC's *Today Show*. She currently resides in Los Angeles, California with her husband, Martin Fink and their two sons.

Although labeled as a Chinese American writer, for Liu, China has no direct influence on her selfhood. She travels freely in both the Western and Eastern hemispheres of the globe. As a third-generation Eurasian removed from China geographically, she reveals no intellectual curiosity about China and Chinese history, confined in the world of her inner torments. Early in 1979, at the age of 23, Aimee Liu published her first book *Solitaire*, which was a memoir. *Solitaire* is a narrative of Liu's own affliction with and recovery from anorexia nervosa.[2] In this book, Liu follows her stream of consciousness and organizes external events according to her internal impulse. Like a modernist exploring the interior pilgrimage of a mind, Liu offers little cultural information, instead she struggles to fulfill the standards of beauty defined by the dominant culture. So to speak, *Solitaire* suggests a new possibility for an ethnic author, the possibility of appealing to audiences without cultural references.[3]

---

1 See http://www.aimeeliu.net/.

2 Anorexia nervosa is an eating disorder that usually strikes young middle- to upper-class women between the ages of thirteen and thirty. Liu suffered from anorexia for eight years, beginning at the age of thirteen and continuing until she was twenty-one. She attributes writing her first book to pulling her out of the final stages of anorexia. With the encouragement from her agent, she turned her energy to magazine editing and co-authoring nonfiction self-help books for the next ten years.

3 In fact, in her own confession, Aimee Liu admits that her cultural identity played a significant role in her anorexia. "Although I did not stress the fact of being Asian-American in the book, I now think that conflicting feelings about my cultural identity did play a significant role in my particular passage through anorexia. I also understand that anorexia is increasingly prevalent among Asian-American high school and college students." See Jid Lee, *From the Promised Land to Home: Trajectories of Selfhood in Asian-American Women's Autobiography* (Las Colinas: Ide House, 1998), 204.

However, with abstinence from cultural information, can an ethnic writer survive in multiethnic, multicultural America? Aimee Liu tried, and it seems that she even has got popularity among the reading public.

> Many of my readers and friends have expressed amazement that I could have exposed such a personal side of my life as I did in *Solitaire*. Their reaction amazed me. The notion that I am so special, so precious that I must not open myself up for scrutiny irks me. We are all the same animal, we human beings. We all share the same feelings, appetites, needs. We differ in our modes of expression, in the traps we create for ourselves and the escape mechanisms we use to free ourselves, but basically we understand each other, or can when we learn the common language.[1]

As a matter of fact, *Solitaire* is not that successful. Liu has confessed that she admires Maxine Hong Kingston, but unlike Kingston who fills her works with cultural references and is popular among readers and critics alike, Liu is critically invisible and obscure to the reading public. While *The Woman Warrior* has continued to appear in *The MLA International Bibliography* and remains in *Books in Print,* 1992-1993, *Solitaire* is neither in print nor in *The MLA International Bibliography* from 1979 through 1987.[2]

Indeed, considering her upbringing and privilege, it is understandable that Aimee Liu sees herself as a privileged American exempted from cultural conflicts and social barriers, not as a Chinese American struggling with her background. In spite of this, Liu also confesses that the issue of growing up with mixed ancestry makes her feel as an "oddball who couldn't fit in." In fact, in *Solitaire,* when portraying an anorexic girl, Liu contains little hint of Eurasian issues. As a Eurasian, Liu resents her short, pudgy Eurasian body, and such a body serves as a factor for her adolescent self-image, which she feels exclusively determined by physical standards. But her Asian physical traits do not cause a problem except in her obsession with having a thin, tall body and she realizes at the end of her autobiography that her adolescent self-image is utterly false

---

1   Quoted from http://voices.cla.umn.edu/artistpages/liu_aimee.php.

2   Despite its lack of cultural references, it was reprinted in 1980 and received four enthusiastic reviews, according to *The Book Review Digest*. These reviews evidence the degree of success a Chinese-American author can achieve without resorting to cultural information. If not high, the degree can exemplify the possibility of violating the rubber-stamp ingredients expected from an ethnic author. Reviewers treat the book as an insightful narrative on anorexia, pay no attention to her Eurasian background, and praise her style. "The brilliant and very moving narrative explores the author's life as a victim of anorexia nervosa…The book's insight, intelligence, and vivid prose make it highly recommended reading." See Marcia G Fuchs, Review of *Solitaire* by Aimme Liu, *Library Journal* (15 June, 1979), 1332.

and her Eurasian features are irrelevant to her selfhood.

Aimee Liu is an author of five books. Besides her autobiography *Solitaire*, she also wrote novels such as *Face* (1994), *Cloud Mountain* (1997), *Flash House* (2003) and *Gaining: The Truth about Life after Eating Disorders* (2008). It is in the first novel *Face* that Liu tracks the female character's struggle to come to terms with an incident of abuse, which is linked to her physical identity as Eurasian. The novel's central themes consist of biracial identity and intermarriage between Chinese and Caucasians. Liu addresses the issues that biracial people face—feelings of inadequacy, being an outsider in one's own community and a loss of one's heritage. Touching on similar territory, Liu's second novel, *Cloud Mountain*, is also about an interracial marriage. She incorporates the story of her grandmother, Jennie Ella Trescott from Fort Dodge, Kansas, and her grandfather, Liu Ch'eng-yu from Canton, China, into a fictional narrative that is "approximately 70% true." In *Cloud Mountain*, the two central characters Hope and Liang Po-yu wed during a time when anti-miscegenation laws were the norm. After receiving racist threats and experiencing prejudice in California, where it was a crime for people of different races to touch in public, Hope and Liang move to China. But in China, Hope finds the same prejudice against intermarriages as she has found in the United States. With most of the novel focused in Shanghai, Liu composes concrete examples of how their status as an interracial couple determines the way others treat them, regardless of their level of education, political power (Liang was a political leader assisting in Dr. Sun Yat-sen's revolutionary plans) or class status. With her last two novels, Aimee Liu still does not offer insight into the author's cultural struggles. *Flash House,* set in 1949 India, tells a story of an American woman who rescues a ten-year-old girl out of prostitution, and the last one, *Gaining: The Truth about Life after Eating Disorders* seemingly is still about the issue of anorexia.

Therefore, Aimee Liu's case is quite different from Diana Chang's. Liu was aware of the inadequacy of cultural information in her first book, so in the second and third books, Liu did try to explore the issues of biraciality and intermarriages from her biracial background. However, Liu still is not so critically visible. In *Negotiating Identities: An Introduction to Asian American Women's Writing*, Helena Grice includes Aimee Liu and her *Face*, discussing the correlation between the politics of body and the dynamics of selfhood. Jid Lee did a survey of Aimee Liu's *Solitaire* in *From the Promised Land to Home: Trajectories of Selfhood in Asian-American Women's Autobiography*, demonstrating Liu's writing of growing pain in *Solitaire*. Hence, readers still have to ponder the question I have asked, as Eurasian authors, Diana Chang and Aimee Liu are technically categorized as Asian (Chinese) Americans, thus accordingly, their literary concerns should have been focused on Asian (Chinese) American issues, culturally and historically. Once they avoid or are totally abstinent from cultural information, it is hard for them to acquire a position in Asian American criticism. Especially, for Aimee Liu, as a third-generation Eurasian, removed from Chinese geographically and biologically, it is much harder to create a text with more appeal to exotica-seeking non-Chinese-American readers. If she could elaborate on her early childhood in India, her feelings of estrangement caused by her French-Chinese name, her sense of inferiority about her short, Eurasian body, and the like, she would have added cultural information to her narrative and possibly attracted more audiences of all colors. She could have given exotica-seeking readers plenty of opportunities to read exotica into her text and earned more visibility among non-Chinese-American readers and critics. "Fulfilling the canonical standard of American autobiography— a narrator's emotional search for inner freedom from the tyrannical outside—it (*Solitaire*) offers few insights into the narrator's cultural and historical struggles, and hence, may not qualify as a Chinese-American woman's autobiography" (Lee 205). Maybe it is owing to her class and privilege that Aimee Liu can easily show such a new authorial position that an ethnic author might consider.

Ⅱ. Question of Biraciality in "Asia If Not in America": *The Frontiers of Love*

Different from the Eaton sisters who explored their Eurasian subjectivity explicitly and implicitly, Diana Chang, in a direct way, specifically probed into the question of Eurasian and Eurasian identity in *The Frontiers of Love* which was considered as the first Chinese American novel.[1] Published in 1956, but set in 1945 wartime Shanghai, *The Frontiers of Love* is an excellent novel in its themes, characters, actions and stylistic textures. It tells of three young Eurasians' search for identity and love in Shanghai at the close of World War Ⅱ. When it first appeared, *The Frontiers of Love* received favorable notice. However, during the1950s, American readers in the main

---

1 The next two Chinese American novels are Louis Chu's *Eat A Bowl of Tea* (1961) and Shawn Wong's *Homebase* (1979). See Chin and others, *Aiiieeeee!*, xiv. But for some other critics, the earliest Asian and Chinese American novels date back to the novels of Winnifred Eaton, even though her forged Japanese identity makes her a controversial figure in the Chinese American/Canadian literary history. Her first novels appeared around the turn of the 20th century, such as *Miss Nume of Japan: A Japanese-American Romance* (1899) and *A Japanese Nightingale* (1901).

were not mindful of issues of diversity. Therefore, Shirley Geok-Lin Lim states that, "nowhere was it hailed then as an Asian American work" (*FL* v). Critics tended to ignore the author's preoccupation with the question of biraciality when acclaiming the novel. Benjamin Lease's review in *Chicago Sun-Times* read the novel within the genre of realism as an expression of private and individual lives. "Remarkably, Chang enters the minds and hearts of her characters, young and old, European and Oriental, reveals them in their strengths and weaknesses, in their moments of self-deception and revelation."[1] Meanwhile, some other reviews at that time defined the novel as "Far East" or "Asia" fiction. Kenneth Rexroth placed the book with several Japanese novels in an article.

> Yet, of all the novels of the Far East published this season, her book, at least for me, has most reality... Not very many first novels are written with as much skill and insight. One Chapter, in which the heroine's Communist lover tries to pump her for information which she doesn't possess by simultaneously making love to her and belaboring her for facts which she doesn't have, is a masterpiece of quiet, mature irony. Whatever we may think of the merits of the Japanese novelists I have been reviewing, Diana Chang is one of ours. She should be around in American literature for some time to come. (Rexroth 272)

Naming *The Frontiers of Love* as a military novel, Rexroth assessed that Chang's achievement is that she has joined the tradition of Ford Maddox Ford, Cummings and Ernest Hemingway by producing a psychological novel of war. Rexroth praised the novel's skill, insight, and "quiet, mature irony." But with respect to the novel's central issue of Eurasian biracial identity, with a bit of boredom, Rexroth underestimated it as "Once again, it is the same message as in so many of these novels, out of this nettle, alienation, we pluck this flower, integrity" (Rexroth 271).

Similar examples existed like Kay Boyle's 1957 "The Far East and Fiction" in *The American Scholar* and Faubion Bowers' 1956 "Asia in Wartime: China" in the *Saturday Review*. Especially, Bowers' review of *The Frontiers of Love* was placed together with a Japanese novel *Zone of Emptiness*, translated into English about enlisted men's life in the Japanese army by Hiroshi Noma on one page. Nevertheless, unlike Kenneth Rexroth, Bowers appreciates that the question of racial identity is central to the novel, describing the Eurasian's life as "trouble, torture, or torment." But what Bowers fails to critique is the racism that Sylvia Chen's father hopes his children will outlive. In Bowers' view, Eurasians are a phenomenon of wartime, not the inevitable result of long-standing racial oppression which most nations preserve, overtly or covertly.

1　See Benjamin Lease, "Review of *The Frontiers of Love*," *Chicago Sun-Times*, 1956.

Thus, compared with her Asian American contemporaries such as Jade Snow Wong whose *Fifth Chinese Daughter* (1945) successfully promoted postwar American values and was translated into several Asian languages by the U.S. State Department, Diana Chang and *The Frontiers of Love* seem not to have received the same attention. There are two reasons. On the one hand, Diana Chang is treated as a foreigner by the American reading public although she is a citizen due to her special life experience. Chang spent her younger years in China. So, unlike many of her Asian American contemporaries, Chang's status seems foreign. Chang herself confessed, "I purchase my citizenship in this land of life from which I feel estranged… I must earn it like an illegitimate child, a stateless person… I create something in order to become all that I was meant to be" (Chang, 1969 1). On the other hand, the special geopolitical milieu of the novel—Japanese occupied Shanghai at the close of the Second World War— impressively set the novel as a foreign text like the Japanese novel *Zone of Emptiness* mentioned above. Hence, Chang and *The Frontiers of Love* were not treated as authentically American. Fortunately, it was precisely because of the "inauthenticity" that Chang was able to escape the severe American ideological attack in the era of the Cold War, when people, especially Americans of Chinese descent, tried all means to disavow everything to do with the Communist China.[1]

The Frontiers of Love is highly considered as Chang's autobiographical novel. Concerning this point, Chang herself also affirmed that "I have not avoided using my own background as a source—two of my novels were informed by my own identity" (Hamalian 32). The two novels she refers to are *The Frontiers of Love* and *The Only Game in Town*. Consistently, identity or selfness is Chang's permanent theme in all her novels. *The Frontiers of Love* is a novel in which Chang directly and explicitly "queried categories of identity—national, racial, class, and gender" (*FL* v). Among the various identities, needless to say, racial identity for Eurasians is the most central one. Chang "explored the Eurasian problem in and through three main characters in order to get a variety of Eurasian identities and responses" (Hamalian 32). Chang demonstrated her knowledge of Eurasian identity through three Eurasian characters—Mimi Lambert, Feng Huang, and Sylvia Chen who symbolically made three different choices as their identity solution.

Gloria Anzaldua defines borderland as a space "where two or more cultures edge each other, where people of different cultures occupy the same territory" (Anzaldua 19). In the novel, Shanghai embodies such a borderland where the protagonists'

---

1   Based on this reason, Amy Ling excused Chang for her non-Asian American theme in later novels. See Ling, *Between Worlds*, 119.

Eurasian consciousness is formed in the process of being oppressed by both cultures. Shirley Geok-Lin Lim has emphasized that "the major characters in *The Frontiers of Love* are bound together in a claustrophobic geographical space… The novel constructs metaphysical problems that cannot be understood apart from their historical and geographical specifics" (*FL* vi). In this sense, it is necessary to illustrate the "historical and geographical specifics." Historically, the story is set just months before and up to the Japanese Imperial Army's surrender after the nuclear holocaust in Hiroshima and Nagasaki in 1945, a time of particular intensity and instability for racialized figures. Usually, war makes people think more about life and doubt the reality and truth they has believed firmly. At the end of the war, people are anxious about their life and future. In *The Frontiers of Love*, war is a formless threat throughout the novel. It begins with a hot and humid summer which predicts the suffocating atmosphere under the war. Liyi instructs his daughter Sylvia, when she is out for a party, to "be sure that you have an escort home" and "go now, before it gets any darker" (*FL* 4). This instruction can be regarded as a father's concern for a daughter, but is also an implication of the dangerous life condition during wartime. Such kind of war menace and anxiety is also pervaded in the party. In the party, where people should be relaxed and happy, they "spoke quietly out of habit as though they were under the monitor of the Japanese soldiers" (*FL* 13). For the Eurasian protagonists in the novel, waiting for the end of the war means endless uncertainty and anxiety over their fate. When the war is over, everything returns to normal, and everything is full of possibilities. Sylvia expresses her depression over the fact that the war is over. For her, the end of the war makes her feel awful. She sighs it is "simply terrifying" when all possibilities return to normal. In this way, *The Frontiers of Love* is enveloped in such a war atmosphere of uncertainty and confusion.

Geographically, the novel is located in Shanghai. Shanghai has functioned as China's major trading port and largest textile center for its good position in the middle of China's east coastline, once known as China's capital in the southeast. However, as Chang said in the *MELUS* interview, Shanghai had been "parceled off in a way that humiliated China" (Hamalian 32). After the first Opium War (1839-1842), Shanghai was forced to open port for foreign trade in 1843, so that Western colonial powers got the chance to control all the river trade up the Yangtze far into China's interior. Gradually, Western colonialist countries, Britain, the United States, and France, one after another, began setting up their concessions in Shanghai which were independent of Chinese law. For almost a hundred years, from 1843 to the end of the Sino-Japanese war in 1945, Shanghai was separated the into the Chinese Section inhabited by the ordinary Chinese, the French Concession and the International Settlement.[1] In Lim's words, "The International Settlement and the French Concession operated as two European areas in Shanghai" (*FL* vii). During the Japanese occupation, this partition was intensified by the internment of the British, American and Dutch in some sections of the International Settlement. The French Concession, where the Eurasian protagonists inhabit, remained separate and better-off.

> The French Concession, in which they all lived, was a borough set apart. Strictly speaking, it could not be called Chinese, though it was inhabited mostly by Chinese—Chinese who either wealthy, Westernized or prayed to a Christian God. In the good old days, before the Japanese occupation, this part of Shanghai had the atmosphere of a suburban area, busy with the comings and goings of foreigners entertaining on their lawns and at the international clubs. It had been a section that had supplied its own aura of well-being. (*FL* 21)

Meanwhile, Shanghai was a city for adventurers of various nationalities, reflected in the novel by the English, American, Swiss, Dutch, Australian, Jewish and the wealthy Chinese, because "from the 1920s to the beginning of World War II, Shanghai became a legendary urban center drawing thousands of Russian refugees fleeing from the Russian Revolution, Japanese traders, a host of European and American capitalist adventurers, and millions of rural Chinese attracted to its opportunities" (*FL* vii). This Westernized cosmopolitan milieu dominates *The Frontiers of Love*.

To sum up, as a frontier, wartime Shanghai is a city whose cosmopolites are "unnamed hybrids." Shanghai is a place where all "boundaries" that define "national, cultural, racial, gender, and other identities are inherently unstable" (*FL* viii). Feng Huang in the novel acknowledges that, it is Shanghai's duplicity, its Westernized colonial culture that contributes to his identity confusion. Shanghai is responsible for the acuteness of his agony.

> People were true to nothing in Shanghai; they belonged only to the surface values of both East and West and leaned heavily toward the exoticism of the West. If one did not hold on carefully to one's sense of self, one might wake up one morning looking for one's face, so easily lost. (*FL* 87)

This is why Chang herself says "Shanghai was a perfect metaphor for the problems of the three Eurasians in my novel" (Hamalian 32). In fact, Chang has elsewhere insisted upon this geographical specificity in the novel. It seems that Chang poses her exploration of Eurasian identity in Asia if not in America. As a matter of fact, it is not real Asia (China), especially the section where the protagonists inhabit. That is also why I use quotation marks in the section title. Shanghai in this novel has

---

1　For a detailed account of Shanghai's colonial history, see G. Lanning and S. Couling, *The History of Shanghai* (Taipei: Ch'eng Wen Publishing Company, 1973).

multiple identities, and as landscape, it dramatizes many of the contestations and struggles of colonialism. On the one hand, although Shanghai is composed politically, economically, and socially of both Chinese and Western people, the social elites that inhabit it are "unnamed hybrids," who are "survivors of a colonialism" (*FL* 86). The French Concession where they live is distinguished from the real Chinese section. While contained by Japanese occupation, the Eurasian characters are further constrained by the world in which they live. Embodying the racism that has underlined Western colonialism in the city, they set themselves apart from the Chinese who live there, confining their "territory" to that which is "circumscribed, uncontaminated, by the Chinese section, which she (Sylvia Chen) had never even visited" (*FL* 85).[1] On the other hand, Shanghai's dividedness and fragmentation reflect the Eurasian characters' disintegration of self. Anzaldua acknowledges the pain and anguish of otherness and seeks to reclaim its latent power by exploring how disempowered subjects labeled as "other" express their identities and resistance.[2] As far as the Eurasian protagonists in the novel are concerned, they are exactly the subjects in Shanghai borderland, where they are tied to both cultures, sharing the feeling that mestizo feels, experiencing the marginality that "tragic" Eurasians experience. Certainly, compared with the Eurasians in the U.S., Shanghai Eurasians are less tragic to a large extent. At least, the Eurasians are enjoying a kind of elite life in the French Concession in the novel.[3]

---

1   According to Herbert Day Lamson, "the cosmopolitanism of Shanghai is not the same as the cosmopolitanism of Chicago." This came down to a matter of the power relations that prevailed in semicolonial Shanghai. As Lamson pointed out, the alien minority in Shanghai perceived itself as a "ruling group," however, the alien minority in Chicago lived with a sense of "being ruled." See Herbert Day Lamson, "The Eurasian in Shanghai" (*American Journal of Sociology* 41.5, 1936), 648.

2   With *Borderlands/La Frontera: The New Mestiza*, Gloria Anzaldua bursts onto the feminist conceptual scene offering new ways of exploring relationships of power and domination, resistance and agency, among women and men hitherto cast as marginalized "others." She coins the term mestiza consciousness to reflect border subjects' expressions of agency that incorporate spiritual transformations and psychic process of exclusion and identification of feeling "in between" cultures, languages, or places. Her theoretical formulation of "borderlands" expounds on the dynamics within material and discursive spaces that transcend geopolitical border areas, where women, men, and youth, straight and queer, adapt, resist, and develop new strategies to negotiate social inequalities. See Gloria Anzaldua, *Borderlands/La Frontera: The New Mestiza* (San Francisco: Spinsters/Aunt Lute, 1987).

3   Shanghai Eurasian is a big research topic in sociology. Generally speaking, the Eurasians in Shanghai occupy an intermediate position biologically, and also are the subjects of social discrimination at the hands of both alien and native groups. On the whole, the native Chinese disapprove of miscegenation and discriminate against the hybrid, especially those who have hybrid-

Amy Ling discussed Americans and Europeans in China, Eurasians in China, saying that the Eurasian's "social status, paradoxically, was higher than that of the Chinese themselves; thus, to follow a Western lifestyle in China was, in certain ways, to be one of the elite" (Ling, 1990 86).

Anyhow, locating her novel in such a geopolitically specific milieu, which shuts a Chinese majority out of the foreground of dramatic action, Chang gave the novel its complicating thematics of race and culture. In this special political and temporal setting of cosmopolitan Shanghai, Chang disclosed the plot of three Eurasians' different paths in search of identity. In "Diana Chang: The Hyphenated Condition," Amy Ling stressed Eurasians' particularity regarding their biracial question, "both races are distinctive and distinguishable but inseparable within herself" (Ling, 1980 71). Thus, Ling generalized three possible directions that Eurasians may take: "she may choose one parent's racial identity and make that her own, rejecting or ignoring the other parent; she may vacillate between the two; or as a hybrid and therefore a member of neither race, she may go her own way, creating herself and improvising as she goes" (71). Likewise, Chang skillfully presented the three main characters' different reactions to their Eurasian identities in *The Frontiers of Love*.

Waiting out the end of the war, three young Eurasian socialites take turns giving and going to parties, each attempting in his or her own way to resolve the inner confusion and pain brought about by their identities as both white and Asian, as both part of and separate from the political conflict that surrounds them. Despite his brown hair and the freckles inherited from his English mother, the twenty-six-year-old Feng Huang chooses to be Chinese. He drops his English name Farthington— the Western part of him, which is given by his mother. Feng's wealthy Chinese father divorced his mother and left the family sixteen years ago. Emotionally very torn by his dependent and somewhat disturbed mother, Feng espouses wholly the cause of the Chinese Communist Party. While attending the parties given by his Eurasian friends, Feng initially seeks to befriend Sylvia Chen in order to gather information about the management of the printing plant where the Communists are secretly planning a strike. Then gradually he falls in love with her. During the planning, Feng betrays the eavesdropping Peiyuan, Sylvia's cousin, which results in Peiyuan's murder as well as the end of the love between him and Sylvia. Feng finally chooses to sacrifice his own humanity in his relentless determination to further the common good. As Diana Chang

---

racial visibility and follow the alien in belittling the native. In the eyes of aliens, a Eurasian is just a "Shanghai boy (girl)." For more sociological studies on Shanghai Eurasians, see Herbert Day Lamson, "The Eurasian in Shanghai," 642-648.

comments, "what he is doing, perhaps unconsciously at some level, is searching for a way to become more Chinese, to be totally Chinese, to deny the English aspect of himself, and thereby to be less conflicted" (Hamilian 32).

Another Eurasian is the nineteen-year-old Mimi Lambert, Sylvia's best friend. Mimi has lost her both parents in the war—her "Australia adventurer" father and her "Chinese socialite" mother, "who had shocked the Peking Hotel populace twenty years before with her décolleté gowns and tennis-playing paramours" (*FL* 11). Orphaned, Mimi is being raised by her Chinese aunt, an upper-class woman, very cosmopolitan in style, yet whose spirit is Chinese. Different from Feng, Mimi prefers the West to China. She vehemently rejects China and Chinese things. She never wears Chinese dresses, and is allowed more freedom that is unusual for young Chinese women. Furthermore, she chooses a Caucasian lover. Beautiful, passionate, lavish with herself, Mimi is astounded to find herself rejected by Robert Bruno, son of the Swiss owner of the printing plant. Robert's decision not to marry her because his father disapproves of her mixed race leaves her searching for some other man, who will take away her confusions about her identity by letting her submit completely, body and soul, to him.

The third Eurasian is the twenty-year-old Sylvia Chen. Daughter of a Chinese man, Liyi, a "cultivated, scholarly, and therefore quiet and restrained gentleman," and an American woman, Helen who is "restless, impatient, outspoken, unhappily detained in China by the war," Sylvia is the most fortunate of the three.[1] She wants to be "both as American as her mother, and as Chinese as her father" (*FL* 19). At home, she often envies her father's Chineseness which from Sylvia's viewpoint simplistically means that "he could afford to forget what he was" (*FL* 55). Additionally, she recoils from her overpowering American mother Helen's aggressiveness which often prompts her to feel "defensive about China" (*FL* 54). Ever since her father brings Peiyuan to Shanghai to look for a job, home becomes a politicized site of racial tension for Sylvia. Through her relationship with Feng, Sylvia seems to find a resolution for her internal struggle, expecting Feng to lead her life. However, Feng's political activities result in the murder of her cousin at last. Disappointed, Sylvia realizes that she can not be American like her mother or be Chinese like her father. She has to be Sylvia Chen. "She must possess her own unique self" (Hamalian 33). As the central Eurasian

---

1　In Lamson's study, Sylvia's parents' marriage represents one of the two types of the Sino-American miscegenation in Shanghai, namely, intermarriage between Chinese returned students from abroad and foreign women. The other type is the mating between alien men and native Chinese women. For more information on the Sino-American miscegenation in Shanghai and its social reactions, see Herbert Day Lamson, "Sino-American Miscegenation in Shanghai."

character of this novel, Sylvia's resolution of her identity dilemma is the most reasonable one. She understands that her self is not a fixed entity but a fluid, changing construct. Swinging between being "so many different people" and questioning and denying herself "a thousand times" (*FL* 146), Sylvia becomes finally resolved to her decision to "speak out for herself—an entity composed of both her parents" (*FL* 237).

III. Identity Is an Ongoing Struggle and "Constant Improvisation"

In *The Frontiers of Love*, all characters, main or minor, are in a quest for selfhood, as Mimi's cynical Aunt Julia remarks, "most people in love are just… trying to rid themselves of themselves, to acquire a new self" (*FL* 173). In one sense, the narrator's preoccupation with selfhood seems very Western. In the novel, the entire group of characters is privileged by both wealth and class. According to Smith Sidonie, such characters should measure themselves against a notion of self as "a web of privileged characteristics in which all 'I's' are rational, agentive, unitary… effectually what Spivak has termed the 'straight white Christian man of property'" (Sidonie xvii). However, none of the characters seems, at least initially, to have any notion of self. Feng Huang sees everyone as "acutely imprisoned" in his own self. Larry (Irish) says of Robert (Swiss) that "Lushes have an urge toward transcendence. They desire a release from selfhood" (*FL* 113). The main character Sylvia is the only one who attempts to wrest the components of selfhood from her environment and construct one for herself, although she too initially is "haunted by doubt of her own existence. She felt a fraud, an illusion, where she should have been" (*FL* 127). Sylvia in particular finally makes some progress toward accepting a heterogeneous concept of selfhood.

The selfhood problem of mixed race characters basically stems from their racial ambivalence. Because they are products of two races and cultures, their struggle for identity is circumscribed by forces quite beyond their control, and each translates a sense of racial displacement into feelings of worthlessness and illegitimacy. Being part Chinese and part Australian, Mimi is a tragic figure whose parents are no longer living. So unlike Sylvia who needs to experience a sort of family-imposed racial conflict which makes her fragmented from interior to exterior, Mimi lives with an ambition and self-confidence—being white. The thoroughly Westernized Mimi takes refuge in a sexually passionate affair with the wealthy, white Robert Bruno, believing that "through her devotion to him she might even acquire a self to call her own" (*FL* 214). Despite her exotic appearance which obviously denies her racial purity, Mimi completely rejects the Chinese part of her biraciality. There is an important moment when upon celebrating the rumor of Japan's surrender on late-night Shanghai's streets, Mimi and her friends are arrested for defying the curfew at eleven. When the Japanese officer interrogates her, Mimi explicitly makes clear her white identity:

> "You are English?" he barked. "Yes or no?"
>
> "Yes—no, I'm Australian."
>
> "Why not in internment camp?" he asked, sucking in his breath.
>
> "I—my aunt, she happens to be Chinese. She is my guardian."
>
> "Ah-so. You are foreigner, but too young. You are Chinese, however not exactly so."
>
> "But my father was Australian," she said firmly. (*FL* 118)

As "exotic" with seemingly "no racial identity at all," Mimi has some wherewithal to construct her racial identity. However, because of the historical contingency of this significant moment in the history of Shanghai and Asia as well as Mimi's individual history, Mimi's construction of identity is limited and always marked by her gender. On the one hand, Mimi is good at taking advantage of her beautiful appearance to allure a man who will in turn give her a sanctuary of self. She is always "incandescent…expending all her charms in challenging Robert" (*FL* 14). In this sense, she is the model of femininity which is accepted unproblematically by American women at that time. Unaware that her selfhood is perplexed by her mixed race identity, Mimi is confident in the power of her beauty. She is "carelessly beautiful, lazily feminine, casually flirtatious" (*FL* 32). Thus she positions herself in terms of the male gaze to negotiate status and her own desire. Her perceptions and desires are feminized in a way to make her most desirable to men. Even when she is twelve, she knows "how to toss her hair back, how to cross her impeccable legs, how to look into a boy's eyes for the maximum results" (*FL* 33). On the other hand, Mimi negotiates her status in men's world through her sexuality. By loving and being loved by Robert, Mimi is "assured of status for herself and a 'society' to which to belong" (*FL* 74). In her introduction to the new edition of *The Frontiers of Love*, Shirley Geok-lin Lim attributes Mimi's failure in achieving an identity to her "replication of patriarchally inscribed sexuality" (xviii). Indeed, Mimi replicates the literary convention of the raced female martyr. In the context of American literary depictions of Asian women, Mimi is recognizable as a sort of fallen Madame Butterfly, a trope with a long history in Anglo-American history. However, in her sexual relationship with Robert Bruno, Mimi usually is not invariably passive.

> Other times, she dared him, provoked him to a male chauvinism, so that he would conquer her,
> so that she would "die" beneath his arrogance. "Do what you will with me!" she had cried one
> afternoon. ...He had taken her violently—as she had so intensely willed and yet so passively
> received. Her utter capitulation had felt like her greatest triumph, and she knew that it was
> Robert, the victor, who had been lovingly used. (*FL* 73-74)

In terms of Mimi's manipulative strategies of passive aggression, it can be seen that she is more than the mere stereotypical fallen Asian woman.

Yet, her racial "contamination" hinders her seemingly successful negotiation of her "white" identity when she becomes pregnant with Robert Bruno's child. Rejected by Robert's authoritative father simply for being a racially inferior Eurasian, Mimi ultimately becomes "a willing victim" to any man invited to "punish her and to find her beautiful" (*FL* 232). Regarding this miserable ending, Lim has stated that Mimi represents a repetition of the "stereotyping of the Eurasian as the subject of conflicting race identities, resulting in self-hatred and sexual confusion and laxity" (*FL* xiii). Eurasian, like birthmark, is the force pressing on Mimi's sense of self. For her, the Eurasian identity is the cross she has to bear all through her life even though she keeps blind eyes to it. Her Chinese aunt laments "nothing will change the fact of her Eurasianness" (*FL* 174). Unfortunately, Mimi has been so preoccupied with using man's power to construct an identity that she has overlooked the implications of her raced body.

Undeniably, Mimi's tragedy calls to mind not only the whole historical discourse of racial discrimination against Eurasians, but also the femininity represented by Mimi. In other words, Mimi becomes a "tragic mulatto" not merely because she is of mixed blood, but also because she wholeheartedly adopts a traditional construction of femininity. She subordinates her self to the aggression of male sexuality, attempts to "place" herself in Robert's truly "paternal" world. It is worth noting that in the opening pages of *The Frontier of Love*, on her way to the party, Sylvia passes by the familiar sight of three beggars near the park who she notes in some detail.

> a blind one who used an oar to tap his way through the city; an albino whose weakness
> extended beyond his pink eyes into his quavering limbs, as though they were held together by
> wires at the joints; and a young, well-shaven Chinese whose legs were missing at the knee. He
> rolled himself along with difficulty on a square platform, a tin can held between his thighs. (*FL* 5)

The image of the albino beggar's exaggerated whiteness exactly represents Mimi's soul state. Mimi's choice of being white, like the albino beggar, is morbid and incomplete as a person of biracial heritage. When mentioning the issue of marriage with Bruno, Mimi only discovers that he has no intention of wedding a Eurasian against his father's wishes. Undone by this rejection, Mimi falls into the stereotype of a sexually licentious Eurasian woman, becoming "as elusive to the grasp as a spirit" (*FL* 231) and barely held together by the fleeting attention of a string of men. Therefore, Mimi's adventures and downfall in Shanghai reflect a typical phenomenon for Eurasian women who usually assume a tragic feminine role due to the alienation caused by racial homelessness.

Like Mimi, Feng is the other tragic Eurasian in the novel, who also suffers a death of self. If there is one positive phrase to describe Feng Huang, it must be a "progressive youth with Communist ideal" (*FL* 182). Feng is passionate, and ultimately destructive, committed to a politically and culturally "pure" Chinese identity through his embrace of an incipient Chinese communism, thereby avoiding a "personal centerlessness" (*FL* 61). Being an essentially homeless Eurasian, Feng Huang is also perplexed by his mixed racial identity. He deliberately hopes he can deny "his own uniqueness" and tries to "force himself into the mold of 'the common man'" (*FL* 8). Feng's discomfort with his birth identity, resulting in his hollow ego, leads him directly to an authoritarian regime for identity security. He not only rejects the name and English culture provided by his English mother, but also rejects the class and race categories assigned to him by this biological bond, becoming an ardent Chinese communist and subordinating everything and everyone to what he believes to be the good of the Party and China, because "He felt more self-respect when he was in custody, in the uniform of a cause" (*FL* 32). Hence, Sylvia is attracted by his idealism and willingness to act. However, in his relationship with Tang, the Chinese foreman of the Bruno printing plant and Communist cell leader, Feng always wants "Tang to find him valuable," because "Tang filled him with a sense of inadequacy" (*FL* 31). It actually means that Tang, a Chinese, never trusts and accepts Feng as a full and real Chinese. "As a Eurasian, he could pass as anything, including a playboy. Eurasians and playboys in Shanghai were suspected of everything, and because of that they were suspected of nothing" (*FL* 32). In spite of this fact, Feng is still willing to be obedient to the communists, because "he was needed, and he felt secure in that way" (*FL* 32).

In order to finish the assignment, Feng initially pursues a relationship with Sylvia to gain access to her father on behalf of the communist resistance. If Mimi's inner self is symbolized by the albino beggar, Feng's inner self is symbolized by the crippled beggar on the square platform. In his collaboration with the Communists, he betrays Sylvia's cousin, Peiyuan, which results in Peiyuan's violent death at the hands of Feng's comrades. Thus, his "well-shaven" Chinese image is symbolically cut off at the knees, and the tin can between the beggar's legs symbolizes Feng's impotence in the face of "the blank wall of self" (*FL* 226). Ultimately, Feng meets his tragic end in leaving Shanghai for the new task. Therefore, in summary, if Mimi's tragedy lies in her attempts to construct herself through a male (Robert), Feng's problem can be ascribed to his escape from his hollow ego to the patriarchal Communist (Tang). To put it metaphorically, Mimi is feminine, and Feng is impotent.

As the central character, Sylvia searches for identity that is much more complicated. At the beginning of the novel, Sylvia's dilemma about what to dress reveals her discomfort with her self.

> She waved and left, walking down the dark stairs in her newest dress, and rebelling inwardly against the sedateness of the tight skirt required of her. That was the trouble with Chinese dresses; they expressed a kind of aristocratic demureness. But foreign clothes didn't suit her entirely either. Their full skirts seemed to stand out from her, making her slighter than she was, orphaned in them. I shall have to design my own kind of clothes, a modified Chinese dress, she thought. I shall do that when the war is over. (*FL* 4)

Sylvia's painful duality, anxiety, or "guilt" of "not knowing who she was" can be traced throughout the text. If the albino and the crippled beggars represent Mimi and Feng respectively, the blind beggar highly symbolizes Sylvia's difficulty with her identity. Like the blind who taps along the street with his oar, Sylvia cannot see her way out of the conflict between her white and Chinese selves—"in despair because she was herself, in despair because she did not know what the self was" (*FL* 236). Sylvia's lack of racial identity leaves her mendicant. At twenty, she seems both "untried and aged, inexperienced and disillusioned" (*FL* 6).

Sylvia's inner conflict and paralysis is apparently revealed by her vision of Shanghai on the way to a party. Making her way through the "dimmed-out curfewed metropolis," Shanghai appears to be deserted, empty of life "as though its inhabitants were away on vacation" (*FL* 4). The only inhabitants she encounters are the three beggars who, to a large extent, define her own instability. The three beggars include a blind who seems to "interpret the signs" of the city by tapping his way, an albino whose literal whiteness leaves "quavering limbs" that seem only "held together by wires at the joints," and a Chinese man with missing legs who holds a tin cup between his thighs (*FL* 5). Factually, taken together, the three beggars are almost exotic in their degradation, weak and quavering, barely wired-together. Their lack of bodily integrity just mirrors Sylvia's stalemate within herself as a Eurasian. Her own existence seems to mean nothing to herself or the world. Hence, on the one hand, unable to bear her sympathetic impulse toward the three impoverished beggars, Sylvia "averts her face" from them; on the other hand, she cannot look directly at her own "disease"—she cannot banish its pain. On her way to the party, although she wears a native gown, her appearance suggests a kind of exoticness, "people never ceased to be curious about her" (*FL* 5). Meanwhile, she walks with all the freedom and impatience of a foreigner, but in her there is something inescapably Oriental. Her "exoticness" and inescapable "Oriental" nature highlight the truth that she has no racial identity at all.

Sylvia's internal fragmentation is intensified by the tense racial encounter within the domestic space. Her American mother Helen is very aggressive and overpowering, who represents the Western racist attitude toward Chinese. Because of her, the family has to speak English at home. For Sylvia, her home is dominated by her mother. Nostalgic for her motherland America, Helen has a racist attitude toward un-Westernized Chinese. The problem becomes intensified when Peiyuan, Liyi's favorite nephew, comes to Shanghai to look for a job and lives together with them. Staring disparagingly at him, Helen finds his features "antagonizingly" Chinese.

> Such small eyes (What's the matter with you Chinese, having such small black eyes?), the kind of Chinese nose that looked stuffed and adenoidal, and such large, uneven white teeth. The cowlick made him look unkempt, indolent, unmannered as only the Chinese could be... (*FL* 54-55)

One day, intolerant with Peiyuan, Helen bursts into a hysterical shout, "Your stupid nephew sleeping in my house. Oh, I tell you I can't stand it … sleeping with his big teeth showing! My house isn't my own, with him around!" (*FL* 53-54).

To some extent, Sylvia internalizes her mother's attitudes, positioning herself with a sense of racial superiority. Sylvia has never visited the Chinese section of Shanghai, though she has lived in Beijing and seen the "squalor" there. "The Shanghai which Sylvia knew was circumscribed, uncontaminated by the Chinese section" (*FL* 85). She respects the "past" China as represented by ruins of stone altars around which the overcrowded peasants maintain a respectful space, but sees the hordes of displaced Chinese as "too many Chinese… it was so easy to claim distinction" (*FL* 86). At the same time, though, she can not accept her mother's irrational racism, sometimes she even interjects herself into her mother's screaming rage against Peiyuan, and becomes defensive about Chinese: "I am Chinese too! 'I-I-I! Chinese, do you understand! …You outsider! …You poor stupid fool!" (*FL* 140). Standing between the two worlds miniaturized in the domestic space, she is threatened by her mother's vigor and worries about her father's reaction. Painfully, Sylvia usually seeks help in church, asking Reverend Ssu-tu to save her from her trinity—her father, her mother, and herself, and save her from her duality. She complains that her spirit belongs to nowhere. As a daughter of Helen and Liyi, Sylvia inherits the conflict inherent like a birthmark, which she cannot do away with. She is deeply tormented by her schizophrenic existence. She complains to Feng, "I think we Orientals are schizophrenic" (*FL* 180). In addition, Sylvia's struggle with her confusing identity can be shown in her sympathy with her Eurasian brother.

> Poor Paul, Sylvia thought, and that was more accurate. My brother, she thought, seeing him as he had been at six, angelic and so beautiful (part porcelain and part flame) he had been painful to look at. At their best, half-breeds who had Chinese blood in them had fine features, thin skins and eyes that caught the light in a blaze. So much tragedy seemed to lie beneath Paul's physical perfection, his puzzling Chinese-Western looks, which seemed like an optical illusion. (*FL* 144)

Painfully self-questioning and constantly wavering between a desire for a secure identity and the knowledge that such security is unattainable, Sylvia envies both her friends' (Mimi and Feng) seeming wholeness. "She longed for a single, comforting bias" (*FL* 18). The yearning for a coherent wholeness accounts for her falling in love with Feng for "his singleness, his pure and masculine identity" (*FL* 148). Like Mimi, Sylvia hopes to acquire self affirmation through the male. Thus, when staying with him, she feels "new born," and her internal struggle with her identity seems to reach a momentary resolution, which nonetheless turns out later to be just an illusion. "She felt she was one at last…She wanted him to lead her life for her" (*FL* 148). Sylvia wants Feng to inflict upon her his aggressiveness because he always makes the truth seem brutal, as opposed to her father whose gentleness keeps her and Paul from the simplest truth. Thus, on that night when the Japanese officer investigates her background, Sylvia readily declares herself Chinese and is waved to stand next to the other "white Chinese" Feng.

However, unlike Mimi, who seems unaware that her ego is perplexed by her mixed racial identity, Sylvia is aware from the beginning. "Sylvia is endowed with the grace of intelligence that resists this replication of patriarchally inscribed sexuality" (*FL* xviii). Therefore, Sylvia overcomes the stereotypical fate for tragic Eurasians. Unlike Mimi who is destroyed by Robert and the white world he represents, Sylvia is activated by Feng and his aggressive Chineseness. In other words, in their relations to males, Mimi is lost, but Sylvia is saved in terms of identity construction. Finally, despite that Sylvia ends her relationship with Feng, she does not want to kill her desire for him. "She wondered how masochistic she was being, enjoying her own pain. It seemed to her that perhaps people created their own pain because only when in pain were they truly sure that they were alive. 'I hurt, therefore I am'" (*FL* 235).

After Peiyuan's death, Sylvia says she was "blind" to trust Feng. She also realizes that it is unreliable to build her identity on others. "She had learned from her dependency the necessity for being separate" (*FL* 236). Sylvia is truly reborn. Her reliance on others to tell who she is ultimately ends. "Like a twig, she had been broken in two, the strong nerve of her attachment and dependency giving way at last" (*FL* 236). She realizes that what she loves about Peiyuan and Feng is their energy, and she makes the eye-opening discovery that she has energy of her own housed in her own body.

> By residing fully and carefully in her own, she would be able to engage her emotions, her mind and her days with pride. Abruptly, she had no longer felt accidental but responsible. She was Sylvia Chen, and she would speak out for herself—**an entity composed of both parents**, but ready to act and not merely react, for **one individual—herself**. She seemed to take her first breath of life. (*FL* 237, emphasis added)

For her, identity is an ongoing struggle. Unlike Feng and Mimi who abandon part of their dual self in the pursuit of coherent self, Sylvia's resistance to being fixed as either the one or the other is an articulation of hybrid identity that shifts in between—Chinese and American, outsider and insider. Unfortunately, Sylvia's search for identity does not achieve a totally satisfactory resolution in terms of "establishing a transgendered, cross-racial, cross-cultural subjectivity that possesses a clear sense of agency" (*FL* xi). At the end of the novel, she is alone but not lonely. She expects a new and sudden vision. Meanwhile, in the conclusion of the novel, walking through the Chinese countryside, Liyi recovers from his guilt and despair at Peiyuan's death, and his love for his children and Helen leads to a life-affirming consciousness, that "life was not to be resolved, but to be lived—a constant improvisation" (*FL* 244-45). For Eurasians, to find a way to negotiate and incorporate the duality or multiplicity lies in "constant improvisation."

To sum up, in "Human Migration and the Marginal Man," Robert Park described one type of "marginal man" as a "cultural hybrid" living between two distinctive groups and never completely accepted by either. Park identified the "mixed blood" as the paradigmatic marginal man, reifying the connection between racial and cultural hybridity. Exactly as Park states, in *The Frontiers of Love*, Diana Chang vividly describes the marginality of Sylvia, Mimi, and Feng which results from the fact that, racially speaking, they are "essentially homeless" in Shanghai that is a very proper metaphor as the "site of violent fragmenting identities, of conflicting evolving and contingent futures" (*FL* ix). In brief, in *The Frontiers of Love*, Diana Chang tackles the themes of psychic exile, alienation, and double consciousness, which are Chang's expressions of Eurasian consciousness. In "Why Do Writers Write," Chang reveals her creative impulse and its relationship with her identity. "With this novel, this play, this poem, this biography, these essays, I purchase my citizenship in this land of life from which I feel estranged… I must earn it like an illegitimate child, a stateless person… I create something in order to become all that I was meant to be" (Chang, 1969 1).

Ⅳ. Insider or Outsider? Identity Quest for a Eurasian in Chinatown: *Face*

As is well known, ever since Chinese immigrants in America began forming communities in the mid-to late-nineteenth century, their residential, business, and cultural space, generally referred to as "Chinatown," has been layered with imagery. These images, largely negative and demeaning, have usually been framed by observers who did not live in Chinatown, and who had little connection to the community. They tended to cluster around a number of common themes, "the physical mysteriousness of Chinatown, unsanitary living conditions, immoral activities, and the general Otherness of the Chinese themselves."[1] Such long-standing stereotypical representations of Chinatown become Chinese American writers' great burden in their writings. Therefore, in her important article, "Ethnic Subject, Ethnic Sign, and the Difficulty of Rehabilitative Representation: Chinatown in Some Works of Chinese American Fiction," Sau-ling Cynthia Wong poses the vexed question: "The Chinese American writer committed to representing Chinatown in a non-stereotypical manner" (Wong 251). In other words, Chinese American writers attempt a rehabilitative representation of Chinatown, even though there is inherent difficulty of this enterprise.[2]

Over a decade after she went public with her account of anorexia nervosa in *Solitaire*, Aimee Liu turns to write fiction with the story of a young Eurasian woman's searching for identity in Chinatown. In *Face*, her second book, Liu seems to understand the trick as an ethnic writer. Though she is culturally and socially

---

1   For a fuller explication of presentations of American Chinatowns, see K. Scott Wong, "Chinatown: Conflicting Images, Contested Terrain," *MELUS*, Vol. 20, No. 1 (Spring 1995), 3-15.

2   For example, Sau-ling Wong uses Frank Chin as an example to demonstrate how difficult it is for writers attempting rehabilitative representations of Chinatown. According to Wong, Chinatown is Chin's focus in work after work, ranging from the much-taught "Food for All His Dead" to the controversial play that made his national reputation, *The Year of the Dragon*, to the short stories written earlier but only recently collected in *The Chinaman Pacific & Frisco R. R. Co.* Frank Chin, fifth-generation Chinese American, sees himself as a word warrior whose mission is to restore Chinese America to historical accuracy, hence its rightful dignity. In spite of this, Chin has certain works which expose the inherent difficulty of rehabilitative writing. For more, see Wong, 255-256.

unfamiliar with Chinese things, she explicitly attempts to add some exotic colors into *Face* in order to attract the reading public. The most exotic in the novel is the description about Chinatown and the life there. Liu always mentions her childhood life in Chinatown hearing the sound of Mahjong, a typical form of entertainment in China. Besides, referring to Chinese New Year, Liu writes, "According to my calculations, it was the Year of the Rooster, but no firecrackers rattled the streets, no lion dancers came forth to welcome me" (*FA* 9). There are more examples like Chinese tongs in Chinatown, old Chinese foot binding, lotus feet, and so on.

Aimee Liu grew up in a predominantly white neighborhood, and her knowledge of Chinatown must be the product of imagination and investigation. However, contrary to Sau-ling Wong's point, Liu's representation of Chinatown is not purely rehabilitative, even to a certain extent, is somewhat stereotypical. Under her pen, Chinatown is a mysterious place where memories, secrets, lies, loss, dreams and nightmares are mingled together. A *Los Angeles Times* review says that "Chinatown becomes a scary, shiny, complicated place where everyone holds some kind of horrific secret."[1] Factually, Liu's representation of Chinatown is complicated. Such complexity is closely related to her character's repressed memory and traumatic past. Sometimes, readers can feel here and there an insider's feeling toward Chinatown—the smell of home; sometimes, Chinatown is a horrific place whose inhabitants see the Eurasian protagonist as a barbarian. As the novel develops, Chinatown is more like a hell which is full of bias and violence.

Face tells the story of a part-American, part-Chinese character Maibelle Chung's search for her identity in New York Chinatown, where she grows up, and finally recollects that she is gang-raped as a child by a group of Chinese boys. As the daughter of a Chinese wartime photojournalist and his American wife, Maibelle is raised in New York Chinatown, but leaves with her family during her teenage years. As an adult, Maibelle is always haunted by an inexplicable compulsion to return to Chinatown, where she is sure that she can uncover the reasons for her ongoing nightmares that hint at a suppressed traumatic past. Maibelle Chung's quest for identity is mapped by her struggle to remember and confront the incident of rape that she has erased from her memory. Generally speaking, the novel is set in a Gothic atmosphere which exerts great influence on readers' mood. "We are so much a part of Maibelle's inner life, so intimate with her pain and frustration, that while readers may root for her to find the truth, there is also a nervous sensation of not really wanting to

---

1　See http://www.aimeeliu.net/.

know."[1] As Maibelle's research comes closer and closer to painful truths, the novel creates a haunting atmosphere of restless, unhappy searching and drifting, heightened by an underlying tone of dread. Structurally, it is episodic, oscillating between the past and the present, thus memory determines the form of the text.

Similar to Diana Chang who posits Eurasian characters' search for identity in a special milieu, Aimee Liu locates it in Chinatown. In this special racial and cultural context, Liu skillfully manipulates the Eurasian character Maibelle's relationship with Chinatown. As a Eurasian, she is both inside and outside of Chinatown. She grows up in Chinatown as a child, later moves out of Chinatown as a teenager. But in her late twenties, she returns repeatedly as a tourist, which renders her an outsider. The novel opens with a recalling of Maibelle's experience growing up in Chinatown psychologically as an insider. In memory, Chinatown is familiar to her.

> I was a child in Chinatown. My earliest memories are filled with strangled ducks and ginseng root, parades of round, worried faces, and babies in pastel colors. Rich lights slants between squeezed buildings, and winter shadows soak the streets tugging warmth from fingers to toes. I hear wailing, chattering, a multitude of tones. A language I can't understand. And *the smells—I know them as well as my name*—the unearthly blend of fishmongers' trash, orange peel, garlic, and sandalwood. Joss sticks lit for the dead. (*FA* 1, emphsis added)[2]

However, little Maibelle's intimacy with Chinatown is always betrayed by her foreign appearance which places her as a non-member.

> I see myself in these memories as a tall, pale, redheaded girl reflected in a storefront window. A narrow face with a broad off-center nose. Too-wide eyes the color of jade and only a vague Oriental cast. Against the rest of the Mott Street crowd I stand out like a vivid flaw in a bolt of jet-black silk. (*FA* 1)

As a Eurasian child living in the Chinese community, Maibelle has strong feelings of inadequacy, and sometimes the feeling is traumatizing. What she admires most is the "Yellow Butterflies"—Chinese girls. In sharp contrast to her foreign looks, the Yellow Butterflies "had the flawless appearance of porcelain dolls. Pale skin. Flying cheekbones. Diminutive noses. Waist-length hair that hung straight, gleaming like cellophane, and those classic almond eyes with their smoothed-down lids, as if carved in a single stroke" (*FA* 1-2). Little Maibelle suffers deep alienation, and always keeps a distance from them. Maibelle is often teased as a foreigner and even bullied by the Yellow Butterflies. "They would pull my hair out strand by strand,

---

1   See http://www.aimeeliu.net/.

2   Aimee Liu, *Face* (New York: Warner Books, Inc., 1994), 1. All further page references are to this edition and are given in parentheses.

they would suck the color from my eyes. They would beat me with their wings until I melted into the pavement" (*FA* 2). Little Maibelle's sufferings in Chinatown echo her father's in a white neighborhood after his marriage with an American woman. Her family moves to Chinatown due to white racism toward her father, a Eurasian too. Maibelle's father, Joe Chung, is a son of a Chinese man who is "a gentleman and a scholar," and an American woman Alyssa Billings, the daughter of a U.S. Navy captain, who was called White Witch by Chinese during their living in China. When living in a white neighborhood, Joe Chung once suffers from an outright racist attack in a store. Because of his yellowness, Joe not only feels that he is not welcome under clerks' "frozen smiles," but also gets malicious personal abuse by a white manager, who sneers at "You yellow bastards" and backs Joe up against the wall, "ramming his large, white thumb into Dad's breastbone" (*FA* 258). Escaping from the attack, Maibelle's parents decide to move to Chinatown, considering Chinatown as a cheap refuge and salvation. However, Maibelle's mother Diana, a midwestern farm girl who fled to New York seeking culture and sophistication, never treats Chinatown as her home although she has lived in Chinatown for nearly twenty years. Both Maibelle's and her father's suffering experiences in Chinatown and the white neighborhood signify the fact that neither wholly Caucasian nor Asian, a Eurasian defines herself/ himself or is defined as a non-member of either racial group, rather than a member of both.

Maibelle's relationship with Chinatown that used to be her home continues to be characterized by ambivalence when she leaves Chinatown as a teenager. Since they move out of it, Maibelle nevertheless has retained a psychological connection with it, partly due to her father, who is Chinese, but also because something repeatedly draws her back. Maibelle's return to Chinatown is initiated by a photographic assignment of her childhood friend Tommy Wah, who plans to write a historical book about the lives of Chinatown residents and needs Maibelle to cooperate with photos. Like her father, Maibelle is also a photojournalist, but she gradually quits it due to her torn terrors of camera which is closely related to her repressed past. Hence, at the very start, Maibelle automatically rejects Tommy Wah's invitation, because subconsciously she evades to return to Chinatown which she makes sure has a certain relationship with her recurring nightmares. She has been tormented by the nightmares for many years which often disturb the nightly peace of her and her neighbors.

> About two this morning I woke, thrashing and sweating, to the crack of billy clubs at my door. I pulled free of my knotted sheets, slowed by breathing to a pinched roar, and stumbled to the peephole. Outside, two overstuffed patrolmen hovered with my neighbor arrayed behind them

> like a geek-show audience. When I opened the door, the police backed away, but Harriet just
> kept coming. She wore a pink hair net and her lips curled down tight over her teeth. Her eyes
> squeezed against the light flooding through my doorway. (*FA* 20)

Repeatedly and finally, Maibelle's landlady Harriet has to issue an ultimatum to her. "I've had it! You either get a grip on yourself or get out. Next time you scream like that, I'm calling Bellevue. Hear me?" (*FA* 20). Like an army deserter, Maibelle always chooses to escape the nightmares by "going away" for many years. In order to get rid of the harassment from nightmares, she even clings to anonymous men one after another, indulging in sensual pleasures. For various reasons, Maibelle is determined to undertake the photographic assignment at last.

> I could say it was Tommy's letter that prompted my return. Or the incident in Pensacola. Or
> Marge. But the truth is, my nightmares have been driving me back for years, as relentlessly as
> they once pushed me away. I came to New York more determined than ever to find the source
> of these nightly terrors, face it down and conquer it. (*FA* 24)

It is these visits that reawaken her contradictory feelings toward the place where she grew up. She returns in the role of an outsider as a tourist. "It's all different, I tell myself. That souvenir sign 'Tourist Welcome,' means you now" (*FA* 133). Sau-ling Wong has suggested that in the gaze of white voyeurs, Chinatown means spectacles. According to Wong, between the spectator and the spectacle, there exists an unequal relationship which renders the spectacle (ethnic subject)'s subjectivity "in danger of being drained from any effort at self-representation" (Wong 252). In other words, in the course of gaze, the spectacle or the minority ethnic subject is objectified. Similarly, in her repeated visits to Chinatown, Maibelle's voyeurism of the Chinatown spectacle means that she herself adopts a racializing gaze when watching other Chinese. For instance, in one scene, Maibelle meets a Chinese. "Suddenly one of the protesters, a man with a ponytail, spins around barking like a seal. The roundness of his face, like a plate, registers. I release the shutter " (*FA* 139).

Gaze is a psychoanalytical term brought into popular usage by Jacques Lacan to describe the anxious state that comes with the awareness that one can be viewed. The psychological effect, Lacan argues, is that the subject loses a degree of autonomy upon realizing that he or she is a visible object. This concept is bound with his theory of the mirror stage, in which a child encountering a mirror realizes that he or she has an external appearance. Michel Foucault first used the term "medical gaze" in *The Birth of the Clinic* to explain the process of medical diagnosis, power dynamics between doctors and patients, and the hegemony of medical knowledge in society. In his *Discipline and Punish*, Foucault elaborated on the gaze to illustrate a particular dynamic in power relations and disciplinary mechanisms, such as surveillance and the function of related disciplinary mechanisms and self-regulation in a prison or school as an apparatus of power. Derrida also elaborated on the relations of animals and humans via the gaze in *The Animal That Therefore I Am*. To summarize, no matter in whose theory, gaze reflects a power relationship, in which the gazer owns power over the gazed-at. In the gaze, which fails to acknowledge individual response, the subjectivity of the individual disappears.

In the process of her spectacular act about Chinatown, Maibelle feels herself to be both the gazed-at and the gazer in Chinatown. Eurasian Maibelle becomes the gazed-at in the way that Wong posits, because she too becomes an object attracting the sight of the Chinese cultural voyeur. The Chinese racializing gaze produces the ethnic subject Maibelle as a spectacle or "otherness." Maibelle significantly feels herself being watched. "I can't shake the feeling that I'm being watched" and "I sense the concealed faces watching" (*FA* 133), as if she is identifying with the angry sentiments of the Chinese she herself has returned to photograph. Paradoxically, she raises her camera—the instrument of spectatorship as a defense against appearing as a spectacle herself, by masking her face, "I hold my circle of glass to my face as if it could protect me" (*FA* 138). As a Eurasian woman and an ethnic subject, Maibelle tries to escape this gaze, which further exposes an anxiety of her self-identity produced and reflected back to her by another. "Self identity ("I" looking at "me") is constituted not only by our looking at ourselves, but also by our looking at others looking at us and our reconstitution of and alternation of these views of others about us" (Ling, 1990 34).

This awareness of gaze is what Du Bois called "double consciousness," which is the sense of watching one's self-image being produced by another. For Eurasian women like Maibelle, gazing is an aspect of racial as well as sexual relations. Frequently, Maibelle is seen in the text trying to evade the gaze, precisely because it signals subordination within a racial and gender hierarchy. She is not only caught in the racializing gaze, but also caught in the gendering gaze. Liu describes Maibelle's self-portrait as a "wall-sized mosaic of one hundred forty-four separate photographs of disconnected body parts" (*FA* 172). This self-portrait expresses the bodily fragmentation she experiences in the face of the racializing and gendering gaze. "As a consequence of their social alienation, women experience their body as parts, 'objects,' rather than integrated wholes" (Waugh 178). In her college years, Maibelle runs into one of the "Yellow Butterflies," a woman whose Asian features she has admired as a child, and finds that she has tried to erase her orientalizing features. "She'd had her eyes done, had the lids lifted, folded, and cut until the almond shape was gone and with it her exotic, imperious beauty. Now she looked innocent. Cute. She could pass for American" (*FA* 2). This woman's attempts to erase the orientalizing signs of her face are the result of the double consciousness of the spectacular act defining her from the outside. For this woman, cosmetic technology is a method to escape racializing gaze.

Essentially, Maibelle is a cultural insider to Chinatown, but she engages herself in such a spectacular act through the lens of her camera when she starts photographing her surroundings. "The cultural insider thus becomes a more extreme voyeur than the visitor from the outside" (Wong 256). In this sense, Maibelle is a white voyeur, no longer an insider to Chinatown. But Maibelle's paradoxical link with Chinatown continues as the plot develops. As a tourist, she shoots the storefronts, the ginseng and strangled ducks, as well as the dancing chickens, all the spectacles to which tourists are attracted when visiting Chinatown. Psychologically, she begins to feel a part of her surroundings once more. "Chinatown wrapped around me as if I'd never left." Maibelle's sense of belonging is so strong that she even begins to assimilate her appearance into her environment. "Even my own reflection—taller, paler, and more out of place than ever—seemed part of the package luring me back, no longer cause to run away" (*FA* 303).

However, finding herself accidentally embroiled in a demonstration against the kind of racial and cultural voyeurism in which she is involved, Maibelle oscillates between the insider and the outsider, the spectator and the spectacle. Not recognizing her as part-Chinese, the round-face Chinese man, who reacts to Maibelle as both spectacle and spectator, asks her, "Come to the Chinatown zoo, lady?" (*FA* 139). Moments later, Maibelle finds herself taunted by a group of young boys who again fail to see her as part-Chinese, calling her "Lou fan," which means "barbarian/outsider" (*FA* 139). Again, Maibelle defends herself against the boys by using her camera as a weapon, so that she turns from the spectacle into the spectator: "I turn quickly, raising the Leica, shoot them once, twice, three times dead on, and start running" (*FA* 140). It is incidents like this that cause her to note "living in Chinatown, things that happened made me feel like an outcast" (*FA* 86). Entangled with her outsider status to Chinatown, to Tommy's disappointment, Maibelle's pictures are "so defensive and tough." When Maibelle attempts to defend herself from her outsider angle, Tommy's words are thought provoking:

> Outsider. Insider. Those are roles. Positions you take in your own life, not in the world around you. Don't you see? The real dividing line has nothing to do with the shape of your eyes or face, what language you speak. It's inside you—are you living your life or just hiding behind that

camera of yours! (*FA* 236)

It is the Chinese boys calling Maibelle "Lou fan" who touch her raw nerves. She begins to recollect the event she has suppressed. She also begins to realize her confusion over her identity and inability to relinquish Chinatown as a psychological influence upon her resulting from her suppression of a rape in Chinatown one night when she returns to take photographs at the age of fourteen. The rape is a very critical moment when the violence and violation of the racializing as well as gendering gaze is explored in most detail. Maibelle recognizes that her attackers are Chinese, they have "so much black. Hair, eyes, clothing, sunglasses" (*FA* 306). For Maibelle, the black hair and eyes that she lacks, and which mark her attackers as Chinese in the dim light, function textually as a trope for threat and evil intent. During their rape, her assailants taunt her, calling her "gui lou fan, Barbarian" and "Bai xiangku, white witch." It is significant that Maibelle refuses to face her attackers. Without looking at them, she "felt rather than saw them closing in" (*FA* 307). However, after the rape, Maibelle shows her defiance over her attackers by gazing at them and facing them, without looking away: "I stared into the flame the fat one kept waving at me. I didn't blink. Again and again, until the muscles around my eyes burned with the effort of keeping them wide" (*FA* 308). Maibelle uses her gazing back as a strong defiance, though it is useless to her hurt. Obviously, the rape is directly linked to her biracial appearance as a Eurasian, because "the girl had red hair, was a teenager. Rumor was, she came from outside" (*FA* 329). In other words, Maibelle's appearance of being part-Chinese and part-American, or not purely Chinese, is the real reason for the abuse. It fully demonstrates the outright bias toward Eurasians in Chinatown. Maibelle deeply understands this point which even makes her very sensitive in her adulthood.

> Aren't you ignoring one fundamental factor? … Looks! Skin color. Hair. Eyes. Body type. Far as most whites are concerned, Chinese are Chinese—for that matter, any Oriental is Chinese—and blacks are black. No difference where they were born or what language they speak. (*FA* 55)

This is also why Aimee Liu titles this novel *Face* though there are not many discussions of face. "Face" can visibly signify a Eurasian's difference from a culturally normalized ethnic or racial majority (Chinese or white). In other words, the ethnic subject is marked by the face, which is the most important signifier of racial identity.

It is her father Joe's story that helps Maibelle face her repressed past courageously. As Maibelle slowly recalls, her father Joe's secret is slowly uncovered too. The two stories are linked through the use of photography as a means of recording the past. Her father tells her that, "the best photographs tell stories better than words" (*FA* 286). Joe Chung is a wartime photojournalist in China whose horrifying pictures of China in the 1940s make him famous. Returning to America, Joe abruptly gives up his photographic career—to his wife's eternal disappointment—for reasons that Maibelle gradually discovers. Joe's photograph results in his father's death in a bombing in Shanghai. What's more, Joe witnesses the whole course of murder. Since then, Joe remains silent about all his life in China and his familial history, submerging himself in his own trauma. Under Maibelle's insistence, Joe finally tells this story in the hope that it will help her to come to terms with her own past. "Only when the question of identity is settled can it do justice to other concerns" (*FA* 292). Maibelle finally recalls the traumatic event. The cathartic process of remembering tracks her reconciliation with her biracial identity.

> The child's eyes are elongated, beautifully carved with the same perfectly smooth, flat lids that I
>
> used to admire in the Yellow Butterflies. But that's where the resemblance ends. As I lean close I
>
> see, this child's eyes are not black or even dark brown. They are flecked with color radiating like
>
> a wheel—silvers of gray, amber, green—but deep in the center, as unearthly and hypnotic as a
>
> summer pool, they are pure blue. (*FA* 356)

Ultimately Maibelle can calmly face the fact that she is biracial, and "began to record what I see" without any internal obstacle (*FA* 356).

To sum up, in *The Frontiers of Love* and *Face*, both Diana Chang and Aimee Liu excellently explore the internal conflict and identity resolution for Eurasians by locating their Eurasian characters' searching for identity in Shanghai and New York Chinatown respectively. In Chang's *The Frontiers of Love*, wartime Shanghai is a very important metaphor. In such a geopolitically specific milieu, the Eurasian characters' internal fragmentation is intensified and highlighted. Living between two races, Eurasian characters tie with both races, but are not accepted by either. Similarly, in Aimee Liu's *Face*, the Eurasian character Maibelle's identity crisis is closely related to her insider/outsider status to Chinatown. More importantly, *Face* reveals Chinese residents' prejudice toward Eurasians in Chinatown, which directly grows into a violent rape. Nonetheless, both novels not only illustrate Eurasians' fragmented sense of self and oscillation between two races, but also point out the notion of Eurasian identity. Existing as a separate entity, Eurasians experience the racialized other's sense of inferiority and the desire for racial wholeness. Meanwhile, regarding identity construction, they have to see identity as a process, rather than a stable entity. In other words, identity is a dynamic construction that is open to internal and external, psychological and historical changes for Eurasians.

Conclusion

This book examines the literary representation of Eurasians in the twentieth century by Eurasian authors. The commonality among these texts is not only based on an assumed transhitoric Eurasian sensibility, but also predicated upon a shared encounter with racism and its concomitant psychoactive effects. With the rise of new fashion for hybridity, mixed race people indeed have acquired much attention in academia, as well as political presence and impact in the U.S. society. At least, the derogatory term for them like "half-caste" has become outdated. People's idea of mixed race shows a change from old essentialist views of biological races to the concepts of "cultural mixing." Even in some idealist statements, mixed race is the perfect race of the future signifying a hybrid vigor. Han Suyin, a Eurasian of Belgian and Chinese ancestry, expressed a sanguine view of Eurasian identity in her famous autobiographical novel *A Many-Splendored Thing*.

> Being Eurasian is not being born of East and of West. It is a state of mind. A state of mind created by false values, prejudice, ignorance. We just get rid of that state of mind. We must carry ourselves with colossal assurance and say: 'Look at us, the Eurasians! Just look. How beautiful we are, more beautiful than either race alone. More clever, more hardy. The meeting of both cultures, the fusion of all that can become a world civilization. Look at us, and envy us, you poor, one-world people, riveted to your limitations. We are the future of the world. Look at us.' (Han 245)

However, in an interview with Amy Ling, Han was a little less sanguine about being a Eurasian. When asked what she believed was the "greatest obstacle" in her life, Han replied that it was "being Eurasian, being unaccepted by both sides, being trivialized all the time and having to prove myself, and having to work three, four times as hard at everything I tried" (Ling, 1986 413-414). In other words, the race problem is still out there in common everyday life.

As textual responses to racism, all four writers illustrate historical, geographical and cultural divergences. But what they unanimously reveal is the neither/nor plight for Eurasians. Stonequist's "Marginal Man" thesis suggests that "those of mixed heritage will suffer undue psychological harm as a result of possible rejection and lack of belonging to a particular culture or race" (Stonequist 4). Hence, from the turn of the century to the end of the twentieth century, "trouble," "horror," "anxiety" are still the dominant themes in the four Euraisan authors' texts. Both Eaton sisters were writing between 1899 and 1925, at the time when virulent anti-miscegenation sentiment specifically targeted the Chinese. Half-Chinese Eurasians were not only rendered invisible in both the master narratives of history and ethnic (Chinese American) history, but also negatively and sensationally described for blurring the color line. Eurasians were portrayed as a "problem," portending racial extinction, the decline of civilization, or social unrest. In this context, Edith Eaton/Sui Sin Far is the first to challenge Anglo writers' negative preoccupation with Eurasian. She is also the first to make the Eurasian voice heard. Sui Sin Far attempted through her works to give shape and meaning to a Eurasian sensibility. In her autobiographical essay, Edith Eaton emphatically demonstrated her "wavering" self-image as neither white nor Chinese and her hope that her resistance to the notion of categorical purity will contribute positively to a mixed race future. Speaking from her personal experience, Edith not only told her lifelong sense of racial displacement, but also expressed a particular Eurasian subjectivity that was simultaneously critical of both white and Chinese prejudice. Sui Sin Far is remembered for her conscientious effort to create a more objective image of Chinese Americans. However, in her short stories, Edith's portrayals of the Chinese are not consistently objective and humane. Some of them sometimes are exotic and even stereotypical. Meanwhile, Sui Sin Far's Eurasian characters find that a wavering identity is too painful to sustain, yet intensifying either side of their identity is not a satisfactory answer.

In contrast to her elder sister Edith, Winnifred Eaton assumed a Japanese pen name in order to bypass the late-nineteenth-century North American Sinophobia and exploit the Japonisme fad, disassociating herself from stereotypes of the Chinese as debased and inassimilable. Hence, Winnifred has been severely criticized by certain critics. However, reading from her expression of Eurasian sensibility, it is less useful to measure Winnifred's level of authenticity and authority. As Edith did, Winnifred engaged with the bigotry she experienced as a Eurasian in her partly fictionalized autobiography *Me* which signals not only a tacit rejection of Onoto Watanna but also a desire to reclaim the real self which stresses "peculiar heredity." In contrast to Edith's racial integrity to stand up to anti-miscegenation feelings and racism, Winnifred chose to express her Eurasian consciousness in an indirect way. In terms of her double ancestries, Winnifred Eaton places her whiteness over her raced side, always expressing her preference of blondeness. She even deliberately depicts a utopian state for all races to live harmoniously without limitations of race. Winnifred's creation of Eurasian characters is much more significant in expanding social awareness of Eurasians. Under her pen, Eurasian characters are positive and non-threatening. Because of the absolute racial distinctions, they are social outcasts but not ruined. They can choose a way out of their conflict by finding a way out of their culture. But being aware of Eurasian vulnerability in a racially divided world and the problems of passing, Winnifred reveals the utopian nature of the fluid identity.

Although Diana Chang's *The Frontiers of Love* is not set in the United States, Westernized Shanghai's racial environment is very much similar to that of the U.S. Each of the Eurasian characters struggles with their confusing racial identity which stems from their racial ambivalence. Chang offers a convincing and interior view of the Eurasian world, literalizing the problematics of Eurasian identity. Similarly, written in the 1990s, Aimee Liu's *Face* still deals with the Eurasian character Maibelle's belonging. Aimee Liu locates Maibelle's struggling experience in Chinatown in order to disclose the inherent prejudice of Chinese Americans toward Eurasians. Maibelle experiences not only the spiritual torment but bodily fragmentation which is closely linked with a suppressed traumatic past.

All in all, this book attempts to theorize Eurasian against the fixed racial identity within current racial dichotomy. It can be seen from the stories in this book that the existence of Eurasians challenges long-held notions about the biological, moral, and social meaning of race. However, racism is highly durable, so a delineation of Eurasian authors' writing on Eurasians from the turn of the twentieth century up to the present day sadly continues to demonstrate both the potency of racist phenomena and the psychological effects of racism upon Eurasians. In fact, the mere existence of racial "mixing" is not enough to overcome racism and prejudice. Despite the tremendous increase in rates of intermarriage in the United States, Americans remain divided on the issue of racial intermixing. A Pew Research Center study issued in 2012 found that while 43 percent of Americans consider the increase to be good for society, another 44 percent say it has "made no difference" (with 11 percent considering it a change for the worse).[1] Therefore, although biracial icons have proved to be powerful public symbols for the desire to heal racial divides, it is overly idealistic. In other words, to expect hybridity alone to do the hard work of anti-racism is idealistic.

However, with the rise of mixed race studies, racial intermixing tends to be considered as a socially progressive and liberal phenomenon. As in postcolonial

---

1   See Wendy Wang, "The Rise of Intermarriage: Rates, Characteristics Vary by Race and Gender," Pew Research Center for Social and Demographic Trends. (Washington, D. C.: Pew Research Center, February 16, 2012), 2.

theory, hybridity is treated as a disruptive or destabilizing force, mixed race identity is claimed to break down racial boundaries and hold the promise toward a multiracial future where indeterminacy, in-betweenness, and ambivalence reign supreme. The exploration of Eurasians in this book directly looks into the issue of racism and the color line. The works of these Eurasian authors are underscored by binary figuration. Hence, mixed race becomes a significant tool in binary reconfiguration. In other words, mixed race can be viewed as a tool or strategy to challenge and perfect American racial categorization. In the era of President Obama, mixed persons are emblems of a new vision. The challenge of the mixed race is whether they can use post-race thinking to provide new spaces for identity within societies for which the concept of race still has real and profound effects.

Works Cited

Ahmed, S. *Strange Encounters: Embodied Others in Post-Coloniality*. London and New York: Routledge, 2000.

Ali, Suki. *Mixed-Race, Post-Race: Gender, New Ethnicities and Cultural Practices*. New York: Berg Publishers, 2003.

Altschuler, Glenn. *Race, Ethnicity, and Class in American Social Thought,* 1865-1919. Arlington Heights, IL: Harlan Davidson, 1982.

Ammons, Elizabeth. *Conflicting Stories: American Women Writers at the Turn into the Twentieth Century*. New York: Oxford University Press, 1992.

Anthia, F., and N. Yuval-Davis *Racialized Boundaries: Race, Nation, Gender, Color and Class, and the Anti-racist Struggle*. London: Routledge, 1993.

Anzaldua, Gloria. *Borderlands/La Frontera: The New Mestiza.* San Francisco: Spinsters/Aunt Lute, 1987.

Arboleda, Teja. *In the Shadow of Race: Growing Up as a Multiethnic, Multicultural, and "Multiracial" American*. New Jersey: Lawrence Erlbaum Associates, Inc., 1998.

Ashcorft, Bill, et al., Eds. *The Post-Colonial Studies Reader*. New York: Routledge, 1995.

Babcock, Winnifred Eaton (Onoto Watanna). *Who Was Who in America with World Notables, Volume VI,* 1974-1976. Chicago: Marquis Who's Who, .

Beck, Louis J. *New York's Chinatown: An Historical Presentation of Its People and Places*. New York: Bohemia Publishing Company, 1898.

Beltran, Mary, and Camilla Fojas, Eds. *Mixed Race Hollywood*. New York: New York University Press, 2008.

Bentley, Nancy. "White Slaves: The Mulatto Hero in Antebellum Fiction." *Subjects and Citizens: Nation, Race, and Gender from Oroonoko to Anita Hill*. Eds. Michael Moon and Cathy N. Davidson. Durham, NC: Duke University Press, 1995.

Berlant, Lauren. "National Brands, National Body." *Comparative American Identities: Race, Sex, and Nationality in Modern Text*. Ed. Hortense J. Spillers. New York: Routledge, 1991.

Berzon, Judith. *Neither White nor Black: The Mulatto Character in American Fiction.*

New York: New York University Press, 1978.

Bhabha, H. K. "The Third Space: Interview with Homi Bhabha." *Identity: Community, Culture, Difference.* Ed. Jonathan Rutherford. London: Lawrence and Wishart, 1990.

---. "Signs Taken for Wonders: Questions of Ambivalence and Authority under a Tree Outside Delhi, May 1817." *Critical Inquiry* 12 (1985): 144-165.

---. *The Location of Culture.* New York: Routledge, 1994.

Birchall, Diana. *Onoto Watanna: The Story of Winnifred Eaton.* Chicago: University of Illinois Press, 2001.

Bloom, Harold. *Asian American Women Writers.* Philadelphia, PA: Chelsea House, 1997.

Botshon, Lisa M. "Cautious Pluralism: Ethnic Women Writers and Early Twentieth-Century United States Popular Culture." Diss., Columbia University, 1997.

Bowers, Faubion. "Asia in Wartime: China." *The Saturday Review.* September 1956: 271.

Boyle, Kay. "The Far East and Fiction." *The American Scholars.* 1957: 222-227.

Bradshaw, C. K. "Beauty and Beast: On Racial Ambiguity." *Racially Mixed People in America.* Ed. Maria P. Root. New York: Sage Publications, 1992.

Brennan, Jonathan. *Mixed Race Literature.* Stanford: Stanford University Press, 2002.

Brown, Melissa. "Changing Authentic Identities: Evidence from Taiwan and China." *Journal of the Royal Anthropological Institute.* 16 (2010): 459-479.

Butler, J. *Bodies That Matter: On the Discursive Limits to Sex.* London: Routledge, 1993.

---. *Feminists Theorize the Political.* New York: Routledge, 1992.

Chan, Sucheng. *Asian Americans: An Interpretive History.* Boston: Twayne Publishers, 1991.

Chang, Diana. *The Frontiers of Love.* Seattle, WA: University of Washington Press, 1994.

---. "An Appearance of Being Chinese." *New York Quarterly.* 1975(17): 65-67.

---. *A Passion for Life.* New York: Random House, 1961.

---. *A Perfect Love.* New York: Jove Books, 1978.

---. *A Woman of Thirty.* New York: Random House, 1959.

---. *Eye to Eye.* New York: Harper and Row, 1974.

---. "In Two." *Ms.* July/August 1988: 83.

---. "Once Upon a Time." *North American Review.* March 1991, 276: 50-51.

---. "Saying Yes." *Asian American Heritage*, ed. David-Hsin-fu Wand. New York:

Washington Square Press, 1978: 30.

---. "Second Nature." *New York Quarterly*. 1972(11):59.

---. *The Horizon Is Definitely Speaking*. Port Jefferson, New York: Backstreet Editions, 1982.

---. *The Only Game in Town*. New York: Signet Books, 1963.

---. *What Matisse Is After*. New York: Contact House Publishers, 1984.

---. "Why Do Writers Write?" *The American Pen* 1 (Summer 1969): 1-3.

Chin, Frank, et al., Eds. *Aiiieeeee: An Anthology of Asian American Writers*. Washington, DC: Howard University Press, 1974.

---. *The Big Aiiieeeee!: An Anthology of Chinese American and Japanese American Literature*. New York: Meridian, 1991.

---. "Who's Afraid of Frank Chin, or Is It Ching?" *Bridge* 2:2 (December 1972): 30-34.

Chu, Patricia P. *Assimilating Asians: Gendered Strategies of Authorship in Asian America*. Durham and London: Duke University Press, 2000.

Chun, Allen. "Fuck Chineseness: On the Ambiguities of Ethnicity as Culture as Identity." *Boundary* 2, 23.2 (1996): 111-138.

Cole, Jean Lee. *The Literary Voices of Winnifred Eaton: Redefining Ethnicity and Authenticity*. New Brunswick: Rutgers University Press, 2002.

Cose, Ellis. *Color-Blind: Seeing Beyond Race in a Race-Obsessed World*. New York: HarperCollins, 1998.

Cotter, Holland. "Beyond Multiculturalism, Freedom?" *New York Times, Arts and Leisure*. July 13, 2001.

Croly, David G. *Miscegenation: The Theory of the Blending of the Races, Applied to the American White Man and Negro*. New York: H. Dexter, Hamilton & Co., 1864.

Crouch, Stanley. "Race is Over." *New York Times*. September 26, 1996.

Cutter, Martha J. "Smuggling Across the Borders of Race, Gender, and Sexuality: Sui Sin Far's *Mrs. Spring Fragrance*." *Mixed Race Literature*. Ed. Jonathan Brennan. Stanford: Stanford University Press, 2002.

DaCosta, Kimberly McClain. *Making Multiracials: State, Family, and Market in the Redrawing of the Color Line*. Stanford, CA: Stanford University Press, 2007.

Daniel, G. Reginald. "Passers and Pluralists: Subverting the Racial Divide." *Racially Mixed People in America*. Ed. Maria P. P. Root. New York: Sage Publications, 1992.

Daniels, Roger. *The Politics of Prejudice: The Anti-Japanese Movement in California and the Struggle for Japanese Exclusion*. New York: Atheneum, 1968.

---. *More than Black? Multiracial Identity and the New Racial Order*. Philadelphia:

Temple University Press, 2001.

Darwin, Charles. *The Variation of Animals and Plants under Domestication.* Vol 2. London: Murray, 1868.

Davis, F. James. *Who is Black?: One Nation's Definition.* Pennsylvania: Pennsylvania State University Press, 1991.

Dawe, W. Carlton. "Yellow and White." *Yellow and White.* Boston, 1895: 7-35.

Derrida, Jacques. *The Animal That Therefore I Am.* Trans. David Wills. New York: Fordham University Press, 2008.

Diana, Vanessa Holford. "Biracial/Bicultural Identity in the Writings of Sui Sin Far." *MELUS* 2 Identities (Summer 2001): 159-186.

Dong, Lorraine, Marlon K. Hom. "Defiance of Perpetuation: An Analysis of Characters in *Mrs. Spring Fragrance.*" *Chinese America: History and Perspectives, 1987.* Eds. Mark Lai, et al. San Francisco: Chinese Historical Society of America, 1987.

Dover, Cedric. *Half-Caste.* London: Martin Secker & Warburg, 1937.

Doyle, James. "Sui Sin Far and Onoto Watanna: Two Early Chinese-Canadian Authors." *Canadian Literature* 140 (Spring 1994): 50-58.

Drachsler, Julius. *Intermarriage in New York City: A Statistical Study of the Amalgamation of European Peoples.* New York: Nabu Press, 1921.

D'Souza, Dinesh. *The End of Racism: Principles for a Multiracial Society.* New York: Free Press, 1995.

Duncan, Patti. *Tell This Silence: Asian American Women Writers and the Politics of Speech.* Iowa: University of Iowa Press, 2004.

Du Bois, W. E. B. *The Souls of Black Folk.* New York: Barnes & Noble Books, 2003.

---. "The Freedom's Bureau." *Atlantic Monthly.* March, 1901.

Eakin, Paul J. *Fictions in Autobiography: Studies in the Art of Self-Invention.* Princeton: Princeton University Press, 1985.

Eaton, Winnifred. *Me: A Book of Remembrance.* Jackson: University of Mississippi Press, 1997.

---. *Marion: The Story of an Artist's Model.* Montreal: McGill-Queens University Press, 2012.

Edwards, Holly. *Noble Dreams, Wicked Pleasures: Orientalism in America* 1870-1930. New Jersey: Princeton University Press, 2000.

Elam, Michele. *The Souls of Mixed Folk: Race, Politics, and Aesthetics in the New Millennium.* Stanford: Stanford University Press, 2011.

Ellison, Ralph. *Shadow and Act.* New York: Vintage House, 1972.

Evrie, John H. Van. *Subgenation: The Theory of the Normal Relation of the Races: An*

Answer to "Miscegenation." 2nd Ed. New York: Bradburn, 1864.

Fadda-Conrey, Carol. "Arab American Literature in the Ethnic Borderland: Cultural Interactions in Diana Abu-Jaber's *Crescent*." *MELUS* 31: 4 (2006): 187-205.

Farley, Reynolds, Walter Allen. *The Color Line and Quality of Life in America.* Newbury Park, Calif.: Sage, 1987.

Felski, Rita. *Beyond Feminist Aesthetics: Feminist Literature and Social Change.* Cambridge, MA: Harvard University Press, 1989.

Ferens, Dominika. *Edith and Winnifred Eaton: Chinatown Missions and Japanese Romances.* Urbana: University of Illinois Press, 2002.

Ferla, Ruth La. "Generation E. A.: Ethnically Ambiguous." *New York Times*. December 28, 2003.

Fernandez, Carlos A. "Government Classification of Multiracial/Multiethnic People." *The Multiracial Experience: Racial Borders as the New Frontier*. Ed. Maria P. P. Root. Thousand Oaks, CA: Sage, 1996.

Fisher, Steve. "Shanghai Butterfly: A Short, Short Story." *Overland Monthly* Nov. 1933: 158.

Foucault, Michel. *The Birth of the Clinic*. Trans. A.M. Sheridan Smith. New York: Vintage Books, 1975.

---. *Discipline and Punish*. Trans. Alan Sheridan. New York: Vintage Books, 1979.

Frankenberg, Ruth. *White Women, Race Matters: The Social Construction of Whiteness*. Minneapolis, MN: University of Minnesota Press, 1993.

Fuchs, Marcia G. "Review of *Solitaire* by Aimee Liu." *Library Journal* 15 June 1979: 1332.

Garrad, Andrew, Robert Kilkenny, Christina Gomez, Eds. *Mixed: Multicultural College Students Tell Their Life Stories*. New York: Cornell University Press, 2013.

Gates, Henry Louis Jr., Kwame Anthony Appiah, Eds. *"Race," Writing, and Difference*. Chicago: University of Chicago Press, 1992.

Giddings, Paula. *When and Where I Enter*. New York: Morrow, 1987.

Gilroy, P. *Between Camps: Nations, Culture and the Allure of Race*. London: Penguin, 2000.

---. *Against Race: Imaging Political Culture Beyond the Color Line*. Cambridge, MA: Belknap Press of Harvard University Press, 2000.

Ginsberg, Elaine K. "The Politics of Passing." *Passing and the Fictions of Identity*. Ed. Elaine K Ginsberg. Durham: Duke University Press, 1996.

Grice, Helena. *Negotiating Identities: An Introduction to Asian American Women's Writing*. Manchester and New York: Manchester University Press, 2002.

Gubar, Susan. *Race Changes: White Skin, Black Face in American Culture*. New York: Oxford University Press, 1997.

Hall, S. "New Ethnicities." *"Race", Culture, Difference*. Eds. J. Donald and A. Rattansi. London: Routledge, 1992.

---, and Paul Du Gay, Eds. *Questions of Cultural Identity*. London: SAGE Publications Ltd., 1996.

Hamalian, Leo. "A *MELUS* Interview: Diana Chang." *MELUS* 20: 4 (1995): 29-43.

Han Suyin. *A Many-Splendored Thing*. St Albans: Panther Books Ltd., 1972.

Haney-Lopez, Ian. *White by Law: The Legal Construction of Race*. New York: New York University Press, 1996.

Harris, Neil. "All the World a Melting Pot: Japan at American Fairs, 1876-1904." *Mutual Images: Essays in American-Japanese Relations*. Ed. Akira Iriye. Cambridge, Mass.: Harvard University Press, 1975.

Harte, Bret. *The Writings of Bret Harte*. Boston: Houghton Mifflin, 1896.

Hawley, John C. *Cross Addressing: Resistance Literature and Cultural Borders*. Albany: State University of New York Press, 1996.

Hollinger, David A. *Postethnic America: Beyond Multiculturalism*. New York: HarperCollins, 1995.

Holt, Hamilton. *The Life Stories of Undistinguished Americans, as Told by Themselves*. New York: J. Pott &Company, 1906.

Horsman, Reginald. *Race and Manifest Destiny: The Origins of American Racial Anglo-Saxonism*. Cambridge: Harvard University Press, 1981.

Howells, William Dean. "The New Historical Romance." *North American Review* (1900) 171: 935-948.

Kaplan, Sidney. "The Miscegenation Issue in the Election of 1864." *Journal of Negro History* 34.3 (July 1949): 274-343.

Kawash, Samira. *Dislocating the Color Line: Identity, Hybridity, and Singularity in African-American Narrative*. Stanford: Stanford University Press, 1997.

Kilcup, Karen. *Nineteenth-Century Women Writers: An Anthology*. London: Blackwell Publishing, 1997.

Kim, Elaine H. *Asian American Literature: An Introduction to the Writings and Their Social Context*. Philadelphia: Temple University Press, 1982.

Kitano, Harry H. L. "The Japanese." *Harvard Encyclopedia of American Ethnic Groups*. Ed. Stephan Thernstrom. Cambridge: Harvard University Press, 1980.

Knox, Robert. *The Races of Men: A Philosophical Enquiry into the Influence of Race over the Destines of Nations*. London: Henry Reushaw, 1862.

Koshy, Susan. *Sexual Naturalization: Asian Americans and Miscegenation*. Stanford: Stanford University Press, 2004.

Kristeva, Julia. *The Powers of Horror: An Essay on Abjection*. New York: Columbia University Press, 1982.

Lacan, Jaques. *The Seminar. Book* XI. *The Four Fundamental Concepts of Psychoanaylsis*, 1964. Trans. Alan Sheridan. London: Hogarth Press and Institute of Psycho-Anaylsis, 1977.

Laing, H. P. and A. R. Lee. *Interpersonal Perception*. London: Tavistock, 1966.

Lamson, Herbert Day. "Sino-American Miscegenation in Shanghai." *Social Forces*. Vol. 14, No.4 (May, 1936): 573-581.

---. "The Eurasian in Shanghai." *American Journal of Sociology* 41.5 (1936): 642-648.

Lanning, G., S. Couling. *The History of Shanghai*. Taipei: Ch'eng Wen Publishing Company, 1973.

---. "The Eurasian in Shanghai." *American Journal of Sociology* 41.5 (1936):642-648.

Lape, Noreen Groover. "West of the Border: Cultural Liminality in the Literature of the Western American Frontiers." Diss., Temple University, 1996.

Lauter, Paul, et al., Eds. *Heath Anthology of American Literature*. Belmont: Wadsworth Publishing, 1995.

Lawrence, Keith, and Floyd Cheung, Eds. *Recovered Legacies: Authority and Identity in Early Asian American Literature*. Philadelphia: Temple University Press, 2005.

Lease, Benjamin. "Review of *The Frontiers of Love*." *Chicago Sun-Times*, 1956.

Lee, Jid. *From the Promised Land to Home: Trajectories of Selfhood in Asian-American Women's Autobiography*. Las Colinas: Ide House, 1998.

Lee, Robert G. *Orientals: Asian Americans in Popular Culture*. Philadelphia: Temple University Press, 1999.

Lewis, Martin W., and Kären Wigen, Eds. *The Myth of Continents: A Critique of Metageography*. Los Angeles: University of California Press, 1997.

Lim, Shirley Geok-lin. "Sibling Hybridities: The Case of Edith Eaton/Sui Sin Far and Winnifred Eaton/Onoto Watanna." *Life Writing* 4-1 (2007): 81-99.

---. Amy Ling, Eds. *Reading the Literatures of Asian America*. Philadelphia: Temple University Press, 1992.

---. Introduction to *The Frontiers of Love*, v-xxiii. Seattle: University of Washington Press, 1994.

---. "Twelve Asian American Writers: In Search of Self-Definition." *Redefining American Literary History*. Eds. A. LaVonne Brown Ruoff and Jerry W. Ward Jr. New York: MLA, 1990.

Ling, Amy. "A Perspective on Chinamerican Literature." *MELUS* 8: 2 (1981) Ethnic Literature and Cultural Nationalism: 76-81.

---, and Annette White-Parks, Eds. *Sui Sin Far: Mrs. Spring Fragrance and Other Writings*. Urbana: University of Illinois Press, 1995.

---. *Between Worlds: Women Writers of Chinese Ancestry*. New York: Pergamon, 1990.

---. "Creating One's Self: The Eaton Sisters." *Reading the Literatures of Asian America*. Eds. Shirley Geok-lin Lim and Amy Ling. Philadelphia: Temple University Press, 1992. 305-18.

---. "Diana Chang: The Hyphenated Condition." *MELUS* 7: 4 (1980): 69-83.

---. "Edith Eaton: Pioneer Chinamerican Writer and Feminist." *American Literary Realism* 16 (Autumn 1983): 287-298.

---. "Winnifred Eaton: Ethnic Chameleon and Popular Success." *MELUS* 11: 3 (1984): 5-15.

---. "Writers with a Cause: Sui Sin Far and Han Suyin." *Women Studies International Forum* 9:4. 1986: 411-419.

Liu, Aimee. *Solitaire: A Narrative*. New York: Barnes & Noble, 1979.

---. *Cloud Mountain*. Boston: Warner Books, 1997.

---. *Face*. New York: Warner Books, 1994.

---. *Flash House*. Boston: Warner Books, 2003.

---. *Gaining: The Truth about Life Eating Disorders*. New York: Grand Central Publishing, 2008.

Lopez, Ian Haney. *White by Law: The Legal Construction of Race*. New York: New York University Press, 1996.

Lowe, Lisa. *Immigrant Acts: On Asian American Cultural Politics*. Durham: Duke University Press, 1996.

Lugones, Maria. "On Borderlands/La Frontera: Interpretive Essay." *Hypatia* 7: 4 (1992): 31-37.

Lui, Ting Yi. *The Chinatown Trunk Mystery: Murder, Miscegenation, and Other Dangerous Encounters in Turn-of-the-Century New York City*. Princeton, NJ: Princeton University Press, 2005.

Lummis, Charles. "In Western Letters." *Outwest* 13 (November 1900): 336.

Lyman, Stanford. "Strangers in the City: The Chinese in the Urban Frontier." *Roots: An Asian American Reader*. Eds. Amy Tachiki, Eddie Wong, Franklin Odo and Buck Wong. Los Angeles: University of California, Los Angeles Asian American Studies Center, 1971: 159-187.

Lynch, Joy M. "'A Distinct Place in America Where All Mestizos Reside': Landscape and Identity in Ana Castillo's *Sapogonia* and Diana Chang's *The Frontier's Love*." *MELUS* 26: 3 (2001): 119-144.

Manlove, Clifford T. "Visual 'Drive' and Cinematic Narrative: Reading Gaze Theory in Lacan, Hitchcock, and Mulvey." *Cinema Journal* 46: 3 (2007): 83-108.

Marchetti, Gina. *Romance and the "Yellow Peril": Race, Sex, and Discursive Strategies in Hollywood Fiction*. Berkeley: University of California Press, 1993.

Matsukawa, Yuko. "Cross-Dressing and Cross-Naming: Decoding Onoto Watanna." *Tricksterism in Turn-of-the-Century American Literature: A Multicultural Perspective*. Eds. Elizabeth Ammons and Annette White-Parks. Hanover: University Press of New English, 1994.

Meech, Julia, and Gabriel P. Weisberg, Eds. *Japonisme Comes to America: The Japanese Impact on American Graphic Arts,* 1876-1925. New York: Harry Abrams, 1990.

Miles, R. *Racism*. London: Routledge, 1989.

Morrison, Toni. "Unspeakable Things Unspoken: The Afro-American Presence in American Literature." *The Norton Anthology of African American Literature*. Eds. Henry Louis Gates, Jr. and Nellie Y. Mckay, 2299-2322. 2nd Ed. New York: W. W. Norton, 2004.

Najmi, Samina. Introduction to *The Heart of Hyacinth*, v-xlvi. Seattle: University of Washington Press, 2000.

---. "Representations of White Women in Works by Selected African American and Asian American Authors." Diss., Tufts University, 1997.

---. "White Woman in Asia: Racial Fluidity as Rebellion in Onoto Watanna's *The Heart of Hyacinth*." *Re-placing America: Conversations and Contestations: Selected Essays*. Eds. Ruth Hsu, Cynthia Franklin and Suzanne Kosanke. Honolulu: University of Hawaii Press, 2000.

Nakamura, Lisa. "Mixedfolks.com: 'Ethnic Ambiguity,' Celebrity Outing, and the Internet," *Mixed Race Hollywood*. Eds. Mary Beltran and Camilla Fojas. New York: New York University Press, 2008.

Nee, Victor G., Brett De Bary. *Longtime Californ': A Documentary Study of an American Chinatown*. New York: Pantheon, 1972.

Newman, Katharine D., ed. *The American Equation: Literature in a Multi-Ethnic Culture*. Boston: Allyn and Bacon, 1971.

Newton, Pauline T. *Transcultural Women of Late-Twentieth-Century U.S. American Literature: First-Generation Migrants from Islands and Peninsulas*. Hampshire, UK: Ashgate, 2005.

New York Times. 1914. "Edith Eaton Dead: Author of Chinese Stories under the Name of Sui Sin Far." Apr. 9, 11.

New York Times Book Review. 1915. "Is Onoto Watanna Author of the Annoymous Novel *Me*?" Oct. 10, 869.

Nobles, Melissa. *Shades of Citizenship: Race and the Census in Modern Politics*. Stanford, CA: Stanford University Press, 2000.

Norris, Frank. *Collected Works of Frank Norris 4*. New York: Kennikatt Press, 1967.

Nott, Josiah. "The Mulatto a Hybrid—Probable Extermination of the Two Races If the Whites and Blacks Are Allowed to Intermarry." *American Journal of the Medical Sciences* (1843): 250-258.

Obama, Barack. *Dreams from My Father: A Story of Race and Inheritance*. New York: Three Rivers Press, Random House, 2004.

Oishi, Eve. Introduction to *Miss Nume of Japan*, xii-xxxi. Baltimore: The Johns Hopkins University Press, 1999.

Osumi, Megumi Dick. "Asians and California's Anti-Miscegenation Laws." *Asian and Pacific American Experiences*. Asian/Pacific Learning Resource Center and General College. Minneapolis: University of Minnesota Press, 1982.

Ouyang, Huining. "Ambivalent Passages: Racial and Cultural Crossings in Onoto Watanna's *The Heart of Hyacinth*." *MELUS* 34. 1 (2009): 211-229.

Palumbo-Liu, David, ed. *The Ethnic Canon: Histories, Institutions, and Interventions*. Minneapolis: University of Minneapolis Press, 1995.

---. *Asian/American: Historical Crossings of a Racial Frontier*. Stanford: Stanford University Press, 1999.

Pan, Lynn. *Sons of the Yellow Emperor: A History of the Chinese Diaspora*. New York: Kodansha International, 1994.

Park, Robert E. "Human Migration and the Marginal Man." *The American Journal of Sociology* 33.6 (1928): 881-893.

Parker, D., and M. Song, Eds. *Rethinking "Mixed Race."* London: Pluto Press, 2001.

Pascal, Roy. *Design and Truth in the Autobiography*. Cambridge: Harvard University Press, 1960.

Pascoe, Peggy. *What Comes Naturally: Miscegenation Law and the Making of Race in America*. New York: Oxford University Press, 2009.

Patterson, Martha. *The American New Woman Revisited: A Reader, 1894-1930*. New Jersey: Rutgers University Press, 2008.

Penn, William S. *As We Are Now: Mixblood Essays on Race and Identity*. New York: University of California Press, 1997.

Perlmann, Joel. "Reflecting the Changing Face of America: Multiracials, Racial Classification, and American Intermarriage." *Interracialism:Black-White Intermarriage in American History, Literature, and Law*. Ed. Werner Sollors. New York: Oxford University Press, 2000.

Pfeiffer, Kathleen. *Race Passing and American Individualism*. Amherst: University of Massachusetts Press, 2003.

Rau, Samantha Ramu. "The Need to Belong." *The New York Times Book Review* 23 September (1956):20-22.

Reuter, Edward Byron. *The Mulatto in the United States: Including a Study of the Role of Mixed-Blood Races Throughout the World*. Stockton: University Press of the Pacific, 1918.

Rev. of *The Heart of Hyacinth*, by Onoto Watanna. *Republican*. 13 Dec. 1903. Reeve file 19.1.

Rev. of *The Heart of Hyacinth*, by Onoto Watanna. *Nashville Banner*. 12 Dec. 1903. Reeve file 19.1.

Rev. of *The Heart of Hyacinth*, by Onoto Watanna. *Public Ledger*, 20 Sep, 1903. Reeve file 19.1

Rexroth, Kenneth. "World ills in the Far East." *Nation* 183 (September 29, 1956): 271-273.

Riddle, Ronald. *Flying Dragons, Flowing Streams: Music in the Life of San Francisco's Chinese*. Westport: Greenwood Press, 1983.

Rody, Caroline. *The Interethnic Imagination: Roots and Passages in Contemporary Asian American Fiction*. New York: Oxford University Press, 2009.

Roh-Spaulding, Carol. "Wavering Images: Mixed-Race Identity in the Stories of Edith Eaton/Sui Sin Far." *Ethnicity and the American Short Story*. Ed. Julic Brown. New York: Garland Publishing, 1997.

---. "Blue-Eyed Asians: Eurasianism in the Work of Edith Eaton/Sui Sin Far, Winnifred Eaton/Onoto Watanna, and Diana Chang." Diss., The University of Iowa, 1996.

---. "Diana Chang (1934-)." *Asian American Novelists: A Bio-Bibliographical Critical Sourcebook*. Ed. Emmanuel S. Nelson. Westport, CT: Greenwood, 2000.

---. "The Go-Between People: Representations of Mixed Race in Twentieth-Century American Literature." *American Mixed Race*. Ed. Naomi Zack. Boston: Rowman & Littlefield Publishers, Inc, 1995.

Root, Maria P. P, Ed. *The Multiracial Experience: Racial Borders as the New Frontier*. Thousand Oaks, CA: Sage, 1996.

---, Ed. *Racially Mixed People in America*. Newbury Park, CA: Sage, 1992.

---. "A Bill of Rights for Racially Mixed People." *The Multicultural Experience: Racial Borders as the New Frontier*. Ed. Maria P. P. Root. Thousand Oaks, CA: Sage, 1995.

---, and Matt Kelley, Eds. *Multiracial Child Resource Book: Living Complex Identities*. Seattle, WA: MAVIN Foundation, 2003.

---. "Within, Between, Beyond Race." *"Mixed Race" Studies: A Reader*. Ed. Jayne O. Ifekwunigwe. New York: Routledge, 2004.

Rosaldo, Renato. *Culture and Truth: The Remaking of Social Analysis*. Boston: Beacon Press, 1989.

Ryan, Mary P. *Womanhood in America*. New York: New Viewpoints, 1975.

Said, Edward. *Orientalism*. New York: Random House, 1979.

San Juan, E. Jr. "Problematiziing Multiculturalism and the 'Common Culture'" *MELUS* 19:2 (Summer 1994): 59-82.

Scheick, William J. *The Half-Blood: A Cultural Symbol in 19th-Century American Fiction*. Lexington, Ky.: University Press of Kentucky, 1979.

Schultz, Alfred. *Race or Mongrel: A Theory That the Fall of Nations Is Due to Intermarriage with Alien Stock: A Demonstration That A Nation's Strength Is Due to Racial Purity*. Montana: Kessinger Publishing, 2010.

Schwartz, Shepard. "Mate Selection among New York City's Chinese Males, 1931-38." *American Journal of Sociology* 56.6 (May 1951): 562-568.

Scott, Joan. "Multiculturalism and the Politics of Identity." *MELUS* 14.2 (Summer 1987): 21-32.

See, Lisa. *On Gold Mountain: The One-Hundred-Year Odyssey of My Chinese-American Family*. New York: Vintage, 1995.

Segura, Denise A., Patricia Zavella. "Gendered Borderlands." *Gender & Society* 22. 5 (2008): 537-544.

Sharfstein, Daniel J. "Crossing the Color Line: Racial Migration and the One-Drop Rule, 1600-1860." *Minnesota Law Review* 91 (2007): 592-656.

Shea, Pat. "Winnifred Eaton and the Politics of Miscegenation in Popular Fiction (Popular Literature and Film)." *MELUS* 22 (Summer 1997): 19-35.

Shih, David. "The Self and Generic Convention." *Recovered Legacies: Authority and Identity in Early Asian American Literature*. Eds. Keith Lawrence and Floyd Cheung. Philadelphia: Temple University Press, 2005.

Shohat, Ella. "Notes on the 'Post-Colonial.'" *Social Text* 31/32 (1992): 99-113.

Sidonie, Smith, Julia Watson, Eds. *De/colonizing the Subject: The Politics of Gender in Women's Autobiography*. Minneapolis: University of Minnesota Press, 1992.

Singh, Amritjit, Joseph T. Skerrett, Jr., Robert E. Hogan, Eds. *Memory, Narrative, and Identity in Ethnic American Literature*. Boston: Northeastern University Press, 1996.

Smith-Rosenberg, Carroll. *Disorderly Conduct: Visions of Gender in Victorian America*. New York: A. Knopf, 1985.

Solberg, S. E. "Eaton Sisters: Sui Sin Far and Onoto Watanna." Paper presented at the Pacific Northwest Asian American Writer's Conferences, Seattle, WA, 1976.

---. "Sui Sin Far/Edith Eaton: First Chinese-American Fictionist." *MELUS* 8 (Spring 1981): 27-39.

---. "Sui, the Storyteller." *Turn Shadows into Light: Art and Culture of the Northwest's Early Asian Community*. Eds. Mayumi Tsutakawa and Alan Chong Lau. Settle: Young Pine Press, 1982.

Sollors, Werner. *Beyond Ethnicity: Consent and Descent in American Culture*. New York: Oxford University Press, 1986.

---. "Intermarriage and Mulattos in the 1920s." *RSA* 5. No.7 (1989):260-271.

---. "The Bluish Tinge in the Halfmoon; or Fingernails as a Racial Sign." *Neither Black nor White yet Both: Thematic Explorations of Interracial Literature*. Ed. Werner Sollors. New York: Oxford University Press, 1997.

Solomon, Robert C. "Subjectivity." *Oxford Companion to Philosophy*. Ed. Ted Honderich. New York: Oxford University Press, 2005.

Spencer, Jon Michael. *The New Colored People: The Mixed-Race Movement in America*. New York: New York University Press, 1997.

Spickard, Paul. *Mixed Blood: Intermarriage and Ethnic Identity in Twentieth-Century America*. Madison: University of Wisconsin Press, 1989.

---. "Who Is an Asian? Who Is a Pacific Islander? Monoracialism, Multiracial People, and Asian American Communities." *The Sum of Our Parts*. Eds. Teresa Williams-Leon and Cynthia L. Nakashima. Philadelphia: Temple University Press, 2001.

---. "The Subject Is Mixed Race: The Boom in Biracial Biography." *Rethinking "Mixed Race."* Eds. David Parker and Miri Song. Sterling, VA: Pluto Press, 2001.

Stonequist, Everett V. *The Marginal Man: A Study in Personality and Culture Conflict*. New York: Russell&Russell, 1961.

Sui Sin Far. *Mrs. Spring Fragrance and Other Writings*. Urbana and Chicago: University of Illinois Press, 1995.

---. "Sweet Sin." *Land of Sunshine* 8 (April 1898): 223-226.

Sung, Betty Lee. *Chinese American Intermarriage*. New York: Center for Migration Studies, 1990.

Takaki, Ronald T. *Iron Cages: Race and Culture in 19th Century America*. Seattle: University of Washington Press, 1979.

Tchen, John Kuo Wei. *New York Before Chinatown: Orientalism and the Shaping of American Culture, 1776-1882*. Baltimore: Johns Hopkins University Press, 1999.

Teng, Emma Jinhua. *Eurasian Mixed Identities in the United States, China, and Hong Kong, 1842-1943*. Berkeley and Los Angeles: University of California Press, 2013.

Usher, R. "Autobiographical Accounts of PhD Students." *Biography and Education: A Reader*. Ed. M. Erben. London: Falmer Press, 1998.

Wald, Alan. "Theorizing Cultural Differences: A Critique of the 'Ethnicity School.'" *MELUS* 14.2 (1987): 21-33.

Wang, Wendy. "The Rise of Intermarriage: Rates, Characteristics Vary by Race and Gender." Pew Research Center for Social and Demographic Trends. Washington, D. C.: Pew Research Center, February 16, 2012.

Watanna, Onoto. *Miss Nume of Japan: A Japanese-American Romance*. Chicago: Rand McNally, 1899.

---. *A Japanese Nightingale*. New York: Harper and Brothers, 1901.

---. *Daughters of Nijo: A Romance of Japan*. New York: Harper and Brothers, 1904.

---. *Tama*. New York: Harper and Brothers, 1910.

---. *The Heart of Hyacinth*. New York: Harper and Brothers, 1903.

---. *The Love of Azalea*. New York: Dodd, Mead, 1904.

---. *His Royal Nibs*. New York: W. J. Watt, 1925.

---. *The Wooing of Wistaria*. New York: Harper and Brothers, 1902.

---. (Anonymously) *Marion: The Story of an Artist's Model*. New York: W. J. Watt, 1916.

---. (Anonymously) *Me: A Book of Remembrance*. New York: Century, 1915.

Watson, Carole McAlpine. *The Novels of Black American Women, 1891-1965*. Westport: Greenwood, 1985.

Waugh, Patricia. *Feminine Fictions: Revisiting the Postmodern*. London: Routledge, 1989.

Weisberg, Gabriel P. "Japonisme: The Commercialization of an Opportunity." *Japonisme Comes to America: The Japanese Impact on American Graphic Arts, 1876-1925*. Eds. Julia Meech and Gabriel P. Weisberg. New York: Harry Abrams, 1990.

White-Parks, Annette. "Sui Sin Far: Writer on the Chinese-Anglo Boarders of North America, 1885-1914." Diss., Washington State University, 1991.

---. "A Reversal of American Concepts of 'Otherness' in the Fiction of Sui Sin Far."

MELUS 20.1 (1995): 17-34.

---. *Sui Sin Far/Edith Maude Eaton: A Literary Biography*. Urbana: University of Illinois Press, 1995.

Williams, Teresa Kay. "Race-ing and Being Raced: The Critical Interrogation of 'Passing'." *Amerasia Journal* 23.1 (1997): 61-65.

Williams-Leon, Teresa, Cynthia L. Nakashimi, Eds. *The Sum of Our Parts: Mixed Heritage Asian Americans*. Philadelphia: Temple University Press, 2001.

Williamson, Joel. *New People: Miscegenation and Mulattoes in the United States*. New York: The Free Press, 1980.

Wong, K. Scott. "Chinatown: Conflicting Images, Contested Terrain." *MELUS* 20. 1 (1995):3-15.

Wong, Sau-ling Cynthia. "Ethnic Subject, Ethnic Sign, and the Difficulty of Rehabilitative Representation: Chinatown in Some Works of Chinese American Fiction." *The Yearbook of English Studies* 24 (1994): 251-262.

Wu, Kitty Wei-hsuing. "Cultural Ideology and Aesthetic Choices: A Study of Three Works by Chinese American Women: Diana Chang, Bette Bao Lord, and Maxine Hong Kingston." Diss., University of Maryland, 1989.

Wu, William F. *Yellow Peril: Chinese Americans in American Fiction,* 1850-1940. Hamden: Archon Books, 1982.

Xicay-Santos, Luis Alfredo. "Reconcilable Differences: Soy Guatemalteco! Soy Mestizo!" *Interrace* (April 1994): 28-30.

Yin, Xiaohuang. *Chinese American Literature since the 1850s*. Urbana and Chicago: University of Illinois Press, 2000.

Young, Robert J. C. *Colonial Desire: Hybridity in Theory, Culture and Race*. London: Routledge, 1995.

Yung, Judy. *Chinese Women of America: A Pictorial History*. Seattle: University of Washington Press, 1986.

Zack, Naomi, Ed. *American Mixed Race: The Culture of Micro-Diversity*. Lanham, MD: Rowman& Littlefield, 1995.

---. *Race and Mixed Race*. Philadelphia: Temple University Press, 1993.

Ziv, Alon. *Breeding Between the Lines: Why Interracial People Are Healthier and More Attractive*. Fort Lee, NJ: Barricade Books, 2006.

"Aimee Liu Fiction," http://www.aimeeliu.net/.

"Artist Pages—Aimee E. Liu," http://voices.cla.umn.edu/artistpages/liu_aimee.php.

后 记

2011年9月，我如愿成为厦门大学外文学院英语语言文学系的一名博士生，在张龙海教授门下专攻美国族裔文学。我深知这种心无旁笃地读书的机会，于我而言是巨大的奢侈，若非张老师的宽容与认可、爱人的谅解与支持，绝不可能成为事实。因此，我异常珍惜这来之不易的读书机会。从踏入厦大课堂的第一天起，我日日如沐春风，意气风发，乐此不疲地奔波在图书馆、孩子幼儿园和家之间。上课，思考，读书，做笔记，再思考，整理归纳，课堂陈述，日子因为繁忙而变得短暂，稍纵即逝。

2012年9月，修满学分后，我又有幸获得国家留学基金委资助，前往美国加利福尼亚大学洛杉矶分校的亚裔研究中心参加联合培养项目1年。UCLA美丽的校园与丰富的藏书，启迪心智的博士生课堂和美方导师凌津奇教授的悉心点拨，又使我再次坠入天堂般的生活。我抓住一切可能的机会走进教授的办公室——不能忘记凌教授在他满墙壁的书柜中爬着梯子寻找适合我阅读的书籍。他无私的付出只为扶持国内慢慢成长起来的青年一代，为祖国的学术繁荣贡献他的绵薄之力。如果说族裔文学值得研究，那么像凌教授这样默默、努力奋战在美国学术界的华裔学者同样值得研究，值得称赞。在UCLA学习一年，我的收获满满当当，感激之情无以言表。

回国后，我把前两年学习、积累的资料整理、分析，选了两个课题找张老师商量博士论文选题。张老师睿智果断，毫不迟疑地让我研究混血作家。因为在全球化的今天，人口的跨国流动使得混血族人口急剧增长，混血儿如何在文学中被体现和他们如何书写文学都值得关注。确定选题后，我回家铺开所有的资料，挥开臂膀，梳理提纲，思路不通畅时就寻求张老师的帮助，与爱人张旭东博士讨论，甚至问问年幼的女儿，孩子天真却富含哲理的话让我一次次眉开眼笑，茅塞顿开。功夫不负有心人，我终于在2014年年底完成了博士论文，并顺利通过答辩，完成了学业，这一年，我33岁，我的学术生命自此开始。

在此，我首先要感谢恩师张龙海教授，是您宽容博大的胸怀让我在宽松自由的环境下，完成了学业；您"做事先做人"的教诲时常回荡于我的耳畔，警醒我激励我，漫长的学术道路我才可以走得扎实走得稳当。其次我要感谢周郁蓓老师，您整整一年的博士课程，让我受益匪浅。与您的讨论以及意见不一致时我藏在心里的不满，都令我回味无穷。感谢周老师，是您逼着我进行的大量阅读与批评史的梳理，使我在博士论文的文献综述部分做得特别轻松顺利。感谢UCLA的凌津奇教授，您无私的帮助与指导，令我无以为报，毕生感激。另外，我要珍重地感谢我的爱人张旭东博士。亲爱的，没有你的支持，我不可能有今天。是你帮我顶住亲友们不让我辞职读博的重重压力，是你坚定不悔、默默无闻的支持使我安心完成了学业。可以说，我的成长是以你的牺牲为代价的。亲爱的，我只有以更多的爱来回报你为我做的一切。感谢我的宝贝女儿玲玲，是你的天真无邪和默默陪伴令妈妈的读书生涯多了一些色彩。感谢婆婆栾秋华女士，在我最困难的时期，她不顾自己身体孱弱远道来到厦门帮助我打理生活、照顾孩子。感谢厦门大学出版社王扬帆老师为本书出版所做的一切。感谢所有的人，谢谢你们。

记得一位年长的学者曾告诉我，人文社科的研究就是在生活中不断思考，随着年龄的增长，感悟不同的感悟。我非常珍惜生命中不同阶段给予我点拨的长者、老师、同辈。因为旁观者清的立场，可以让身在其中的我幡然醒悟，拔高思想。今天，这本以我的博士论文为基础的书即将付梓，我同样期待学界同仁、师长同学能够给予批评指正，助我成长。本书的部分章节已以中文论文的形式刊登于《外国文学评论》，编辑部老师的修改意见对于本书的后续修改起到了很大的作用。书中如有错漏之处，文责均由本人承担。

2016年12月14日
于厦门厦港